LAW, CRIME AND LAW ENFORCEMENT

FEDERAL FORFEITURE LAW

PROVISIONS, ISSUES AND REFORM PROPOSALS

LAW, CRIME AND LAW ENFORCEMENT

Additional books in this series can be found on Nova's website under the Series tab.

Additional e-books in this series can be found on Nova's website under the e-book tab.

LAW, CRIME AND LAW ENFORCEMENT

FEDERAL FORFEITURE LAW

PROVISIONS, ISSUES AND REFORM PROPOSALS

JERALD DIAZ
EDITOR

nova publishers
New York

NOTICE TO THE READER

Library of Congress Cataloging-in-Publication Data

ISBN: 978-1-63483-310-3

Published by Nova Science Publishers, Inc. † New York

CONTENTS

PREFACE

Forfeiture has long been an effective law enforcement tool. Congress and state legislatures have authorized its use for over 200 years. Every year, it redirects property worth billions of dollars from criminal to lawful uses. Forfeiture law has always been somewhat unique. By the close of the 20th century, however, legislative bodies, commentators, and the courts had begun to examine its eccentricities in greater detail because under some circumstances it could be not only harsh but unfair. The Civil Asset Forfeiture Reform Act was a product of that reexamination. This book is an overview of federal forfeiture law. It sketches the origins and general attributes of forfeiture, describes the distribution of the hundreds of millions of dollars it generates, and identifies some of the constitutional issues it raises. Furthermore, the book provides an overview of selected legal issues and reforms surrounding asset forfeiture, including the burden-of-proof standard and innocent-owner defense in civil asset forfeiture cases, access to counsel in both civil and criminal forfeiture cases, allocation of profits from confiscated assets, and DOJ's equitable sharing program.

In: Federal Forfeiture Law
Editor: Jerald Diaz
ISBN: 978-1-63483-310-3

Chapter 1

CRIME AND FORFEITURE*

Charles Doyle

SUMMARY

Forfeiture has long been an effective law enforcement tool. Congress and state legislatures have authorized its use for over 200 years. Every year, it redirects property worth billions of dollars from criminal to lawful uses. Forfeiture law has always been somewhat unique. By the close of the 20th century, however, legislative bodies, commentators, and the courts had begun to examine its eccentricities in greater detail because under some circumstances it could be not only harsh but unfair. The Civil Asset Forfeiture Reform Act (CAFRA), P.L. 106-185, 114 Stat. 202 (2000), was a product of that reexamination.

Modern forfeiture follows one of two procedural routes. Although crime triggers all forfeitures, they are classified as civil forfeitures or criminal forfeitures according to the nature of the procedure which ends in confiscation. Civil forfeiture is an in rem proceeding. The property is the defendant in the case. Unless the statute provides otherwise, the innocence of the owner is irrelevant—it is enough that the property was involved in a violation to which forfeiture attaches. As a matter of expedience and judicial economy, Congress often allows administrative forfeiture in uncontested civil confiscation cases. Criminal forfeiture is an in personam proceeding, and confiscation is possible only upon the conviction of the owner of the property.

---

* This is an edited, reformatted and augmented version of a Congressional Research Service publication, No. 97-139, dated January 22, 2015.

The Supreme Court has held that authorities may seize moveable property without prior notice or an opportunity for a hearing but that real property owners are entitled as a matter of due process to preseizure notice and a hearing. As a matter of due process, innocence may be irrelevant in the case of an individual who entrusts his or her property to someone who uses the property for criminal purposes. Although some civil forfeitures may be considered punitive for purposes of the Eighth Amendment's excessive fines clause, civil forfeitures do not implicate the Fifth Amendment's double jeopardy clause unless they are so utterly punitive as to belie remedial classification.

The statutes governing the disposal of forfeited property may authorize its destruction, its transfer for governmental purposes, or deposit of the property or of the proceeds from its sale in a special fund. Intra- and intergovernmental transfers and the use of special funds are hallmarks of federal forfeiture. Every year, federal agencies share among themselves the proceeds of jointly conducted forfeitures. They also transfer hundreds of millions of dollars and property to state, local, and foreign law enforcement officials as compensation for their contribution to joint enforcement efforts.

INTRODUCTION

This is an overview of federal forfeiture law.[1] It sketches the origins and general attributes of forfeiture, describes the distribution of the hundreds of millions of dollars it generates, and identifies some of the constitutional issues it raises.

BACKGROUND

Congress and state legislatures have authorized the use of forfeiture for over 200 years. Forfeiture law has always been somewhat unique. Its increased use has highlighted its eccentricities and attendant policy concerns.

Present forfeiture law has its roots in early English law. It is reminiscent of three early English procedures: deodands, forfeiture of estate or common law forfeiture, and statutory or commercial forfeiture.[2]

At early common law, the object that caused the death of a human being—the ox that gored, the knife that stabbed, or the cart that crushed—was confiscated as a deodand.[3] Coroners' inquests and grand juries, bound with the duty to determine the cause of death, were obligated to identify the offending object and determine its value.[4] The Crown distributed the proceeds realized from the confiscation of the animal or deadly object for religious and charitable purposes in the name of the deceased.[5]

Although deodands were not unknown in the American colonies,[6] they appear to have fallen into disuse or been abolished by the time of the American Revolution or shortly thereafter.[7] In spite of their limited use in this country, deodands and the practice of treating the offending animal or object as the defendant have frequently been cited to illustrate the characteristics of modern civil forfeiture.[8]

Forfeiture of estate or common law forfeiture, unlike deodands, focused solely on a human offender. At common law, anyone, convicted and attained for treason or a felony, forfeited all his lands and personal property.[9] Attainder, the judicial declaration of civil death, occurred as a consequence of the pronouncement of final sentence for treason or felony.[10] In colonial America, common law forfeitures were rare.[11] After the Revolution, the Constitution restricted the use of common law forfeiture in cases of treason, and Congress restricted its use, by statute, in the case of other crimes.[12]

The third antecedent of modern forfeiture, statutory or commercial forfeiture, figured prominently in cases in admiralty and on the revenue side of the Exchequer in pre-colonial England.[13] It was used fairly extensively against smuggling and other revenue evasion schemes in the American colonies and has been used ever since.[14] In most instances, the statutes called for *in rem* confiscation proceedings in which, as with deodands, the offending object was the defendant; occasionally, they established *in personam* procedures where confiscation occurred as the result of the conviction of the owner of the property.[15]

Although contemporary American forfeiture law owes much to the law of deodands and the law of forfeiture of estate, it is clearly a descendant of English statutory or commercial forfeiture.[16]

MODERN FORFEITURE LAW

Property and Trigger Crimes

Modern forfeiture is a creature of statute. While there are some common themes and general patterns concerning the crimes that trigger forfeiture, the property subject to confiscation, and the procedures associated with forfeiture, federal forfeiture statutes are matters of legislative choice and can vary greatly.[17]

Virtually every kind of property, real or personal, tangible or intangible, may be subject to confiscation under the appropriate circumstances.[18] The laws that call for the confiscation of contraband per se, property whose very possession has been outlawed, were at one time the most prevalent and can still be found.[19] Property—particularly vehicles—used to facilitate the commission of a crime and without which violation would be less likely, has long been the target of confiscatory statutes as well.[20]

In some instances, Congress has focused upon the profits of crime and authorized the confiscation of the direct and indirect proceeds of illegal activities.[21] And under some circumstances, it has authorized the forfeiture of substitute assets, when the tainted property subject to confiscation under a particular statute has become unavailable.[22]

Traditionally, the crimes which triggered forfeiture were (1) those that threatened the government's revenue interest, for example, smuggling, tax evasion, hunting or fishing without a license, or (2) those crimes that because of their perceived threat to public health or morals might have been considered public nuisances subject to abatement, for example, gambling, or dealing in obscene material, or illicit drug use.

Beginning with the racketeering statutes, a number of jurisdictions have created another category of forfeiture warranting offenses—crimes that involve substantial economic gain for the defendant even if not at the expense of government revenues, but which may greatly enhance government revenues, for example, racketeering and money laundering.[23] A prime example of this approach is the Civil Asset Forfeiture Reform Act (CAFRA),[24] which makes forfeitable, among other things, the proceeds from any of the crimes upon which a money laundering or RICO prosecution might be based.[25]

Following the terrorist attacks on September 11, 2001, Congress authorized the confiscation of another type of crime-related property—property owned by certain terrorists regardless of whether the property is traceable, used to facilitate, or connected in any other way to any practical crime.[26]

Federal confiscation ordinarily begins with a federal crime. Federal law, however, permits the confiscation of property located in the United States, derived from or used to facilitate various crimes committed in violation of foreign law overseas.[27] The qualifying felonies include public corruption, crimes of violence, drug trafficking, gun running, bank fraud, and child prostitution.[28]

Civil Forfeiture

Forfeiture follows one of two procedural routes: criminal or civil. Although crime triggers all forfeitures, they are classified as civil forfeitures or criminal forfeitures according to the nature of the judicial procedure which ends in confiscation. Criminal forfeitures are part of the criminal proceedings against the property owner, and confiscation is possible only upon the conviction of the owner of the property[29] and only to the extent of defendant's interest in the property.[30]

Civil forfeitures are accomplished using civil procedure. Civil forfeiture is ordinarily the product of a civil, in rem proceeding in which the property is treated as the offender.[31] Within the confines of due process and the language of the applicable statutes, the guilt or innocence of the property owner is irrelevant; it is enough that the property was involved in a crime to which forfeiture attaches in the manner in which statute demands.[32] Some civil forfeitures are accomplished administratively; some are not. Administrative forfeitures are, in oversimplified terms, uncontested civil forfeitures.

Historically, most forfeiture statutes called for civil forfeiture. The procedure for forfeiture varies according to the statute which authorizes confiscation. Although each usually contains a few procedural features, the drug, money laundering, and several other civil forfeiture statutes fill in their procedural gaps by cross-reference to the regime established under the customs laws.[33] CAFRA contains generally applicable procedures and thus reduces the extent to which civil forfeiture procedural matters are resolved by reference solely to the customs laws.[34]

As a general rule, since the proceedings are in rem, actual or constructive possession of the property by the court is a necessary first step in any confiscation proceeding.[35] The arrest of the property may be accomplished either by warrant under the Federal Rules of Criminal Procedure; or, if judicial proceedings have been filed, by a warrant under the Supplemental Rules of Certain Admiralty and Maritime Claims; or without warrant, if there is probable cause and other grounds under which the Fourth Amendment permits a warrantless arrest; or pursuant to equivalent authority under state law.[36] Because realty cannot ordinarily be seized until after the property owner has been given an opportunity for a hearing,[37] the procedure differs slightly in the case of real property.[38]

Where the seizure of the property causes an undue hardship, CAFRA affords an owner the opportunity to petition the court for release of the property pending the completion of forfeiture proceedings.[39] Conversely, the government may be entitled to a restraining or protective order to preserve the property pending the completion of forfeiture proceedings.[40]

Administrative Forfeitures

In the interests of expediency and judicial economy, Congress has sometimes authorized the use of administrative forfeiture as the first step after seizure in "uncontested" cases.[41] It may be somewhat misleading to characterize administrative forfeitures as uncontested forfeitures, given the procedural obstacles that the government and claimants must overcome before the government is put to its burden in a judicial proceeding.

For the government the procedure begins with seizure of the property.[42] It must notify anyone with an interest in the property and provide an opportunity to request judicial forfeiture proceedings.[43] Notice of the seizure alone, but without notice of the government's intent to seek confiscation, is not in itself sufficient.[44] Anyone with an interest in the property may contest confiscation with a verified claim under the Supplemental Rules.[45] Property owners have 30 days after the government's filing to submit a claim,[46] and 20 days thereafter to tender their answer.[47]

The period within which a claimant must register his or her intent to contest can be a fairly narrow window. Moreover, the courts may consider time of the essence, as long as the government has made reasonable efforts to notify interested parties.[48] Even if the government sustains no appreciable damage, a claim not promptly filed may be a claim lost.[49] The government may petition the court to dismiss a claim for want of statutory standing, which in turn may require the claimant to establish that he lawfully obtained the targeted property.[50]

If there are no viable claims, the property is summarily declared forfeited.[51] If the government has failed to provide adequate notice or failed to honor some other due process obligation, the declaration of administrative forfeiture may be set aside.[52] When an administrative forfeiture is set aside for want of notice, section 983(e) gives the government 60 days to initiate judicial forfeiture proceedings notwithstanding the expiration of an otherwise applicable statute of limitations.[53]

CAFRA establishes a timetable for administrative forfeitures under which the government must notify those with a property interest of its intent to confiscate within 60 days of seizure.[54] Thereafter, the property owner has at least 35 days within which to file a claim and request a judicial hearing.[55] The government has 90 days within which to initiate judicial proceedings after the receipt of a claim.[56] In customs or tax cases or cases that predate the passage of CAFRA, due process dictates the speed with which the government must act to initiate forfeiture proceedings following seizure of the property.[57]

When administrative forfeiture is unavailable, or when a claimant has successfully sought judicial proceedings, or when the government has elected not to proceed administratively, the government may begin civil judicial proceedings by filing either a complaint or a libel against the property.[58]

In money laundering and other civil forfeitures governed by CAFRA, the government must establish that the property is subject to confiscation by a preponderance of the evidence.[59] In cases such as those arising under the customs laws and cases filed before the effective date of CAFRA amendments, the government must establish probable cause to believe that the property is subject to forfeiture.[60]

If the government overcomes the initial obstacle, a claimant may successfully challenge confiscation on several grounds. He or she may be able to show that the predicate criminal offense did not occur or that his or her property lacks the statutorily required nexus to the crime.[61] For example, when the government claims that property is forfeitable because it was used to commit or to facilitate the commission of a crime, it must "establish that there was a substantial connection between the property and the offense."[62] A claimant's innocence or even acquittal only bars civil forfeiture to the extent that a statute permits or due process requires.[63]

For most civil forfeitures, other than those arising under the tax or customs laws,[64] CAFRA establishes two "innocent owner" defenses—one for claimants with an interest in the property at the time the forfeiture-triggering offense occurred and the other for claimants with an interest acquired after the forfeiture-triggering offense occurred.[65] The first is available to claimants either who were unaware that their property was being criminally used or who did all that could be reasonably expected of them to prevent criminal use of their property.[66] The second is for good faith purchasers who did not know of the taint on the property at the time they acquired their interest.[67] Even when the government establishes that property is subject to civil forfeiture, CAFRA affords a claimant the right to a judicial reduction of the amount of the confiscation, if the court determines the extent of the forfeiture is excessive in view of the gravity of the offense and claimant's culpability.[68]

When the court determines that the property is not subject to forfeiture, it must be released to its owner, assuming the property can be lawfully possessed by its owner.[69] Regardless of the statutory procedure initially invoked, prevailing claimants may be entitled to compensation for damages to the property incurred while in federal custody,[70] attorneys' fees,[71] post-judgment interest, and in some instances pre-judgment interest.[72]

Criminal Forfeiture

Once less frequently invoked than civil forfeiture, criminal forfeiture appears to have become the procedure of choice when judicial proceedings are required.[73] CAFRA added to the federal crimes punishable by criminal forfeiture, various offenses involving unlawful money transmission,[74] counterfeiting,[75] identify fraud,[76] credit card fraud,[77] computer fraud,[78] theft related to motor vehicles,[79] health care fraud,[80] telemarketing fraud,[81] bank fraud,[82] and immigration-related offenses.[83] Perhaps more significantly, a bridge statute, 28 U.S.C. 2461(c), exists which permits confiscation using criminal forfeiture procedures whenever civil forfeiture is authorized elsewhere.[84]

Like civil forfeiture, criminal forfeiture is a creature of statute.[85] Unlike civil forfeiture, criminal forfeiture follows as a consequence of conviction.[86] It is punishment,[87] even though it may also serve remedial purposes very effectively.[88] While civil forfeiture treats the property as the defendant, confiscating the interests of the innocent and guilty alike, criminal forfeiture traditionally consumes only the property interests of the convicted defendant,[89] and only with respect to the crime for which he is convicted.[90] When the property subject to confiscation is unavailable following the defendant's conviction, however, the court may order the confiscation of other property belonging to the defendant in its stead (substitute assets).[91]

The indictment or information upon which the conviction is based must list the property which the government asserts is subject to confiscation.[92] When the trial is conducted before a jury, either party may insist upon a jury determination of the forfeiture issue.[93] Since the court's jurisdiction does not depend upon initial control of the res, it need not be seized before forfeiture is declared.[94] Although the courts are authorized to issue pretrial restraining orders to prevent depletion or transfer of property which the government contends is subject to confiscation,[95] many are hesitant to issue pre-trial restraining orders covering substitute property.[96] And there may be some lingering uncertainty as to whether such orders can be issued when the government has opted to use the good offices of the bridge statute[97] to accomplish what would otherwise be a civil forfeiture in conjunction with the criminal prosecution of the property owner.

Originally, section 2461(c) permitted criminal forfeiture under statutes that authorized civil forfeiture but that made no provision for criminal forfeiture.[98] In such cases, it declared that "upon conviction, the court shall order the forfeiture of the property in accordance with the procedures set forth in section 413 of the Controlled Substances Act (21 U.S.C. 853), other than subsection (d) of that section."[99] The current version of section 2461(c) appeared, unexplained, in the conference report on the bill subsequently enacted as the USA PATRIOT Improvement and Reauthorization Act.[100] The new language permits criminal forfeiture under the procedures of section 2461(c) whenever a civil forfeiture is authorized, regardless of whether the statute that authorizes the civil forfeiture also authorizes criminal forfeiture under different procedures.[101] It allows the government to elect to use section 2461(c)'s criminal forfeiture procedures even where alternative criminal forfeiture procedures were already available, hence perhaps its "uniform procedures" caption in the act.

In any event, the defense to criminal forfeiture differs somewhat from the defense to civil forfeiture. For example, since conviction is a prerequisite to confiscation, an overturned conviction or an acquittal will ordinarily preclude forfeiture.[102] Third party interests are less likely to be cut off by virtue of the property's proximity to criminal conduct simply because only the defendant's interest in the property is subject to confiscation and because bona fide purchaser exceptions are more common. Bona fide purchaser exceptions protect a good faith purchaser who acquired the property after commission of the offense—at which time title to the property vested in the United States—but before the declaration of forfeiture.[103]

After conviction of the defendant and after it has met its burden of establishing forfeitability by a preponderance of the evidence,[104] the government may elect to seek either confiscation of forfeitable property or a money judgment in the amount of its value.[105] If the government seeks confiscation, the court must determine whether the statutory nexus between the property and the crime of conviction exists.[106] If the government instead seeks a money judgment, the court must determine the amount the defendant must pay.[107] At that point, the court issues a preliminary forfeiture order or order for a money judgment against the defendant in favor of the government.[108] Upon the issuance of a preliminary forfeiture order, the government must proclaim its intent to dispose of the property and notify any third parties known to have an interest in the property.[109] Third parties with a legal interest in the forfeited property, other than the defendant, are then entitled to a judicial hearing,[110] provided they file a timely petition asserting their claims.[111] The court may amend its forfeiture order at any time, even a number of years after its initial entry.[112]

Third party claims may be grounded either in an assertion that they possessed a superior interest in the property at the time confiscation-trigger misconduct occurred or that they are good faith purchasers.[113] The courts will not recognize the unsecured claims of general creditors to the property,[114] but will look to state law to determine whether a third party has the requisite superior interest in the property.[115] Regardless of whether third parties assert a superior interest or the status of a good faith purchaser, they bear the burden of establishing their claim by a preponderance of the evidence.[116]

When the government is awarded a money judgment, it is not limited to the forfeitable assets the defendant has on hand at the time but may enforce the judgment against future assets as well.[117] In such cases, the courts are divided over the question of whether the government may enforce the judgment like any other judgment creditor or instead is limited to substitute assets and then only if the tainted assets are unavailable.[118]

Disposition of Forfeited Assets

Disposal of forfeited property is ordinarily a matter of statute. The pertinent statute may require that the proceeds of a confiscation be devoted to a single purpose, such as the support of education or deposit in the general fund. The statute may call for the destruction of property that cannot be lawfully possessed;[119] or authorize rewards, the settlement of claims against the property; or remission or mitigation.[120] It may permit distribution of the proceeds or a portion thereof as victim restitution.[121] Intergovernmental transfers and the use of special funds, however, are the hallmarks of the more prominent federal forfeiture statutes. The Attorney General and the Secretary of the Treasury enjoy wide latitude to transfer confiscated property to federal, state, local, and foreign law enforcement agencies to the extent of their participation in the case.[122] Nevertheless, both must be assured that the transfers will encourage law enforcement cooperation.[123]

Equitable Sharing and Adoptive Forfeitures

At one time, this "equitable sharing" transfer authority could not be used unless the Attorney General was convinced that confiscated property "[was] not so transferred to circumvent any requirement of State law that prohibits forfeiture or limits use or disposition of property forfeited to State or local agencies."[124] The restriction addressed sometimes controversial adoptive forfeitures.[125]

Adoptive forfeiture occurs when property is forfeitable under federal law because of its relation to conduct, such as drug trafficking, which violates both federal and state law. The Department of Justice "adopts," for processing under federal law, a forfeiture case brought to it by state or local law enforcement officials and in which the United States is not otherwise involved. Federal adoption is sometimes attractive because of the speed afforded by federal administrative forfeiture. It may also be attractive because forfeiture would be impossible or more difficult under state law or because law enforcement agencies would not share as extensively in the bounty of a successful forfeiture under state law.

The circumvention restriction is no longer in effect, but the Treasury and Justice Departments insist that state and local law enforcement agencies indicate the law enforcement purposes to which the transferred property is to be devoted and that the transfer will increase and not supplant law enforcement resources.[126] Moreover, the Attorney General has prohibited adoption subject to narrow exceptions.[127]

Federal Funds

The direct lion's share of confiscated cash or the proceeds from the sale of confiscated property, however, is now deposited in either the Department of Justice Asset Forfeiture Fund,[128] or the Department of the Treasury Forfeiture Fund.[129] The Comprehensive Crime Control Act of 1984 changed the way in which the federal government deals with revenues realized from the collection of fines and forfeitures.[130] Prior to the Crime Control legislation, virtually all of the money realized from fines and forfeitures, like most federal revenues, was deposited in the general fund of the United States Treasury. Through the enactment of annual appropriation bills, Congress permitted the money in the general fund to be spent to finance the activities it had authorized by statute.[131]

The Crime Control legislation created three new funds to receive revenues collected as part of the federal criminal law enforcement process, and Congress added a fourth a few years later. The Customs Forfeiture Fund, which became the Department of the Treasury Forfeiture Fund, and the Department of Justice Asset Forfeiture Fund collect confiscated cash and the proceeds from other forfeitures which are available for federal and state law enforcement purposes. The Treasury and Justice Department Funds together receive over $2 billion per year.[132]

Department of Justice Asset Forfeiture Fund

Congress created the Department of Justice Asset Forfeiture Fund[133] as part of the Comprehensive Crime Control Act of 1984.[134] The Department of Justice administers the Fund, which receives confiscated cash and the proceeds from forfeitures conducted under the laws enforced or administered by the Department of Justice and the Department of Justice's equitable share of forfeitures conducted by other state, federal, or foreign law enforcement agencies.[135]

Before confiscated cash or the proceeds from the sale of other confiscated property is paid into the Fund, the Attorney General may often authorize it to be transferred to or shared with other federal, state, local, or foreign law enforcement agencies who have participated in the investigation or proceedings that resulted in confiscation.[136]

After money has been paid into the Fund, the Attorney General may use it to pay:

- forfeiture related expenses,
- rewards to informants in illicit drug cases,[137]
- rewards to informants in forfeiture cases,[138]
- liens and mortgages against forfeited property,
- remission and mitigation in forfeiture cases,
- to equip cars, boats and planes for law enforcement purposes,[139]
- to purchase evidence of money laundering or of federal drug crimes,
- to pay state and local real estate taxes on forfeited property,
- to pay overtime, travel, training and the like for assisting state and local law enforcement personnel,
- federal correctional construction costs,
- the Special Forfeiture Fund,[140] and
- to pay for joint state, local and federal cooperative law enforcement operations.[141]

In the past, Congress has occasionally directed that the Fund be made available during a particular year and for a specific law enforcement purpose in anticipation of a surplus in the Fund after the statutory purposes had been served.[142] More recently, however, it has authorized the Attorney General to tap this "super surplus" for any law enforcement or Justice Department purpose.[143]

Although once money has been appropriated it may be spent in any fiscal year, access to the Fund is subject to annual appropriation for purposes of awarding rewards, purchasing evidence, and refitting of law enforcement vehicles.[144] For other purposes, Congress has enacted a permanent appropriation.[145]

Record-keeping functions are performed under contract paid out of the Fund. Originally, the Department of Justice did not use the Fund to pay the salaries and expenses of the United States Marshals Service personnel responsible for management of the seized assets and thc Fund. Except in the case of equitable sharing where they were covered by the administrative fee, those costs were generally handled through the overall salaries and expenses appropriation for the Marshals Service.[146] More recently, however, the Department has used the Fund to pay the salaries and other administrative costs of forfeiture-related personnel in the Marshals Service, the Department's Management Division's Asset Forfeiture Management Staff, and its Criminal Division's Asset Forfeiture and Money Laundering Section.[147]

Department of the Treasury Forfeiture Fund

The Department of the Treasury Forfeiture Fund began as the Customs Forfeiture Fund.[148] It is administered by the Secretary of the Treasury and receives deposits of currency and proceeds from forfeitures under laws enforced or administered by the Department of the Treasury or the Coast Guard, amounts received by the Department of the Treasury or the Coast Guard as an equitable share of a forfeiture conducted by other authorities, or income realized from investments on behalf of the Fund.[149] Earlier plans to merge the Justice and Treasury Department Funds[150] have never been acted upon.[151]

Before confiscated cash or the proceeds from the sale of other confiscated property are paid into the Fund, the Secretary of the Treasury may also authorize transfer of the property to other federal, state, local, or foreign law enforcement agencies who assisted in its forfeiture.[152]

After money has been paid into the Fund, the Secretary of the Treasury makes one portion available to the Coast Guard in an amount reflecting its contributions.[153] The moneys available for the Coast Guard may be used to equip cars, boats and planes for law enforcement purposes, to pay overtime and similar expenses for state and local law enforcement officers in a joint operation, and to satisfy environmental requirements before sinking hazards to navigation.[154]

The Fund is otherwise available to the Secretary of the Treasury for a number of purposes, including paying:

- expenses associated with the forfeiture,[155]
- claims against the property,[156]
- liens and mortgages against forfeited property,[157]
- remission and mitigation,[158]
- rewards for information concerning violations of the customs laws,[159]
- rewards for information or assistance resulting in a Department of Treasury forfeiture,[160]
- to equip cars, boats and planes for law enforcement purposes,[161]
- to purchase evidence of various crimes traditionally within the jurisdiction of the Department,[162]
- to reimburse the expenses of private individuals associated with Department law enforcement activities,[163]
- for equitable sharing, if not accomplished prior to deposit in the Fund,[164]
- for "overtime salaries, travel, fuel, training, equipment, and other similar costs of State and local law enforcement officers that are incurred in joint law enforcement operations,"[165] and
- to train foreign law enforcement personnel in Department forfeiture related matters.[166]

Congress has established a permanent appropriation to pay for forfeiture-related expenses, for the settlement of claims, liens, and mortgages, for remission and mitigation, rewards under the customs laws, and equitable sharing.[167]

Special Forfeiture Fund

The Special Forfeiture Fund originally financed the Office of National Drug Control Policy (the "drug czar"),[168] and fed off the Department of Justice Asset Forfeiture Fund. The Special Forfeiture Fund has since been abolished.[169]

Crime Victims Fund

The Justice Department's Office for Victims of Crime in the Office of Justice Programs administers the Crime Victims Fund created by the Crime Control Act.[170] The Fund receives revenues collected as fines for violations of federal criminal law, as special assessments against misdemeanor offenders, as a consequence of jumping bail,[171] and from the operation of the espionage provisions,[172] and the "Son of Sam" forfeiture provisions.[173] The Fund is available for grants to the States for crime victim compensation and assistance programs, for HHS child-abuse prevention and treatment grants, and to reimburse the courts for administrative costs.[174]

CONSTITUTIONAL CONSIDERATIONS

At one time, it could safely be said that the Constitution afforded state and federal governments extraordinary latitude to enact and enforce forfeiture statutes; forfeiture often seemed unusual, sometimes severe, and occasionally unfair, yet with rare exceptions it was not unconstitutional. In 1993, the Court handed down a series of decisions that seemed to signal its uneasiness with the trends in forfeiture law.[175] Yet thereafter, it seems to deny any inclination to totally repudiate the government's broad forfeiture authority,[176] although it incrementally began to define the constitutional borders of that authority.[177]

Eighth Amendment

The Eighth Amendment states in its entirety that "[e]xcessive bail shall not be required, nor excessive fines imposed, nor cruel and unusual punishments inflicted." The lower courts had on several occasions held that criminal forfeitures are subject to Eighth Amendment analysis,[178] but Eighth Amendment concerns were generally considered irrelevant in civil forfeiture cases because the Amendment was thought to be limited to criminal punishments while civil forfeitures were remedial and thus neither criminal nor punishments.[179]

This changed in 1993 when the Supreme Court announced that the Eighth Amendment's excessive fines clause applies not only to criminal forfeitures but to some civil forfeitures as well.[180] The full impact of those decisions remained uncertain initially, because the Court declined to articulate a test by which to measure particular forfeitures against the clause's proscriptions.[181] Then in *Bajakajian* it selected the standard used as the measure under the parallel cruel and unusual punishment clause of the Eighth Amendment: "a punitive forfeiture violates the Excessive Fines Clause if it is grossly disproportionate to the gravity of a defendant's offense."[182]

Later federal appellate courts tend to measure the facts before them against those in *Bajakajian*. Several circuits begin with a standard distilled from the factors there;[183] others simply point to the stark factual differences between *Bajakajian* and the cases before them.[184] In either case, a punitive forfeiture ordinarily will not be considered an excessive fine, if it is distinguishable on one or more of the grounds *Bajakajian* mentioned as indicative of gross disproportionality, for example, a single crime, unrelated to any other criminality, causing relatively little harm, but resulting in a forfeiture greatly disproportionate to the authorized fine.[185]

Double Jeopardy

Historically, the procedure used to accomplish forfeiture made a difference for purposes of the Fifth Amendment's double jeopardy clause.[186] Where confiscation was accomplished through civil, in rem proceedings against the property, a prior trial of the property owner resulting in either acquittal or conviction was no bar to subsequent forfeiture proceedings.[187] Where conviction was a prerequisite to forfeiture, if double jeopardy precluded further trial and conviction, it likewise precluded forfeiture.

The Supreme Court's conclusion in *Austin* that certain civil forfeitures might be considered punitive for purposes of the Eighth Amendment's excessive fines clause seemed to have obvious double jeopardy implications. In fact, the Court went so far as to note that its past decisions declining to apply the double jeopardy clause to civil forfeitures arose "only in cases where the forfeiture could properly be characterized as remedial."[188] Yet, the Court in *United States v. Ursery* reaffirmed its faith in the traditional tests.[189] Forfeitures that Congress has designated as remedial civil sanctions do not implicate double jeopardy concerns unless "the statutory scheme [is] so punitive either in purpose or effect as to negate Congress' intention to establish a civil remedial mechanism."[190]

Sixth Amendment

The Sixth Amendment assures the accused in criminal proceedings the right to a jury trial, to the assistance of counsel, and to confrontation of accusers. The Supreme Court long ago held that the right to confrontation does not apply in civil forfeiture cases and has not revisited the issue.[191] The right to the assistance of counsel in criminal cases does not prevent the government from confiscating tainted fees paid to counsel;[192] or, upon a probable cause showing, from obtaining a restraining order to freeze assets preventing the payment of attorneys' fees;[193] or entitle an otherwise indigent property owner to the appointment of counsel for substitute asset forfeiture proceedings.[194] The Amendment is by its terms only applicable "in all criminal prosecutions," and consequently there is no constitutionally required right to assistance of counsel in civil forfeiture cases.[195]

The Court's opinion in *Libretti,* to the effect that there is no right to a jury trial on disputed factual issues in criminal forfeiture, rests on a somewhat battered foundation. At the time, it was thought that "there [was] no Sixth Amendment right to jury sentencing, even where the sentence turns on specific finding of fact."[196] Thereafter, the Court explained that *McMillan* impermissibly slighted the right to have certain sentencing factors decided by the jury. "Any fact that increases the penalty for a crime beyond the prescribed statutory maximum," the Court declared in *Apprendi v. New Jersey*, 530 U.S. 466, 490 (2000), "must be submitted to a jury, and proved beyond a reasonable doubt." The erosion of *McMillan* notwithstanding, the fact that criminal forfeiture is a penalty *within* "the prescribed statutory maximum" and that Rule 32.2 of the Federal Rules of Criminal Procedure affords an expanded jury determination right would seem to shield federal criminal forfeiture procedures from *Apprendi*-based attacks. Although *Apprendi*'s implications for the preponderance standard might appear slightly more ominous, particularly after the Court found that the *Apprendi* rule applies to fines as well as terms of imprisonment,[197] the federal appellate courts have either explicitly or implicitly declined to apply *Apprendi* to criminal forfeitures.[198]

Due Process

Due process objections can come in such a multitude of variations that general statements are hazardous. That said, the courts have acknowledged that due process demands that those with an interest in the property which the government seeks to confiscate be given notice and opportunity for a hearing to contest.[199] Actual notice is not required but the government's efforts must be "reasonably calculated, under all the circumstances, to apprise" of the opportunity to contest.[200] In some instances, due process permits the initiation of forfeiture proceedings by seizing the personal property in question without first giving the property owner either notice or the prior opportunity of a hearing to contest the seizure and confiscation.[201] But absent exigent circumstances, the owner is entitled to the opportunity for a pre-seizure hearing in the case of real property where there is no real danger that the property will be spirited away in order to frustrate efforts to secure in rem jurisdiction over it.[202]

Due process also requires a probable cause determination of the forfeitability of property made subject to a post-seizure, pretrial restraining order designed to prevent dissipation.[203] Due process does not require an adversarial determination of the existence of probable cause; a grand jury indictment will do.[204]

While due process clearly limits at some point the circumstances under which the property of an innocent owner may be confiscated,[205] the Court has declined the opportunity to broadly assert that due process uniformly precludes confiscation of the property of an innocent owner, *Bennis v. Michigan.*[206] *Bennis*, however, is a 5-4 decision in which Justice Ginsburg joined the majority but filed a concurring opinion in which she emphasized the importance of the case's somewhat individualistic facts.[207]

Any delay between seizure and hearing offends due process only when it fails to meet the test applied in speedy trial cases: Is the delay unreasonable given the length of delay, the reasons for the delay, the claimant's assertion of his or her rights, and prejudice to the claimant?[208]

In other challenges, the lower federal courts have found that due process permits: the procedure of shifting the burden of proof to a forfeiture claimant after the government has shown probable cause and allows use of a probable cause standard in civil forfeitures;[209] postponement of the determination of third-party interests in criminal forfeiture cases until after trial in the main;[210] an 11-year delay between issuance of a criminal forfeiture order and amendment of the original order to reach overseas assets;[211] and fugitive disentitlement under 28 U.S.C. 2466.[212] On the other hand, a court may not order the criminal forfeiture of defendant's property if it has totally failed to honor the procedural requirements of Rule 32.2(b) of the Federal Rules of Criminal Procedure.[213]

Whether in cases occasioned by delay, failure of notice, or want of predeprivational hearing for real property, the lower courts became somewhat ensnarled in the consequences that flow from a finding that the government has violated due process demands in a civil forfeiture context. Some concluded that the lack of due process voided the purported administrative or judicial forfeiture even if an intervening statute of limitations barred relitigation of confiscation proceedings;[214] others determined that the forfeiture need not be vacated[215] although they sometimes held that the property owner might be entitled to disgorgement or interest.[216] CAFRA resolved the conflict by establishing a timetable within which the government must restart forfeiture proceedings following a claimant's successful motion setting aside an earlier confiscation declaration.[217]

Finally, counsel in *Monsanto* and *Caplin & Drysdale*, challenged on both Sixth Amendment right to counsel and Fifth Amendment due process grounds the confiscation of property paid for, and destined to pay for, the services of defense counsel. The Supreme Court rejected both assertions.[218] The Court left open, however, the question of whether due process requires notice and the opportunity for a hearing before a restraining order may be issued.[219] At least two circuits have concluded that absent extraordinary circumstances due process requires notice and an opportunity to be heard prior to the issuance of a restraining order.[220] In the presence of extraordinary circumstances, notice and hearing may be postponed until soon after issuance of the order as long as the opportunity is afforded before trial.[221]

Article III

Section 3 of Article III of the United States Constitution does not appear to threaten most contemporary forfeiture statutes. It provides in part that "no attainder of treason shall work corruption of blood, or forfeiture except during the life of the person attainted." The section on its face seems to restrict forfeiture only in treason cases, but at least one court has suggested a broader scope.[222]

Even if Article III when read in conjunction with the due process clause reaches not only treason but all crimes, its prohibitions run only to forfeiture of estate. They do not address statutory forfeitures of the type currently found in state and federal law. The critical distinction between forfeiture of estate and statutory forfeiture is that in the first all of the defendant's property, related or unrelated to the offense and acquired before, during, or after the crime, is confiscated. In the second, confiscation is possible only if the property is related to the criminal conduct in the manner defined by the statute. Some have suggested that Congress intended to revive forfeiture of estate when it crafted the RICO criminal forfeiture provisions.[223] The courts have nevertheless upheld the RICO provisions in the face of Article III challenges.[224]

Article III also declares that the judicial power of the United States extends to certain cases and controversies.[225] If a litigant has no judicially recognized interest in the outcome of such a case or controversy, he is said to lack standing and the court lacks jurisdiction to proceed.[226] In some instances, a statute or rule imposes additional, more demanding standing requirements. So it is with civil forfeiture.[227] As a threshold matter, however, a claimant must satisfy Article III standing requirements.

In order to meet the case-or-controversy requirement of Article III, a plaintiff (including a civil forfeiture claimant) must establish the three elements of standing, namely, that the plaintiff suffered an injury in fact, that there is a causal connection between the injury and conduct complained of, and that it is likely the injury will be redressed by a favorable decision. Claimants in civil forfeiture actions can satisfy this test by showing that they have a colorable interest in the property, which includes an ownership interest or a possessory interest. Article III's standing requirement is thereby satisfied because the owner or possessor of property that has been seized necessarily suffers an injury that can be redressed at least in part by the return of the seized property.[228]

Fourth Amendment

The Fourth Amendment condemns unreasonable search and seizures.[229] The hallmark of a seizure which is not unreasonable is the presence of warrant issued upon probable cause. Nevertheless, warrantless seizures or those grounded in less than probable cause are not unreasonable under all circumstances.[230] For example, authorities may seize property without a warrant based on exceptions recognized for searches incident to arrest or for the search of vehicles.[231] Moreover, several of the older civil forfeiture statutes, particularly those arising in a customs or maritime context, reflected the traditional view that contraband and other forfeitable property may be seized without observing the normal demands of the Amendment's requirements.[232] Some question may persist over whether warrantless seizures or seizures with less than probable cause are generally permissible in forfeiture cases, regardless of the want of any customs or maritime connection.[233]

In any event, unlawfully seized evidence may not be used in the forfeiture proceedings,[234] but unlawful seizure of the res does not doom the proceedings as long as there is sufficient untainted evidence to support the confiscation.[235]

Ex Post Facto

Neither the states nor the federal government may enact ex post facto laws.[236] The prohibition applies both to laws which make criminal conduct which was innocent when committed and laws which increase the penalties for a crime over those which attached when a crime was committed.[237] The ex post facto bar, however, poses no impediment to the application of a new sanction such as forfeiture to a continuing crime which straddles the date of enactment.[238]

First Amendment

When confiscation involves material entitled to First Amendment protection, more demanding standards must be met. In *Fort Wayne Books, Inc. v. Indiana*,[239] the Court held that while a single book or film might be seized upon an ex parte probable cause showing, books or films could not be taken completely out of circulation until after an adversary hearing on their obscenity. On the other hand, the First Amendment stands as no bar to the use of criminal forfeiture to punish those convicted of engaging in the commercial exploitation of obscenity,[240] nor to the use of civil forfeiture to confiscate equipment used by an unlicensed radio station.[241]

ATTACHMENTS

18 U.S.C. 981. Civil Forfeiture (text)

(a)(1) The following property is subject to forfeiture to the United States:

(A) Any property, real or personal, involved in a transaction or attempted transaction in violation of section 1956, 1957 or 1960 of this title, or any property traceable to such property.

(B) Any property, real or personal, within the jurisdiction of the United States, constituting, derived from, or traceable to, any proceeds obtained directly or indirectly from an offense against a foreign nation, or any property used to facilitate such an offense, if the offense—

(i) involves trafficking in nuclear, chemical, biological, or radiological weapons technology or material, or the manufacture, importation, sale, or distribution of a controlled substance (as that term is defined for purposes of the Controlled Substances Act), or any other conduct described in section 1956(c)(7)(B);

(ii) would be punishable within the jurisdiction of the foreign nation by death or imprisonment for a term exceeding 1 year; and

(iii) would be punishable under the laws of the United States by imprisonment for a term exceeding 1 year, if the act or activity constituting the offense had occurred within the jurisdiction of the United States.

(C) Any property, real or personal, which constitutes or is derived from proceeds traceable to a violation of section 215, 471, 472, 473, 474, 476, 477, 478, 479, 480, 481, 485, 486, 487, 488, 501, 502, 510, 542, 545, 555, 656, 657, 670, 842, 844, 1005, 1006, 1007, 1014, 1028, 1029, 1030, 1032, or 1344 of this title or any offense constituting "specified unlawful activity" (as defined in section 1956(c)(7) of this title), or a conspiracy to commit such offense.

(D) Any property, real or personal, which represents or is traceable to the gross receipts obtained, directly or indirectly, from a violation of—

(i) section 666(a)(1) (relating to Federal program fraud);

(ii) section 1001 (relating to fraud and false statements);

(iii) section 1031 (relating to major fraud against the United States);

(iv) section 1032 (relating to concealment of assets from conservator or receiver of insured financial institution);

(v) section 1341 (relating to mail fraud); or

(vi) section 1343 (relating to wire fraud),

if such violation relates to the sale of assets acquired or held by the Federal Deposit Insurance Corporation, as conservator or receiver for a financial institution, or any other conservator for a financial institution appointed by the Office of the Comptroller of the Currency or the National Credit Union Administration, as conservator or liquidating agent for a financial institution.

(E) With respect to an offense listed in subsection (a)(1)(D) committed for the purpose of executing or attempting to execute any scheme or artifice to defraud, or for obtaining money or property by means of false or fraudulent statements, pretenses, representations or promises, the gross receipts of such an offense shall include all property, real or personal, tangible or intangible, which thereby is obtained, directly or indirectly.

(F) Any property, real or personal, which represents or is traceable to the gross proceeds obtained, directly or indirectly, from a violation of—

(i) section 511 (altering or removing motor vehicle identification numbers);

(ii) section 553 (importing or exporting stolen motor vehicles);

(iii) section 2119 (armed robbery of automobiles);

(iv) section 2312 (transporting stolen motor vehicles in interstate commerce); or

(v) section 2313 (possessing or selling a stolen motor vehicle that has moved in interstate commerce).

(G) All assets, foreign or domestic—

(i) of any individual, entity, or organization engaged in planning or perpetrating any Federal crime of terrorism (as defined in section 2332b(g)(5)) against the United States, citizens or residents of the United States, or their property, and all assets, foreign or domestic, affording any person a source of influence over any such entity or organization;

(ii) acquired or maintained by any person with the intent and for the purpose of supporting, planning, conducting, or concealing Federal crime of terrorism (as defined in section 2332b(g)(5)) against the United States, citizens or residents of the United States, or their property; or

(iii) derived from, involved in, or used or intended to be used to commit any Federal crime of terrorism (as defined in section 2332b(g)(5)) against the United States, citizens or residents of the United States, or their property.

(iv) of any individual, entity, or organization engaged in planning or perpetrating any act of international terrorism (as defined in section 2331) against an international organization (as defined in section 209 of the State Department Basic Authorities Act of 1956 (22 U.S.C. 4309(b)) or against any foreign Government. Where the property sought for forfeiture is located beyond the territorial boundaries of the United States, an act in furtherance of such planning or perpetration must have occurred within the jurisdiction of the United States.

(H) Any property, real or personal, involved in a violation or attempted violation, or which constitutes or is derived from proceeds traceable to a violation, of section 2339C of this title.

(2) For purposes of paragraph (1), the term "proceeds" is defined as follows:

(A) In cases involving illegal goods, illegal services, unlawful activities, and telemarketing and health care fraud schemes, the term "proceeds" means property of any kind obtained directly or indirectly, as the result of the commission of the offense giving rise to forfeiture, and any property traceable thereto, and is not limited to the net gain or profit realized from the offense.

(B) In cases involving lawful goods or lawful services that are sold or provided in an illegal manner, the term "proceeds" means the amount of money acquired through the illegal transactions resulting in the forfeiture, less the direct costs incurred in providing the goods or services. The claimant shall have the burden of proof with respect to the issue of direct costs. The direct costs shall not include any part of the overhead expenses of the entity providing the goods or services, or any part of the income taxes paid by the entity.

(C) In cases involving fraud in the process of obtaining a loan or extension of credit, the court shall allow the claimant a deduction from the forfeiture to the extent that the loan was repaid, or the debt was satisfied, without any financial loss to the victim.

(b)(1) Except as provided in section 985, any property subject to forfeiture to the United States under subsection (a) may be seized by the Attorney General and, in the case of property involved in a violation investigated by the Secretary of the Treasury or the United States Postal Service, the property may also be seized by the Secretary of the Treasury or the Postal Service, respectively.

(2) Seizures pursuant to this section shall be made pursuant to a warrant obtained in the same manner as provided for a search warrant under the Federal Rules of Criminal Procedure, except that a seizure may be made without a warrant if—

(A) a complaint for forfeiture has been filed in the United States district court and the court issued an arrest warrant in rem pursuant to the Supplemental Rules for Certain Admiralty and Maritime Claims;

(B) there is probable cause to believe that the property is subject to forfeiture and—

(i) the seizure is made pursuant to a lawful arrest or search; or

(ii) another exception to the Fourth Amendment warrant requirement would apply; or

(C) the property was lawfully seized by a State or local law enforcement agency and transferred to a Federal agency.

(3) Notwithstanding the provisions of rule 41(a) of the Federal Rules of Criminal Procedure, a seizure warrant may be issued pursuant to this subsection by a judicial officer in any district in which a forfeiture action against the property may be filed under section 1355(b) of title 28, and may be executed in any district in which the property is found, or transmitted to the central authority of any foreign state for service in accordance with any treaty or other international agreement. Any motion for the return of property seized

under this section shall be filed in the district court in which the seizure warrant was issued or in the district court for the district in which the property was seized.

(4)(A) If any person is arrested or charged in a foreign country in connection with an offense that would give rise to the forfeiture of property in the United States under this section or under the Controlled Substances Act, the Attorney General may apply to any Federal judge or magistrate judge in the district in which the property is located for an ex parte order restraining the property subject to forfeiture for not more than 30 days, except that the time may be extended for good cause shown at a hearing conducted in the manner provided in rule 43(e) of the Federal Rules of Civil Procedure.

(B) The application for the restraining order shall set forth the nature and circumstances of the foreign charges and the basis for belief that the person arrested or charged has property in the United States that would be subject to forfeiture, and shall contain a statement that the restraining order is needed to preserve the availability of property for such time as is necessary to receive evidence from the foreign country or elsewhere in support of probable cause for the seizure of the property under this subsection.

(c) Property taken or detained under this section shall not be repleviable, but shall be deemed to be in the custody of the Attorney General, the Secretary of the Treasury, or the Postal Service, as the case may be, subject only to the orders and decrees of the court or the official having jurisdiction thereof. Whenever property is seized under this subsection, the Attorney General, the Secretary of the Treasury, or the Postal Service, as the case may be, may—

(1) place the property under seal;

(2) remove the property to a place designated by him; or

(3) require that the General Services Administration take custody of the property and remove it, if practicable, to an appropriate location for disposition in accordance with law.

(d) For purposes of this section, the provisions of the customs laws relating to the seizure, summary and judicial forfeiture, condemnation of property for violation of the customs laws, the disposition of such property or the proceeds from the sale of such property under this section, the remission or mitigation of such forfeitures, and the compromise of claims (19 U.S.C. 1602 et seq.), insofar as they are applicable and not inconsistent with the provisions of this section, shall apply to seizures and forfeitures incurred, or alleged to have been incurred, under this section, except that such duties as are imposed upon the customs officer or any other person with respect to the seizure and forfeiture of property under the customs laws shall be performed with respect to seizures and forfeitures of property under this section by such officers, agents, or other persons as may be authorized or designated for that purpose by the Attorney General, the Secretary of the Treasury, or the Postal Service, as the case may be. The Attorney General shall have sole responsibility for disposing of petitions for remission or mitigation with respect to property involved in a judicial forfeiture proceeding.

(e) Notwithstanding any other provision of the law, except section 3 of the Anti Drug Abuse Act of 1986, the Attorney General, the Secretary of the Treasury, or the Postal Service, as the case may be, is authorized to retain property forfeited pursuant to this section, or to transfer such property on such terms and conditions as he may determine—

(1) to any other Federal agency;

(2) to any State or local law enforcement agency which participated directly in any of the acts which led to the seizure or forfeiture of the property;

(3) in the case of property referred to in subsection (a)(1)(C), to any Federal financial institution regulatory agency—

(A) to reimburse the agency for payments to claimants or creditors of the institution; and

(B) to reimburse the insurance fund of the agency for losses suffered by the fund as a result of the receivership or liquidation;

(4) in the case of property referred to in subsection (a)(1)(C), upon the order of the appropriate Federal financial institution regulatory agency, to the financial institution as restitution, with the value of the property so transferred to be set off against any amount later recovered by the financial institution as compensatory damages in any State or Federal proceeding;

(5) in the case of property referred to in subsection (a)(1)(C), to any Federal financial institution regulatory agency, to the extent of the agency's contribution of resources to, or expenses involved in, the seizure and forfeiture, and the investigation leading directly to the seizure and forfeiture, of such property;

(6) as restoration to any victim of the offense giving rise to the forfeiture, including, in the case of a money laundering offense, any offense constituting the underlying specified unlawful activity; or

(7) In the case of property referred to in subsection (a)(1)(D), to the Resolution Trust Corporation, the Federal Deposit Insurance Corporation, or any other Federal financial institution regulatory agency (as defined in section 8(e)(7)(D) of the Federal Deposit Insurance Act).

The Attorney General, the Secretary of the Treasury, or the Postal Service, as the case may be, shall ensure the equitable transfer pursuant to paragraph

(2) of any forfeited property to the appropriate State or local law enforcement agency so as to reflect generally the contribution of any such agency participating directly in any of the acts which led to the seizure or forfeiture of such property. A decision by the Attorney General, the Secretary of the Treasury, or the Postal Service pursuant to paragraph (2) shall not be subject to review. The United States shall not be liable in any action arising out of the use of any property the custody of which was transferred pursuant to this section to any non-Federal agency. The Attorney General, the Secretary of the Treasury, or the Postal Service may order the discontinuance of any forfeiture proceedings under this section in favor of the institution of forfeiture proceedings by State or local authorities under an appropriate State or local statute. After the filing of a complaint for forfeiture under this section, the Attorney General may seek dismissal of the complaint in favor of forfeiture proceedings under State or local law. Whenever forfeiture proceedings are discontinued by the United States in favor of State or local proceedings, the United States may transfer custody and possession of the seized property to the appropriate State or local official immediately upon the initiation of the proper actions by such officials. Whenever forfeiture proceedings are discontinued by the United States in favor of State or local proceedings, notice shall be sent to all known interested parties advising them of the discontinuance or dismissal. The United States shall not be liable in any action arising out of the seizure, detention, and transfer of seized property to State or local officials. The United States shall not be liable in any action arising out of a transfer under paragraph (3), (4), or (5) of this subsection.

(f) All right, title, and interest in property described in subsection (a) of this section shall vest in the United States upon commission of the act giving rise to forfeiture under this section.

(g)(1) Upon the motion of the United States, the court shall stay the civil forfeiture proceeding if the court determines that civil discovery will adversely affect the ability of the Government to conduct a related criminal investigation or the prosecution of a related criminal case.

(2) Upon the motion of a claimant, the court shall stay the civil forfeiture proceeding with respect to that claimant if the court determines that—

(A) the claimant is the subject of a related criminal investigation or case;

(B) the claimant has standing to assert a claim in the civil forfeiture proceeding; and

(C) continuation of the forfeiture proceeding will burden the right of the claimant against self-incrimination in the related investigation or case.

(3) With respect to the impact of civil discovery described in paragraphs (1) and (2), the court may determine that a stay is unnecessary if a protective order limiting discovery would protect the interest of one party without unfairly limiting the ability of the opposing party to pursue the civil case.

In no case, however, shall the court impose a protective order as an alternative to a stay if the effect of such protective order would be to allow one party to pursue discovery while the other party is substantially unable to do so.

(4) In this subsection, the terms "related criminal case" and "related criminal investigation" mean an actual prosecution or investigation in progress at the time at which the request for the stay, or any subsequent motion to lift the stay is made. In determining whether a criminal case or investigation is "related" to a civil forfeiture proceeding, the court shall consider the degree of similarity between the parties, witnesses, facts, and circumstances involved in the two proceedings, without requiring an identity with respect to any one or more factors.

(5) In requesting a stay under paragraph (1), the Government may, in appropriate cases, submit evidence ex parte in order to avoid disclosing any matter that may adversely affect an ongoing criminal investigation or pending criminal trial.

(6) Whenever a civil forfeiture proceeding is stayed pursuant to this subsection, the court shall enter any order necessary to preserve the value of the property or to protect the rights of lienholders or other persons with an interest in the property while the stay is in effect.

(7) A determination by the court that the claimant has standing to request a stay pursuant to paragraph (2) shall apply only to this subsection and shall not preclude the Government from objecting to the standing of the claimant by dispositive motion or at the time of trial.

(h) In addition to the venue provided for in section 1395 of title 28 or any other provision of law, in the case of property of a defendant charged with a violation that is the basis for forfeiture of the property under this section, a proceeding for forfeiture under this section may be brought in the judicial district in which the defendant owning such property is found or in the judicial district in which the criminal prosecution is brought.

(*i*)(1) Whenever property is civilly or criminally forfeited under this chapter, the Attorney General or the Secretary of the Treasury, as the case may be, may transfer the forfeited personal property or the proceeds of the sale of any forfeited personal or real property to any foreign country which participated directly or indirectly in the seizure or forfeiture of the property, if such a transfer—

(A) has been agreed to by the Secretary of State;

(B) is authorized in an international agreement between the United States and the foreign country; and

(C) is made to a country which, if applicable, has been certified under section 481(h) of the Foreign Assistance Act of 1961.

A decision by the Attorney General or the Secretary of the Treasury pursuant to this paragraph shall not be subject to review. The foreign country shall, in the event of a transfer of property or proceeds of sale of property under this subsection, bear all expenses incurred by the United States in the seizure, maintenance, inventory, storage, forfeiture, and disposition of the property, and all transfer costs. The payment of all such expenses, and the transfer of assets pursuant to this paragraph, shall be upon such terms and conditions as the Attorney General or the Secretary of the Treasury may, in his discretion, set.

(2) The provisions of this section shall not be construed as limiting or superseding any other authority of the United States to provide assistance to a foreign country in obtaining property related to a crime committed in the foreign country, including property which is sought as evidence of a crime committed in the foreign country.

(3) A certified order or judgment of forfeiture by a court of competent jurisdiction of a foreign country concerning property which is the subject of forfeiture under this section and was determined by such court to be the type of property described in subsection (a)(1)(B) of this section, and any certified recordings or transcripts of testimony taken in a foreign judicial proceeding concerning such order or judgment of forfeiture, shall be admissible in evidence in a proceeding brought pursuant to this section. Such certified order or judgment of forfeiture, when admitted into evidence, shall constitute probable cause that the property forfeited by such order or judgment of forfeiture is subject to forfeiture under this section and creates a rebuttable presumption of the forfeitability of such property under this section.

(4) A certified order or judgment of conviction by a court of competent jurisdiction of a foreign country concerning an unlawful drug activity which gives rise to forfeiture under this section and any certified recordings or transcripts of testimony taken in a foreign judicial proceeding concerning such order or judgment of conviction shall be admissible in evidence in a proceeding brought pursuant to this section. Such certified order or judgment of conviction, when admitted into evidence, creates a rebuttable presumption that the unlawful drug activity giving rise to forfeiture under this section has occurred.

(5) The provisions of paragraphs (3) and (4) of this subsection shall not be construed as limiting the admissibility of any evidence otherwise admissible, nor shall they limit the ability of the United States to establish probable cause that property is subject to forfeiture by any evidence otherwise admissible.

(j) For purposes of this section—

(1) the term "Attorney General" means the Attorney General or his delegate; and

(2) the term "Secretary of the Treasury" means the Secretary of the Treasury or his delegate.

(k) (k) Interbank accounts.—

(1) In general.—

(A) In general.—For the purpose of a forfeiture under this section or under the Controlled Substances Act (21 U.S.C. 801 et seq.), if funds are deposited into an account at a foreign bank, and that foreign bank has an interbank account in the United States with a covered financial institution (as defined in section 5318(j)(1) of title 31), the funds shall be deemed to have been deposited into the interbank account in the United States, and any restraining order, seizure warrant, or arrest warrant in rem regarding the funds may be served on the covered financial institution, and funds in the interbank account, up to the value of the funds deposited into the account at the foreign bank, may be restrained, seized, or arrested.

(B) Authority to suspend.—The Attorney General, in consultation with the Secretary of the Treasury, may suspend or terminate a forfeiture under this section if the Attorney General determines that a conflict of law exists between the laws of the jurisdiction in which the foreign bank is located and the laws of the United States with respect to liabilities arising from the restraint, seizure, or arrest of such funds, and that such suspension or termination would be in the interest of justice and would not harm the national interests of the United States.

(2) No requirement for Government to trace funds.—If a forfeiture action is brought against funds that are restrained, seized, or arrested under paragraph (1), it shall not be necessary for the Government to establish that the funds are directly traceable to the funds that were deposited into the foreign bank, nor shall it be necessary for the Government to rely on the application of section 984.

(3) Claims brought by owner of the funds.—If a forfeiture action is instituted against funds restrained, seized, or arrested under paragraph (1), the owner of the funds deposited into the account at the foreign bank may contest the forfeiture by filing a claim under section 983.

(4) Definitions.—For purposes of this subsection, the following definitions shall apply:

(A) Interbank account.—The term "interbank account" has the same meaning as in section 984(c)(2)(B).

(B) Owner.—

(i) In general.—Except as provided in clause (ii), the term "owner"—

(I) means the person who was the owner, as that term is defined in section 983(d)(6), of the funds that were deposited into the foreign bank at the time such funds were deposited; and

(II) does not include either the foreign bank or any financial institution acting as an intermediary in the transfer of the funds into the interbank account.

(ii) Exception.—The foreign bank may be considered the "owner" of the funds (and no other person shall qualify as the owner of such funds) only if—

(I) the basis for the forfeiture action is wrongdoing committed by the foreign bank; or

(II) the foreign bank establishes, by a preponderance of the evidence, that prior to the restraint, seizure, or arrest of the funds, the foreign bank had discharged all or part of its obligation to the prior owner of the funds, in which case the foreign bank shall be deemed the owner of the funds to the extent of such discharged obligation.

18 U.S.C. 982. Criminal Forfeiture (text)

(a)(1) The court, in imposing sentence on a person convicted of an offense in violation of section 1956, 1957, or 1960 of this title, shall order that the person forfeit to the United States any property, real or personal, involved in such offense, or any property traceable to such property.

(2) The court, in imposing sentence on a person convicted of a violation of, or a conspiracy to violate—

(A) section 215, 656, 657, 1005, 1006, 1007, 1014, 1341, 1343, or 1344 of this title, affecting a financial institution, or

(B) section 471, 472, 473, 474, 476, 477, 478, 479, 480, 481, 485, 486, 487, 488, 501, 502, 510, 542, 545, 555, 842, 844, 1028, 1029, or 1030 of this title, shall order that the person forfeit to the United States any property constituting, or derived from, proceeds the person obtained directly or indirectly, as the result of such violation.

(3) The court, in imposing a sentence on a person convicted of an offense under—

(A) section 666(a)(1) (relating to Federal program fraud);

(B) section 1001 (relating to fraud and false statements);

(C) section 1031 (relating to major fraud against the United States);

(D) section 1032 (relating to concealment of assets from conservator, receiver, or liquidating agent of insured financial institution);

(E) section 1341 (relating to mail fraud); or

(F) section 1343 (relating to wire fraud), involving the sale of assets acquired or held by the Federal Deposit Insurance Corporation, as conservator or receiver for a financial institution or any other conservator for a financial institution appointed by the Office of the Comptroller of the Currency or the National Credit Union Administration, as conservator or liquidating agent for a financial institution, shall order that the person forfeit to the United States any property, real or personal, which represents or is traceable to the gross receipts obtained, directly or indirectly, as a result of such violation.

(4) With respect to an offense listed in subsection (a)(3) committed for the purpose of executing or attempting to execute any scheme or artifice to defraud, or for obtaining money or property by means of false or fraudulent statements, pretenses, representations, or promises, the gross receipts of such an offense shall include any property, real or personal, tangible or intangible, which is obtained, directly or indirectly, as a result of such offense.

(5) The court, in imposing sentence on a person convicted of a violation or conspiracy to violate—

(A) section 511 (altering or removing motor vehicle identification numbers);

(B) section 553 (importing or exporting stolen motor vehicles);

(C) section 2119 (armed robbery of automobiles);

(D) section 2312 (transporting stolen motor vehicles in interstate commerce); or

(E) section 2313 (possessing or selling a stolen motor vehicle that has moved in interstate commerce); shall order that the person forfeit to the United States any property, real or personal, which represents or is traceable to the gross proceeds obtained, directly or indirectly, as a result of such violation. (6)(A) The court, in imposing sentence on a person convicted of a violation of, or conspiracy to violate, section 274(a), 274A(a)(1), or 274A(a)(2) of the Immigration and Nationality Act or section 554, 1425, 1426, 1427, 1541, 1542, 1543, 1544, or 1546 of this title, or a violation of, or conspiracy to violate, section 1028 of this title if committed in connection with passport or visa issuance or use, shall order that the person forfeit to the United States, regardless of any provision of State law—

(i) any conveyance, including any vessel, vehicle, or aircraft used in the commission of the offense of which the person is convicted; and

(ii) any property real or personal—

(I) that constitutes, or is derived from or is traceable to the proceeds obtained directly or indirectly from the commission of the offense of which the person is convicted; or

(II) that is used to facilitate, or is intended to be used to facilitate, the commission of the offense of which the person is convicted.

(B) The court, in imposing sentence on a person described in subparagraph (A), shall order that the person forfeit to the United States all property described in that subparagraph.

(7) The court, in imposing sentence on a person convicted of a Federal health care offense, shall order the person to forfeit property, real or personal, that constitutes or is derived, directly or indirectly, from gross proceeds traceable to the commission of the offense.

(8) The court, in sentencing a defendant convicted of an offense under section 1028, 1029, 1341, 1342, 1343, or 1344, or of a conspiracy to commit such an offense, if the offense involves telemarketing (as that term is defined in section 2325), shall order that the defendant forfeit to the United States any real or personal property—

(A) used or intended to be used to commit, to facilitate, or to promote the commission of such offense; and

(B) constituting, derived from, or traceable to the gross proceeds that the defendant obtained directly or indirectly as a result of the offense.

(b)(1) The forfeiture of property under this section, including any seizure and disposition of the property and any related judicial or administrative proceeding, shall be governed by the provisions of section 413 (other than subsection (d) of that section) of the Comprehensive Drug Abuse Prevention and Control Act of 1970 (21 U.S.C. 853).

(2) The substitution of assets provisions of subsection 413(p) shall not be used to order a defendant to forfeit assets in place of the actual property laundered where such defendant acted merely as an intermediary who handled but did not retain the property in the course of the money laundering offense unless the defendant, in committing the offense or offenses giving rise to the forfeiture, conducted three or more separate transactions involving a total of $100,000 or more in any twelve month period.

18 U.S.C. 983. General Rules for Civil Forfeiture Proceedings (text)

(a) *Notice; claim; complaint.—*

(1)(A)(i) Except as provided in clauses (ii) through (v), in any nonjudicial civil forfeiture proceeding under a civil forfeiture statute, with respect to which the Government is required to send written notice to interested parties, such notice shall be sent in a manner to achieve proper notice as soon as practicable, and in no case more than 60 days after the date of the seizure.

(ii) No notice is required if, before the 60-day period expires, the Government files a civil judicial forfeiture action against the property and provides notice of that action as required by law.

(iii) If, before the 60-day period expires, the Government does not file a civil judicial forfeiture action, but does obtain a criminal indictment containing an allegation that the property is subject to forfeiture, the Government shall either—

(I) send notice within the 60 days and continue the nonjudicial civil forfeiture proceeding under this section; or

(II) terminate the nonjudicial civil forfeiture proceeding, and take the steps necessary to preserve its right to maintain custody of the property as provided in the applicable criminal forfeiture statute.

(iv) In a case in which the property is seized by a State or local law enforcement agency and turned over to a Federal law enforcement agency for the purpose of forfeiture under Federal law, notice shall be sent not more than 90 days after the date of seizure by the State or local law enforcement agency.

(v) If the identity or interest of a party is not determined until after the seizure or turnover but is determined before a declaration of forfeiture is entered, notice shall be sent to such interested party not later than 60 days after the determination by the Government of the identity of the party or the party's interest.

(B) A supervisory official in the headquarters office of the seizing agency may extend the period for sending notice under subparagraph (A) for a period not to exceed 30 days (which period may not be further extended except by a court), if the official determines that the conditions in subparagraph (D) are present.

(C) Upon motion by the Government, a court may extend the period for sending notice under subparagraph

(A) for a period not to exceed 60 days, which period may be further extended by the court for 60-day periods, as necessary, if the court determines, based on a written certification of a supervisory official in the headquarters office of the seizing agency, that the conditions in subparagraph (D) are present.

(D) The period for sending notice under this paragraph may be extended only if there is reason to believe that notice may have an adverse result, including—

(i) endangering the life or physical safety of an individual;

(ii) flight from prosecution;

(iii) destruction of or tampering with evidence;

(iv) intimidation of potential witnesses; or

(v) otherwise seriously jeopardizing an investigation or unduly delaying a trial.

(E) Each of the Federal seizing agencies conducting nonjudicial forfeitures under this section shall report periodically to the Committees on the Judiciary of the House of Representatives and the Senate the number of occasions when an extension of time is granted under subparagraph (B).

(F) If the Government does not send notice of a seizure of property in accordance with subparagraph (A) to the person from whom the property was seized, and no extension of time is granted, the Government shall return the property to that person without prejudice to the right of the Government to commence a forfeiture proceeding at a later time. The Government shall not be required to return contraband or other property that the person from whom the property was seized may not legally possess.

(2)(A) Any person claiming property seized in a nonjudicial civil forfeiture proceeding under a civil forfeiture statute may file a claim with the appropriate official after the seizure.

(B) A claim under subparagraph (A) may be filed not later than the deadline set forth in a personal notice letter (which deadline may be not earlier than 35 days after the date the letter is mailed), except that if that letter is not received, then a claim may be filed not later than 30 days after the date of final publication of notice of seizure.

A claim shall—

(i) identify the specific property being claimed;

(ii) state the claimant's interest in such property; and

(iii) be made under oath, subject to penalty of perjury.

(D) A claim need not be made in any particular form. Each Federal agency conducting nonjudicial forfeitures under this section shall make claim forms generally available on request, which forms shall be written in easily understandable language.

(E) Any person may make a claim under subparagraph (A) without posting bond with respect to the property which is the subject of the claim.

(3)(A) Not later than 90 days after a claim has been filed, the Government shall file a complaint for forfeiture in the manner set forth in the Supplemental Rules for Certain Admiralty and Maritime Claims or return the property pending the filing of a complaint, except that a court in the district in which the complaint will be filed may extend the period for filing a complaint for good cause shown or upon agreement of the parties.

(B) If the Government does not—

(i) file a complaint for forfeiture or return the property, in accordance with subparagraph (A); or

(ii) before the time for filing a complaint has expired—

(I) obtain a criminal indictment containing an allegation that the property is subject to forfeiture; and

(II) take the steps necessary to preserve its right to maintain custody of the property as provided in the applicable criminal forfeiture statute, the Government shall promptly release the property pursuant to regulations promulgated by the Attorney General, and may not take any further action to effect the civil forfeiture of such property in connection with the underlying offense.

(C) In lieu of, or in addition to, filing a civil forfeiture complaint, the Government may include a forfeiture allegation in a criminal indictment. If criminal forfeiture is the only forfeiture proceeding commenced by the Government, the Government's right to continued possession of the property shall be governed by the applicable criminal forfeiture statute.

(D) No complaint may be dismissed on the ground that the Government did not have adequate evidence at the time the complaint was filed to establish the forfeitability of the property.

(4)(A) In any case in which the Government files in the appropriate United States district court a complaint for forfeiture of property, any person claiming an interest in the seized property may file a claim asserting such person's interest in the property in the manner set forth in the Supplemental Rules for Certain Admiralty and Maritime Claims, except that such claim may be filed not later than 30 days after the date of service of the Government's complaint or, as applicable, not later than 30 days after the date of final publication of notice of the filing of the complaint.

(B) A person asserting an interest in seized property, in accordance with subparagraph (A), shall file an answer to the Government's complaint for forfeiture not later than 20 days after the date of the filing of the claim.

(b) *Representation.*—

(1)(A) If a person with standing to contest the forfeiture of property in a judicial civil forfeiture proceeding under a civil forfeiture statute is financially unable to obtain representation by counsel, and the person is represented by counsel appointed under section 3006A of this title in connection with a related criminal case, the court may authorize counsel to represent that person with respect to the claim.

(B) In determining whether to authorize counsel to represent a person under subparagraph (A), the court shall take into account such factors as—

(i) the person's standing to contest the forfeiture; and

(ii) whether the claim appears to be made in good faith.

(2)(A) If a person with standing to contest the forfeiture of property in a judicial civil forfeiture proceeding under a civil forfeiture statute is financially unable to obtain representation by counsel, and the property subject to forfeiture is real property that is being used by the person as a primary residence, the court, at the request of the person, shall insure that the person is represented by an attorney for the Legal Services Corporation with respect to the claim.

(B)(i) At appropriate times during a representation under subparagraph (A), the Legal Services Corporation shall submit a statement of reasonable attorney fees and costs to the court.

(ii) The court shall enter a judgment in favor of the Legal Services Corporation for reasonable attorney fees and costs submitted pursuant to clause (i) and treat such judgment as payable under section 2465 of title 28, United States Code, regardless of the outcome of the case.

(3) The court shall set the compensation for representation under this subsection, which shall be equivalent to that provided for court-appointed representation under section 3006A of this title.

(c) *Burden of proof.*—In a suit or action brought under any civil forfeiture statute for the civil forfeiture of any property—

(1) the burden of proof is on the Government to establish, by a preponderance of the evidence, that the property is subject to forfeiture;

(2) the Government may use evidence gathered after the filing of a complaint for forfeiture to establish, by a preponderance of the evidence, that property is subject to forfeiture; and

(3) if the Government's theory of forfeiture is that the property was used to commit or facilitate the commission of a criminal offense, or was involved in the commission of a criminal offense, the Government shall establish that there was a substantial connection between the property and the offense.

(d) *Innocent owner defense.*—

(1) An innocent owner's interest in property shall not be forfeited under any civil forfeiture statute. The claimant shall have the burden of proving that the claimant is an innocent owner by a preponderance of the evidence.

(2)(A) With respect to a property interest in existence at the time the illegal conduct giving rise to forfeiture took place, the term "innocent owner" means an owner who—

(i) did not know of the conduct giving rise to forfeiture; or

(ii) upon learning of the conduct giving rise to the forfeiture, did all that reasonably could be expected under the circumstances to terminate such use of the property.

(B)(i) For the purposes of this paragraph, ways in which a person may show that such person did all that reasonably could be expected may include demonstrating that such person, to the extent permitted by law—

(I) gave timely notice to an appropriate law enforcement agency of information that led the person to know the conduct giving rise to a forfeiture would occur or has occurred; and

(II) in a timely fashion revoked or made a good faith attempt to revoke permission for those engaging in such conduct to use the property or took reasonable actions in consultation with a law enforcement agency to discourage or prevent the illegal use of the property.

(ii) A person is not required by this subparagraph to take steps that the person reasonably believes would be likely to subject any person (other than the person whose conduct gave rise to the forfeiture) to physical danger.

(3)(A) With respect to a property interest acquired after the conduct giving rise to the forfeiture has taken place, the term "innocent owner" means a person who, at the time that person acquired the interest in the property—

(i) was a bona fide purchaser or seller for value (including a purchaser or seller of goods or services for value); and

(ii) did not know and was reasonably without cause to believe that the property was subject to forfeiture.

(B) An otherwise valid claim under subparagraph (A) shall not be denied on the ground that the claimant gave nothing of value in exchange for the property if—

(i) the property is the primary residence of the claimant;

(ii) depriving the claimant of the property would deprive the claimant of the means to maintain reasonable shelter in the community for the claimant and all dependents residing with the claimant;

(iii) the property is not, and is not traceable to, the proceeds of any criminal offense; and

(iv) the claimant acquired his or her interest in the property through marriage, divorce, or legal separation, or the claimant was the spouse or legal dependent of a person whose death resulted in the transfer of the property to the claimant through inheritance or probate, except that the court shall limit the value of any real property interest for which innocent ownership is recognized under this subparagraph to the value necessary to maintain reasonable shelter in the community for such claimant and all dependents residing with the claimant.

(4) Notwithstanding any provision of this subsection, no person may assert an ownership interest under this subsection in contraband or other property that it is illegal to possess.

(5) If the court determines, in accordance with this section, that an innocent owner has a partial interest in property otherwise subject to forfeiture, or a joint tenancy or tenancy by the entirety in such property, the court may enter an appropriate order—

(A) severing the property;

(B) transferring the property to the Government with a provision that the Government compensate the innocent owner to the extent of his or her ownership interest once a final order of forfeiture has been entered and the property has been reduced to liquid assets; or

(C) permitting the innocent owner to retain the property subject to a lien in favor of the Government to the extent of the forfeitable interest in the property.

(6) In this subsection, the term "owner"—

(A) means a person with an ownership interest in the specific property sought to be forfeited, including a leasehold, lien, mortgage, recorded security interest, or valid assignment of an ownership interest; and

(B) does not include—

(i) a person with only a general unsecured interest in, or claim against, the property or estate of another;

(ii) a bailee unless the bailor is identified and the bailee shows a colorable legitimate interest in the property seized; or

(iii) a nominee who exercises no dominion or control over the property.

(e) *Motion to set aside forfeiture.*—

(1) Any person entitled to written notice in any nonjudicial civil forfeiture proceeding under a civil forfeiture statute who does not receive such notice may file a motion to set aside a declaration of forfeiture with respect to that person's interest in the property, which motion shall be granted if—

(A) the Government knew, or reasonably should have known, of the moving party's interest and failed to take reasonable steps to provide such party with notice; and

(B) the moving party did not know or have reason to know of the seizure within sufficient time to file a timely claim.

(2)(A) Notwithstanding the expiration of any applicable statute of limitations, if the court grants a motion under paragraph (1), the court shall set aside the declaration of forfeiture as to the interest of the moving party without prejudice to the right of the Government to commence a subsequent forfeiture proceeding as to the interest of the moving party.

(B) Any proceeding described in subparagraph (A) shall be commenced—

(i) if nonjudicial, within 60 days of the entry of the order granting the motion; or

(ii) if judicial, within 6 months of the entry of the order granting the motion.

(3) A motion under paragraph (1) may be filed not later than 5 years after the date of final publication of notice of seizure of the property.

(4) If, at the time a motion made under paragraph (1) is granted, the forfeited property has been disposed of by the Government in accordance with law, the Government may institute proceedings against a substitute sum of money equal to the value of the moving party's interest in the property at the time the property was disposed of.

(5) A motion filed under this subsection shall be the exclusive remedy for seeking to set aside a declaration of forfeiture under a civil forfeiture statute.

(f) *Release of seized property.*—

(1) A claimant under subsection (a) is entitled to immediate release of seized property if—

(A) the claimant has a possessory interest in the property;

(B) the claimant has sufficient ties to the community to provide assurance that the property will be available at the time of the trial;

(C) the continued possession by the Government pending the final disposition of forfeiture proceedings will cause substantial hardship to the claimant, such as preventing the functioning of a business, preventing an individual from working, or leaving an individual homeless;

(D) the claimant's likely hardship from the continued possession by the Government of the seized property outweighs the risk that the property will be destroyed, damaged, lost, concealed, or transferred if it is returned to the claimant during the pendency of the proceeding; and

(E) none of the conditions set forth in paragraph (8) applies.

(2) A claimant seeking release of property under this subsection must request possession of the property from the appropriate official, and the request must set forth the basis on which the requirements of paragraph (1) are met.

(3)(A) If not later than 15 days after the date of a request under paragraph (2) the property has not been released, the claimant may file a petition in the district court in which the complaint has been filed or, if no complaint has been filed, in the district court in which the seizure warrant was issued or in the district court for the district in which the property was seized.

(B) The petition described in subparagraph (A) shall set forth—

(i) the basis on which the requirements of paragraph (1) are met; and

(ii) the steps the claimant has taken to secure release of the property from the appropriate official.

(4) If the Government establishes that the claimant's claim is frivolous, the court shall deny the petition. In responding to a petition under this subsection on other grounds, the Government may in appropriate cases submit evidence ex parte in order to avoid disclosing any matter that may adversely affect an ongoing criminal investigation or pending criminal trial.

(5) The court shall render a decision on a petition filed under paragraph (3) not later than 30 days after the date of the filing, unless such 30-day limitation is extended by consent of the parties or by the court for good cause shown.

(6) If—

(A) a petition is filed under paragraph (3); and

(B) the claimant demonstrates that the requirements of paragraph (1) have been met, the district court shall order that the property be returned to the claimant, pending completion of proceedings by the Government to obtain forfeiture of the property.

(7) If the court grants a petition under paragraph (3)—

(A) the court may enter any order necessary to ensure that the value of the property is maintained while the forfeiture action is pending, including

(i) permitting the inspection, photographing, and inventory of the property;

(ii) fixing a bond in accordance with rule E(5) of the Supplemental Rules for Certain Admiralty and Maritime Claims; and

(iii) requiring the claimant to obtain or maintain insurance on the subject property; and

(B) the Government may place a lien against the property or file a lis pendens to ensure that the property is not transferred to another person.

(8) This subsection shall not apply if the seized property—

(A) is contraband, currency, or other monetary instrument, or electronic funds unless such currency or other monetary instrument or electronic funds constitutes the assets of a legitimate business which has been seized;

(B) is to be used as evidence of a violation of the law;

(C) by reason of design or other characteristic, is particularly suited for use in illegal activities; or

(D) is likely to be used to commit additional criminal acts if returned to the claimant.

(g) *Proportionality.*—

(1) The claimant under subsection (a)(4) may petition the court to determine whether the forfeiture was constitutionally excessive.

(2) In making this determination, the court shall compare the forfeiture to the gravity of the offense giving rise to the forfeiture.

(3) The claimant shall have the burden of establishing that the forfeiture is grossly disproportional by a preponderance of the evidence at a hearing conducted by the court without a jury.

(4) If the court finds that the forfeiture is grossly disproportional to the offense it shall reduce or eliminate the forfeiture as necessary to avoid a violation of the Excessive Fines Clause of the Eighth Amendment of the Constitution.

(h) *Civil fine.*—

(1) In any civil forfeiture proceeding under a civil forfeiture statute in which the Government prevails, if the court finds that the claimant's assertion of an interest in the property was frivolous, the court may impose a civil fine on the claimant of an amount equal to 10 percent of the value of the forfeited property, but in no event shall the fine be less than $250 or greater than $5,000.

(2) Any civil fine imposed under this subsection shall not preclude the court from imposing sanctions under rule 11 of the Federal Rules of Civil Procedure.

(3) In addition to the limitations of section 1915 of title 28, United States Code, in no event shall a prisoner file a claim under a civil forfeiture statute or appeal a judgment in a civil action or proceeding based on a civil forfeiture statute if the prisoner has, on three or more prior occasions, while incarcerated or detained in any facility, brought an action or appeal in a court of the United States that was dismissed on the grounds that it is frivolous or malicious, unless the prisoner shows extraordinary and exceptional circumstances.

(i) *Civil forfeiture statute defined.*—In this section, the term "civil forfeiture statute"—

(1) means any provision of Federal law providing for the forfeiture of property other than as a sentence imposed upon conviction of a criminal offense; and

(2) does not include—

(A) the Tariff Act of 1930 or any other provision of law codified in title 19;

(B) the Internal Revenue Code of 1986;

(C) the Federal Food, Drug, and Cosmetic Act (21 U.S.C. 301 et seq.);

(D) the Trading with the Enemy Act (50 U.S.C. App. 1 et seq.) or the International Emergency Economic Powers Act (IEEPA) (50 U.S.C. 1701 et seq.); or

(E) section 1 of title VI of the Act of June 15, 1917 (40 Stat. 233; 22 U.S.C. 401).

(j) *Restraining orders; protective orders.*—

(1) Upon application of the United States, the court may enter a restraining order or injunction, require the execution of satisfactory performance bonds, create receiverships, appoint conservators, custodians, appraisers, accountants, or trustees, or take any other action to seize, secure, maintain, or preserve the availability of property subject to civil forfeiture—

(A) upon the filing of a civil forfeiture complaint alleging that the property with respect to which the order is sought is subject to civil forfeiture; or

(B) prior to the filing of such a complaint, if, after notice to persons appearing to have an interest in the property and opportunity for a hearing, the court determines that—

(i) there is a substantial probability that the United States will prevail on the issue of forfeiture and that failure to enter the order will result in the property being destroyed, removed from the jurisdiction of the court, or otherwise made unavailable for forfeiture; and

(ii) the need to preserve the availability of the property through the entry of the requested order outweighs the hardship on any party against whom the order is to be entered.

(2) An order entered pursuant to paragraph (1)(B) shall be effective for not more than 90 days, unless extended by the court for good cause shown, or unless a complaint described in paragraph (1)(A) has been filed.

(3) A temporary restraining order under this subsection may be entered upon application of the United States without notice or opportunity for a hearing when a complaint has not yet been filed with respect to the property, if

the United States demonstrates that there is probable cause to believe that the property with respect to which the order is sought is subject to civil forfeiture and that provision of notice will jeopardize the availability of the property for forfeiture. Such a temporary order shall expire not more than 14 days after the date on which it is entered, unless extended for good cause shown or unless the party against whom it is entered consents to an extension for a longer period. A hearing requested concerning an order entered under this paragraph shall be held at the earliest possible time and prior to the expiration of the temporary order.

(4) The court may receive and consider, at a hearing held pursuant to this subsection, evidence and information that would be inadmissible under the Federal Rules of Evidence.

Federal Rules of Civil Procedure, Supplemental Rules for Certain Admiralty and Maritime Claims. Rule G. Forfeiture Actions in Rem (text)

(1) Scope. This rule governs a forfeiture action in rem arising from a federal statute. To the extent that this rule does not address an issue, Supplemental Rules C and E and the Federal Rules of Civil Procedure also apply.

(2) Complaint. The complaint must:

(a) be verified;

(b) state the grounds for subject-matter jurisdiction, in rem jurisdiction over the defendant property, and venue;

(c) describe the property with reasonable particularity;

(d) if the property is tangible, state its location when any seizure occurred and—if different—its location when the action is filed;

(e) identify the statute under which the forfeiture action is brought; and

(f) state sufficiently detailed facts to support a reasonable belief that the government will be able to meet its burden of proof at trial.

(3) Judicial Authorization and Process.

(a) *Real Property*. If the defendant is real property, the government must proceed under 18 U.S.C. §985.

(b) *Other Property; Arrest Warrant*. If the defendant is not real property:

(i) the clerk must issue a warrant to arrest the property if it is in the government's possession, custody, or control;

(ii) the court—on finding probable cause—must issue a warrant to arrest the property if it is not in the government's possession, custody, or control and is not subject to a judicial restraining order; and

(iii) a warrant is not necessary if the property is subject to a judicial restraining order.

(c) *Execution of Process.*

(i) The warrant and any supplemental process must be delivered to a person or organization authorized to execute it, who may be: (A) a marshal or any other United States officer or employee; (B) someone under contract with the United States; or (C) someone specially appointed by the court for that purpose.

(ii) The authorized person or organization must execute the warrant and any supplemental process on property in the United States as soon as practicable unless:

(A) the property is in the government's possession, custody, or control; or

(B) the court orders a different time when the complaint is under seal, the action is stayed before the warrant and supplemental process are executed, or the court finds other good cause.

(iii) The warrant and any supplemental process may be executed within the district or, when authorized by statute, outside the district.

(iv) If executing a warrant on property outside the United States is required, the warrant may be transmitted to an appropriate authority for serving process where the property is located.

(4) Notice.

(a) *Notice by Publication.*

(i) *When Publication Is Required.* A judgment of forfeiture may be entered only if the government has published notice of the action within a reasonable time after filing the complaint or at a time the court orders. But notice need not be published if:

(A) the defendant property is worth less than $1,000 and direct notice is sent under Rule G(4)(b) to every person the government can reasonably identify as a potential claimant; or

(B) the court finds that the cost of publication exceeds the property's value and that other means of notice would satisfy due process.

(ii) *Content of the Notice.* Unless the court orders otherwise, the notice must:

(A) describe the property with reasonable particularity;

(B) state the times under Rule G(5) to file a claim and to answer; and

(C) name the government attorney to be served with the claim and answer.

(iii) *Frequency of Publication.* Published notice must appear:

(A) once a week for three consecutive weeks; or

(B) only once if, before the action was filed, notice of nonjudicial forfeiture of the same property was published on an official internet government forfeiture site for at least 30 consecutive days, or in a newspaper of general circulation for three consecutive weeks in a district where publication is authorized under Rule G(4)(a)(iv).

(iv) *Means of Publication.* The government should select from the following options a means of publication reasonably calculated to notify potential claimants of the action:

(A) if the property is in the United States, publication in a newspaper generally circulated in the district where the action is filed, where the property was seized, or where property that was not seized is located;

(B) if the property is outside the United States, publication in a newspaper generally circulated in a district where the action is filed, in a newspaper generally circulated in the country where the property is located, or in legal notices published and generally circulated in the country where the property is located; or

(C) instead of (A) or (B), posting a notice on an official internet government forfeiture site for at least 30 consecutive days.

(b) *Notice to Known Potential Claimants.*

(i) *Direct Notice Required.* The government must send notice of the action and a copy of the complaint to any person who reasonably appears to be a potential claimant on the facts known to the government before the end of the time for filing a claim under Rule G(5)(a)(ii)(B).

(ii) *Content of the Notice.* The notice must state:

(A) the date when the notice is sent;

(B) a deadline for filing a claim, at least 35 days after the notice is sent;

(C) that an answer or a motion under Rule 12 must be filed no later than 21 days after filing the claim; and

(D) the name of the government attorney to be served with the claim and answer.

(iii) *Sending Notice.*

(A) The notice must be sent by means reasonably calculated to reach the potential claimant.

(B) Notice may be sent to the potential claimant or to the attorney representing the potential claimant with respect to the seizure of the property or in a related investigation, administrative forfeiture proceeding, or criminal case.

(C) Notice sent to a potential claimant who is incarcerated must be sent to the place of incarceration.

(D) Notice to a person arrested in connection with an offense giving rise to the forfeiture who is not incarcerated when notice is sent may be sent to the address that person last gave to the agency that arrested or released the person.

(E) Notice to a person from whom the property was seized who is not incarcerated when notice is sent may be sent to the last address that person gave to the agency that seized the property.

(iv) *When Notice Is Sent.* Notice by the following means is sent on the date when it is placed in the mail, delivered to a commercial carrier, or sent by electronic mail.

(v) *Actual Notice.* A potential claimant who had actual notice of a forfeiture action may not oppose or seek relief from forfeiture because of the government's failure to send the required notice.

(5) Responsive Pleadings.

(a) *Filing a Claim.*

(i) A person who asserts an interest in the defendant property may contest the forfeiture by filing a claim in the court where the action is pending. The claim must:

(A) identify the specific property claimed;

(B) identify the claimant and state the claimant's interest in the property;

(C) be signed by the claimant under penalty of perjury; and

(D) be served on the government attorney designated under Rule G(4)(a)(ii)(C) or (b)(ii)(D).

(ii) Unless the court for good cause sets a different time, the claim must be filed: (A) by the time stated in a direct notice sent under Rule G(4)(b);

(B) if notice was published but direct notice was not sent to the claimant or the claimant's attorney, no later than 30 days after final publication of newspaper notice or legal notice under Rule G(4)(a) or no later than 60 days after the first day of publication on an official internet government forfeiture site; or

(C) if notice was not published and direct notice was not sent to the claimant or the claimant's attorney:

(1) if the property was in the government's possession, custody, or control when the complaint was filed, no later than 60 days after the filing, not counting any time when the complaint was under seal or when the action was stayed before execution of a warrant issued under Rule G(3)(b); or

(2) if the property was not in the government's possession, custody, or control when the complaint was filed, no later than 60 days after the

government complied with 18 U.S.C. §985(c) as to real property, or 60 days after process was executed on the property under Rule G(3). (iii) A claim filed by a person asserting an interest as a bailee must identify the bailor, and if filed on the bailor's behalf must state the authority to do so.

(b) *Answer.* A claimant must serve and file an answer to the complaint or a motion under Rule 12 within 21 days after filing the claim. A claimant waives an objection to in rem jurisdiction or to venue if the objection is not made by motion or stated in the answer.

(6) Special Interrogatories.

(a) Time and Scope. The government may serve special interrogatories limited to the claimant's identity and relationship to the defendant property without the court's leave at any time after the claim is filed and before discovery is closed. But if the claimant serves a motion to dismiss the action, the government must serve the interrogatories within 21 days after the motion is served.

(b) Answers or Objections. Answers or objections to these interrogatories must be served within 21 days after the interrogatories are served.

(c) Government's Response Deferred. The government need not respond to a claimant's motion to dismiss the action under Rule G(8)(b) until 21 days after the claimant has answered these interrogatories.

(7) Preserving, Preventing Criminal Use, and Disposing of Property; Sales.

(a) Preserving and Preventing Criminal Use of Property. When the government does not have actual possession of the defendant property the court, on motion or on its own, may enter any order necessary to preserve the property, to prevent its removal or encumbrance, or to prevent its use in a criminal offense.

(b) Interlocutory Sale or Delivery.

(i) *Order to Sell.* On motion by a party or a person having custody of the property, the court may order all or part of the property sold if:

(A) the property is perishable or at risk of deterioration, decay, or injury by being detained in custody pending the action;

(B) the expense of keeping the property is excessive or is disproportionate to its fair market value;

(C) the property is subject to a mortgage or to taxes on which the owner is in default; or

(D) the court finds other good cause.

(ii) *Who Makes the Sale.* A sale must be made by a United States agency that has authority to sell the property, by the agency's contractor, or by any person the court designates.

(iii) *Sale Procedures.* The sale is governed by 28 U.S.C. §§2001, 2002, and 2004, unless all parties, with the court's approval, agree to the sale, aspects of the sale, or different procedures.

(iv) *Sale Proceeds.* Sale proceeds are a substitute res subject to forfeiture in place of the property that was sold. The proceeds must be held in an interest-bearing account maintained by the United States pending the conclusion of the forfeiture action.

(v) *Delivery on a Claimant's Motion.* The court may order that the property be delivered to the claimant pending the conclusion of the action if the claimant shows circumstances that would permit sale under Rule G(7)(b)(i) and gives security under these rules.

(c) *Disposing of Forfeited Property.* Upon entry of a forfeiture judgment, the property or proceeds from selling the property must be disposed of as provided by law.

(8) Motions.

(a) *Motion To Suppress Use of the Property as Evidence.* If the defendant property was seized, a party with standing to contest the lawfulness of the seizure may move to suppress use of the property as evidence. Suppression does not affect forfeiture of the property based on independently derived evidence.

(b) *Motion To Dismiss the Action.*

(i) A claimant who establishes standing to contest forfeiture may move to dismiss the action under Rule 12(b).

(ii) In an action governed by 18 U.S.C. §983(a)(3)(D) the complaint may not be dismissed on the ground that the government did not have adequate evidence at the time the complaint was filed to establish the forfeitability of the property. The sufficiency of the complaint is governed by Rule G(2).

(c) *Motion To Strike a Claim or Answer.*

(i) At any time before trial, the government may move to strike a claim or answer:

(A) for failing to comply with Rule G(5) or (6), or

(B) because the claimant lacks standing.

(ii) The motion:

(A) must be decided before any motion by the claimant to dismiss the action; and

(B) may be presented as a motion for judgment on the pleadings or as a motion to determine after a hearing or by summary judgment whether the claimant can carry the burden of establishing standing by a preponderance of the evidence.

(d) *Petition To Release Property.*

(i) If a United States agency or an agency's contractor holds property for judicial or nonjudicial forfeiture under a statute governed by 18 U.S.C. §983(f), a person who has filed a claim to the property may petition for its release under §983(f).

(ii) If a petition for release is filed before a judicial forfeiture action is filed against the property, the petition may be filed either in the district where the property was seized or in the district where a warrant to seize the property issued. If a judicial forfeiture action against the property is later filed in another district-or if the government shows that the action will be filed in another district-the petition may be transferred to that district under 28 U.S.C. §1404.

(e) *Excessive Fines.* A claimant may seek to mitigate a forfeiture under the Excessive Fines Clause of the Eighth Amendment by motion for summary judgment or by motion made after entry of a forfeiture judgment if:

(i) the claimant has pleaded the defense under Rule 8; and

(ii) the parties have had the opportunity to conduct civil discovery on the defense.

(9) Trial. Trial is to the court unless any party demands trial by jury under Rule 38.

18 U.S.C. 984. Civil Forfeiture of Fungible Property (text)

(a)(1) In any forfeiture action in rem in which the subject property is cash, monetary instruments in bearer form, funds deposited in an account in a financial institution (as defined in section 20 of this title), or precious metals—

(A) it shall not be necessary for the Government to identify the specific property involved in the offense that is the basis for the forfeiture; and

(B) it shall not be a defense that the property involved in such an offense has been removed and replaced by identical property.

(2) Except as provided in subsection (b), any identical property found in the same place or account as the property involved in the offense that is the basis for the forfeiture shall be subject to forfeiture under this section.

(b) No action pursuant to this section to forfeit property not traceable directly to the offense that is the basis for the forfeiture may be commenced more than 1 year from the date of the offense.

(c)(1) Subsection (a) does not apply to an action against funds held by a financial institution in an interbank account unless the account holder knowingly engaged in the offense that is the basis for the forfeiture. (2) In this subsection—

(A) the term "financial institution" includes a foreign bank (as defined in section 1(b)(7) of the International Banking Act of 1978 (12 U.S.C. 3101(b)(7))); and

(B) the term "interbank account" means an account held by one financial institution at another financial institution primarily for the purpose of facilitating customer transactions.

(d) Nothing in this section may be construed to limit the ability of the Government to forfeit property under any provision of law if the property involved in the offense giving rise to the forfeiture or property traceable thereto is available for forfeiture.

18 U.S.C. 985. Civil Forfeiture of Real Property (text)

(a) Notwithstanding any other provision of law, all civil forfeitures of real property and interests in real property shall proceed as judicial forfeitures.

(b)(1) Except as provided in this section—

(A) real property that is the subject of a civil forfeiture action shall not be seized before entry of an order of forfeiture; and

(B) the owners or occupants of the real property shall not be evicted from, or otherwise deprived of the use and enjoyment of, real property that is the subject of a pending forfeiture action.

(2) The filing of a lis pendens and the execution of a writ of entry for the purpose of conducting an inspection and inventory of the property shall not be considered a seizure under this subsection.

(c)(1) The Government shall initiate a civil forfeiture action against real property by—

(A) filing a complaint for forfeiture;

(B) posting a notice of the complaint on the property; and

(C) serving notice on the property owner, along with a copy of the complaint.

(2) If the property owner cannot be served with the notice under paragraph (1) because the owner—

(A) is a fugitive;

(B) resides outside the United States and efforts at service pursuant to rule 4 of the Federal Rules of Civil Procedure are unavailing; or

(C) cannot be located despite the exercise of due diligence, constructive service may be made in accordance with the laws of the State in which the property is located.

(3) If real property has been posted in accordance with this subsection, it shall not be necessary for the court to issue an arrest warrant in rem, or to take any other action to establish in rem jurisdiction over the property.

(d)(1) Real property may be seized prior to the entry of an order of forfeiture if—

(A) the Government notifies the court that it intends to seize the property before trial; and

(B) the court—

(i) issues a notice of application for warrant, causes the notice to be served on the property owner and posted on the property, and conducts a hearing in which the property owner has a meaningful opportunity to be heard; or

(ii) makes an ex parte determination that there is probable cause for the forfeiture and that there are exigent circumstances that permit the Government to seize the property without prior notice and an opportunity for the property owner to be heard.

(2) For purposes of paragraph (1)(B)(ii), to establish exigent circumstances, the Government shall show that less restrictive measures such as a lis pendens, restraining order, or bond would not suffice to protect the Government's interests in preventing the sale, destruction, or continued unlawful use of the real property.

(e) If the court authorizes a seizure of real property under subsection (d)(1)(B)(ii), it shall conduct a prompt post-seizure hearing during which the property owner shall have an opportunity to contest the basis for the seizure.

(f) This section—

(1) applies only to civil forfeitures of real property and interests in real property;

(2) does not apply to forfeitures of the proceeds of the sale of such property or interests, or of money or other assets intended to be used to acquire such property or interests; and

(3) shall not affect the authority of the court to enter a restraining order relating to real property.

18 U.S.C. 987. Anti-Terrorist Forfeiture Protection (text)

(a) Right to contest.—An owner of property that is confiscated under any provision of law relating to the confiscation of assets of suspected international terrorists, may contest that confiscation by filing a claim in the manner set forth in the Federal Rules of Civil Procedure (Supplemental Rules for Certain Admiralty and Maritime Claims), and asserting as an affirmative defense that—

(1) the property is not subject to confiscation under such provision of law; or

(2) the innocent owner provisions of section 983(d) of title 18, United States Code, apply to the case.

(b) Evidence.—In considering a claim filed under this section, a court may admit evidence that is otherwise inadmissible under the Federal Rules of Evidence, if the court determines that the evidence is reliable, and that compliance with the Federal Rules of Evidence may jeopardize the national security interests of the United States.

(c) Clarifications.—

(1) Protection of rights.—The exclusion of certain provisions of Federal law from the definition of the term "civil forfeiture statute" in section 983(i) of title 18, United States Code, shall not be construed to deny an owner of property the right to contest the confiscation of assets of suspected international terrorists under—

(A) subsection (a) of this section;

(B) the Constitution; or

(C) subchapter II of chapter 5 of title 5, United States Code (commonly known as the "Administrative Procedure Act").

(2) Savings clause.—Nothing in this section shall limit or otherwise affect any other remedies that may be available to an owner of property under section 983 of title 18, United States Code, or any other provision of law.

21 U.S.C. 881. Civil Forfeitures (Controlled Substances) (text)

(a) Subject property

The following shall be subject to forfeiture to the United States and no property right shall exist in them:

(1) All controlled substances which have been manufactured, distributed, dispensed, or acquired in violation of this subchapter.

(2) All raw materials, products, and equipment of any kind which are used, or intended for use, in manufacturing, compounding, processing, delivering, importing, or exporting any controlled substance or listed chemical in violation of this subchapter.

(3) All property which is used, or intended for use, as a container for property described in paragraph (1), (2), or (9).

(4) All conveyances, including aircraft, vehicles, or vessels, which are used, or are intended for use, to transport, or in any manner to facilitate the transportation, sale, receipt, possession, or concealment of property described in paragraph (1), (2), or (9).

(5) All books, records, and research, including formulas, microfilm, tapes, and data which are used, or intended for use, in violation of this subchapter.

(6) All moneys, negotiable instruments, securities, or other things of value furnished or intended to be furnished by any person in exchange for a controlled substance or listed chemical in violation of this subchapter, all proceeds traceable to such an exchange, and all moneys, negotiable instruments, and securities used or intended to be used to facilitate any violation of this subchapter.

(7) All real property, including any right, title, and interest (including any leasehold interest) in the whole of any lot or tract of land and any appurtenances or improvements, which is used, or intended to be used, in any manner or part, to commit, or to facilitate the commission of, a violation of this subchapter punishable by more than one year's imprisonment.

(8) All controlled substances which have been possessed in violation of this subchapter.

(9)All listed chemicals, all drug manufacturing equipment, all tableting machines, all encapsulating machines, and all gelatin capsules, which have been imported, exported, manufactured, possessed, distributed, dispensed, acquired, or intended to be distributed, dispensed, acquired, imported, or exported, in violation of this subchapter or subchapter II of this chapter.

(10) Any drug paraphernalia (as defined in section 863 of this title).

(11) Any firearm (as defined in section 921 of Title 18) used or intended to be used to facilitate the transportation, sale, receipt, possession, or concealment of property described in paragraph (1) or (2) and any proceeds traceable to such property.

(b) Seizure procedures

Any property subject to forfeiture to the United States under this section may be seized by the Attorney General in the manner set forth in section 981(b) of Title 18.

(c) Custody of Attorney General

Property taken or detained under this section shall not be repleviable, but shall be deemed to be in the custody of the Attorney General, subject only to the orders and decrees of the court or the official having jurisdiction thereof. Whenever property is seized under any of the provisions of this subchapter, the Attorney General may—

(1) place the property under seal;

(2) remove the property to a place designated by him; or

(3) require that the General Services Administration take custody of the property and remove it, if practicable, to an appropriate location for disposition in accordance with law.

(d) Other laws and proceedings applicable

The provisions of law relating to the seizure, summary and judicial forfeiture, and condemnation of property for violation of the customs laws; the disposition of such property or the proceeds from the sale thereof; the remission or mitigation of such forfeitures; and the compromise of claims shall apply to seizures and forfeitures incurred, or alleged to have been incurred, under any of the provisions of this subchapter, insofar as applicable and not inconsistent with the provisions hereof; except that such duties as are imposed upon the customs officer or any other person with respect to the seizure and forfeiture of property under the customs laws shall be performed with respect to seizures and forfeitures of property under this subchapter by such officers, agents, or other persons as may be authorized or designated for that purpose by the Attorney General, except to the extent that such duties arise from seizures and forfeitures effected by any customs officer.

(e) Disposition of forfeited property

(1) Whenever property is civilly or criminally forfeited under this subchapter the Attorney General may—

(A) retain the property for official use or, in the manner provided with respect to transfers under section 1616a of Title 19, transfer the property to any Federal agency or to any State or local law enforcement agency which participated directly in the seizure or forfeiture of the property;

(B) except as provided in paragraph (4), sell, by public sale or any other commercially feasible means, any forfeited property which is not required to be destroyed by law and which is not harmful to the public;

(C) require that the General Services Administration take custody of the property and dispose of it in accordance with law;

(D) forward it to the Drug Enforcement Administration for disposition (including delivery for medical or scientific use to any Federal or State agency under regulations of the Attorney General); or

(E) transfer the forfeited personal property or the proceeds of the sale of any forfeited personal or real property to any foreign country which participated directly or indirectly in the seizure or forfeiture of the property, if such a transfer—

(i) has been agreed to by the Secretary of State;

(ii) is authorized in an international agreement between the United States and the foreign country; and

(iii) is made to a country which, if applicable, has been certified under section 2291j(b) of Title 22.

(2)(A) The proceeds from any sale under subparagraph (B) of paragraph (1) and any moneys forfeited under this title shall be used to pay—

(i) all property expenses of the proceedings for forfeiture and sale including expenses of seizure, maintenance of custody, advertising, and court costs; and

(ii) awards of up to $100,000 to any individual who provides original information which leads to the arrest and conviction of a person who kills or kidnaps a Federal drug law enforcement agent.

Any award paid for information concerning the killing or kidnaping of a Federal drug law enforcement agent, as provided in clause (ii), shall be paid at the discretion of the Attorney General.

(B) The Attorney General shall forward to the Treasurer of the United States for deposit in accordance with section 524(c) of Title 28, any amounts of such moneys and proceeds remaining after payment of the expenses provided in subparagraph (A), except that, with respect to forfeitures conducted by the Postal Service, the Postal Service shall deposit in the Postal Service Fund, under section 2003(b)(7) of Title 39, such moneys and proceeds.

(3) The Attorney General shall assure that any property transferred to a State or local law enforcement agency under paragraph (1)(A)—

(A) has a value that bears a reasonable relationship to the degree of direct participation of the State or local agency in the law enforcement effort resulting in the forfeiture, taking into account the total value of all property forfeited and the total law enforcement effort with respect to the violation of law on which the forfeiture is based; and

(B) will serve to encourage further cooperation between the recipient State or local agency and Federal law enforcement agencies.

(4)(A) With respect to real property described in subparagraph (B), if the chief executive officer of the State involved submits to the Attorney General a request for purposes of such subparagraph, the authority established in such subparagraph is in lieu of the authority established in paragraph (1)(B).

(B) In the case of property described in paragraph (1)(B) that is civilly or criminally forfeited under this subchapter, if the property is real property that is appropriate for use as a public area reserved for recreational or historic purposes or for the preservation of natural conditions, the Attorney General, upon the request of the chief executive officer of the State in which the property is located, may transfer title to the property to the State, either without charge or for a nominal charge, through a legal instrument providing that—

(i) such use will be the principal use of the property; and

(ii) title to the property reverts to the United States in the event that the property is used otherwise.

(f) Forfeiture and destruction of schedule I and II substances

(1) All controlled substances in schedule I or II that are possessed, transferred, sold, or offered for sale in violation of the provisions of this subchapter; all dangerous, toxic, or hazardous raw materials or products subject to forfeiture under subsection (a)(2) of this section; and any equipment or container subject to forfeiture under subsection (a)(2) or (3) of this section which cannot be separated safely from such raw materials or products shall be deemed contraband and seized and summarily forfeited to the United States. Similarly, all substances in schedule I or II, which are seized or come into the possession of the United States, the owners of which are unknown, shall be deemed contraband and summarily forfeited to the United States.

(2) The Attorney General may direct the destruction of all controlled substances in schedule I or II seized for violation of this subchapter; all dangerous, toxic, or hazardous raw materials or products subject to forfeiture under subsection (a)(2) of this section; and any equipment or container subject to forfeiture under subsection (a)(2) or (3) of this section which cannot be separated safely from such raw materials or products under such circumstances as the Attorney General may deem necessary.

(g) Plants

(1) All species of plants from which controlled substances in schedules I and II may be derived which have been planted or cultivated in violation of this subchapter, or of which the owners or cultivators are unknown, or which are wild growths, may be seized and summarily forfeited to the United States.

(2) The failure, upon demand by the Attorney General or his duly authorized agent, of the person in occupancy or in control of land or premises upon which such species of plants are growing or being stored, to produce an appropriate registration, or proof that he is the holder thereof, shall constitute authority for the seizure and forfeiture.

(3) The Attorney General, or his duly authorized agent, shall have authority to enter upon any lands, or into any dwelling pursuant to a search warrant, to cut, harvest, carry off, or destroy such plants.

(h) Vesting of title in United States

All right, title, and interest in property described in subsection (a) of this section shall vest in the United States upon commission of the act giving rise to forfeiture under this section.

(i) Stay of civil forfeiture proceedings; applicability

The provisions of section 981(g) of title 18, United States Code, regarding the stay of a civil forfeiture proceeding shall apply to forfeitures under this section.

(j) Venue

In addition to the venue provided for in section 1395 of Title 28 or any other provision of law, in the case of property of a defendant charged with a violation that is the basis for forfeiture of the property under this section, a proceeding for forfeiture under this section may be brought in the judicial district in which the defendant owning such property is found or in the judicial district in which the criminal prosecution is brought.

(l) Agreement between Attorney General and Postal Service for performance of functions

The functions of the Attorney General under this section shall be carried out by the Postal Service pursuant to such agreement as may be entered into between the Attorney General and the Postal Service.

21 U.S.C. 853. Criminal Forfeiture (Controlled Substances) (text)

(a) Property subject to criminal forfeiture

Any person convicted of a violation of this subchapter or subchapter II of this chapter punishable by imprisonment for more than one year shall forfeit to the United States, irrespective of any provision of State law—

(1) any property constituting, or derived from, any proceeds the person obtained, directly or indirectly, as the result of such violation;

(2) any of the person's property used, or intended to be used, in any manner or part, to commit, or to facilitate the commission of, such violation; and

(3) in the case of a person convicted of engaging in a continuing criminal enterprise in violation of section 848 of this title, the person shall forfeit, in addition to any property described in paragraph (1) or (2), any of his interest in, claims against, and property or contractual rights affording a source of control over, the continuing criminal enterprise.

The court, in imposing sentence on such person, shall order, in addition to any other sentence imposed pursuant to this subchapter or subchapter II of this chapter, that the person forfeit to the United States all property described in this subsection. In lieu of a fine otherwise authorized by this part, a defendant who derives profits or other proceeds from an offense may be fined not more than twice the gross profits or other proceeds.

(b) Meaning of term "property"

Property subject to criminal forfeiture under this section includes—

(1) real property, including things growing on, affixed to, and found in land; and

(2) tangible and intangible personal property, including rights, privileges, interests, claims, and securities.

(c) Third party transfers

All right, title, and interest in property described in subsection (a) of this section vests in the United States upon the commission of the act giving rise to forfeiture under this section. Any such property that is subsequently transferred to a person other than the defendant may be the subject of a special verdict of forfeiture and thereafter shall be ordered forfeited to the United States, unless the transferee establishes in a hearing pursuant to subsection (n) of this section that he is a bona fide purchaser for value of such property who at the time of purchase was reasonably without cause to believe that the property was subject to forfeiture under this section.

(d) Rebuttable presumption

There is a rebuttable presumption at trial that any property of a person convicted of a felony under this subchapter or subchapter II of this chapter is subject to forfeiture under this section if the United States establishes by a preponderance of the evidence that—

(1) such property was acquired by such person during the period of the violation of this subchapter or subchapter II of this chapter or within a reasonable time after such period; and

(2) there was no likely source for such property other than the violation of this subchapter or subchapter II of this chapter.

(e) Protective orders

(1) Upon application of the United States, the court may enter a restraining order or injunction, require the execution of a satisfactory performance bond, or take any other action to preserve the availability of property described in subsection (a) of this section for forfeiture under this section—

(A) upon the filing of an indictment or information charging a violation of this subchapter or subchapter II of this chapter for which criminal forfeiture may be ordered under this section and alleging that the property with respect to which the order is sought would, in the event of conviction, be subject to forfeiture under this section; or

(B) prior to the filing of such an indictment or information, if, after notice to persons appearing to have an interest in the property and opportunity for a hearing, the court determines that—

(i) there is a substantial probability that the United States will prevail on the issue of forfeiture and that failure to enter the order will result in the property being destroyed, removed from the jurisdiction of the court, or otherwise made unavailable for forfeiture; and

(ii) the need to preserve the availability of the property through the entry of the requested order outweighs the hardship on any party against whom the order is to be entered:

Provided, however, That an order entered pursuant to subparagraph (B) shall be effective for not more than ninety days, unless extended by the court for good cause shown or unless an indictment or information described in subparagraph (A) has been filed.

(2) A temporary restraining order under this subsection may be entered upon application of the United States without notice or opportunity for a hearing when an information or indictment has not yet been filed with respect to the property, if the United States demonstrates that there is probable cause to believe that the property with respect to which the order is sought would, in the event of conviction, be subject to forfeiture under this section and that provision of notice will jeopardize the availability of the property for forfeiture. Such a temporary order shall expire not more than fourteen days after the date on which it is entered, unless extended for good cause shown or unless the party against whom it is entered consents to an extension for a longer period. A hearing requested concerning an order entered under this

paragraph shall be held at the earliest possible time and prior to the expiration of the temporary order.

(3) The court may receive and consider, at a hearing held pursuant to this subsection, evidence and information that would be inadmissible under the Federal Rules of Evidence.

(f) Warrant of seizure

The Government may request the issuance of a warrant authorizing the seizure of property subject to forfeiture under this section in the same manner as provided for a search warrant. If the court determines that there is probable cause to believe that the property to be seized would, in the event of conviction, be subject to forfeiture and that an order under subsection (e) of this section may not be sufficient to assure the availability of the property for forfeiture, the court shall issue a warrant authorizing the seizure of such property.

(g) Execution

Upon entry of an order of forfeiture under this section, the court shall authorize the Attorney General to seize all property ordered forfeited upon such terms and conditions as the court shall deem proper. Following entry of an order declaring the property forfeited, the court may, upon application of the United States, enter such appropriate restraining orders or injunctions, require the execution of satisfactory performance bonds, appoint receivers, conservators, appraisers, accountants, or trustees, or take any other action to protect the interest of the United States in the property ordered forfeited. Any income accruing to or derived from property ordered forfeited under this section may be used to offset ordinary and necessary expenses to the property which are required by law, or which are necessary to protect the interests of the United States or third parties.

(h) Disposition of property

Following the seizure of property ordered forfeited under this section, the Attorney General shall direct the disposition of the property by sale or any other commercially feasible means, making due provision for the rights of any innocent persons. Any property right or interest not exercisable by, or transferable for value to, the United States shall expire and shall not revert to the defendant, nor shall the defendant or any person acting in concert with him or on his behalf be eligible to purchase forfeited property at any sale held by the United States. Upon application of a person, other than the defendant or a person acting in concert with him or on his behalf, the court may restrain or stay the sale or disposition of the property pending the conclusion of any appeal of the criminal case giving rise to the forfeiture, if the applicant demonstrates that proceeding with the sale or disposition of the property will result in irreparable injury, harm, or loss to him.

(i) Authority of the Attorney General

With respect to property ordered forfeited under this section, the Attorney General is authorized to—

(1) grant petitions for mitigation or remission of forfeiture, restore forfeited property to victims of a violation of this subchapter, or take any other action to protect the rights of innocent persons which is in the interest of justice and which is not inconsistent with the provisions of this section;

(2) compromise claims arising under this section;

(3) award compensation to persons providing information resulting in a forfeiture under this section;

(4) direct the disposition by the United States, in accordance with the provisions of section 881(e) of this title, of all property ordered forfeited under this section by public sale or any other commercially feasible means, making due provision for the rights of innocent persons; and

(5) take appropriate measures necessary to safeguard and maintain property ordered forfeited under this section pending its disposition.

(j) Applicability of civil forfeiture provisions

Except to the extent that they are inconsistent with the provisions of this section, the provisions of section 881(d) of this title shall apply to a criminal forfeiture under this section.

(k) Bar on intervention

Except as provided in subsection (n) of this section, no party claiming an interest in property subject to forfeiture under this section may—

(1) intervene in a trial or appeal of a criminal case involving the forfeiture of such property under this section; or

(2) commence an action at law or equity against the United States concerning the validity of his alleged interest in the property subsequent to the filing of an indictment or information alleging that the property is subject to forfeiture under this section.

(l) Jurisdiction to enter orders

The district courts of the United States shall have jurisdiction to enter orders as provided in this section without regard to the location of any property which may be subject to forfeiture under this section or which has been ordered forfeited under this section.

(m) Depositions

In order to facilitate the identification and location of property declared forfeited and to facilitate the disposition of petitions for remission or mitigation of forfeiture, after the entry of an order declaring property forfeited to the United States, the court may, upon application of the United States, order that the testimony of any witness relating to the property forfeited be taken by deposition and that any designated book, paper, document, record, recording, or other material not privileged be produced at the same time and place, in the same manner as provided for the taking of depositions under Rule 15 of the Federal Rules of Criminal Procedure.

(n) Third party interests

(1) Following the entry of an order of forfeiture under this section, the United States shall publish notice of the order and of its intent to dispose of the property in such manner as the Attorney General may direct. The Government may also, to the extent practicable, provide direct written notice to any person known to have alleged an interest in the property that is the subject of the order of forfeiture as a substitute for published notice as to those persons so notified.

(2) Any person, other than the defendant, asserting a legal interest in property which has been ordered forfeited to the United States pursuant to this section may, within thirty days of the final publication of notice or his receipt of notice under paragraph (1), whichever is earlier, petition the court for a hearing to adjudicate the validity of his alleged interest in the property. The hearing shall be held before the court alone, without a jury.

(3) The petition shall be signed by the petitioner under penalty of perjury and shall set forth the nature and extent of the petitioner's right, title, or interest in the property, the time and circumstances of the petitioner's acquisition of the right, title, or interest in the property, any additional facts supporting the petitioner's claim, and the relief sought.

(4) The hearing on the petition shall, to the extent practicable and consistent with the interests of justice, be held within thirty days of the filing of the petition. The court may consolidate the hearing on the petition with a hearing on any other petition filed by a person other than the defendant under this subsection.

(5) At the hearing, the petitioner may testify and present evidence and witnesses on his own behalf, and cross examine witnesses who appear at the hearing. The United States may present evidence and witnesses in rebuttal and in defense of its claim to the property and cross-examine witnesses who appear at the hearing. In addition to testimony and evidence presented at the hearing, the court shall consider the relevant portions of the record of the criminal case which resulted in the order of forfeiture.

(6) If, after the hearing, the court determines that the petitioner has established by a preponderance of the evidence that—

(A) the petitioner has a legal right, title, or interest in the property, and such right, title, or interest renders the order of forfeiture invalid in whole or in part because the right, title, or interest was vested in the petitioner rather than the defendant or was superior to any right, title, or interest of the defendant at the time of the commission of the acts which gave rise to the forfeiture of the property under this section; or

(B) the petitioner is a bona fide purchaser for value of the right, title, or interest in the property and was at the time of purchase reasonably without cause to believe that the property was subject to forfeiture under this section;

the court shall amend the order of forfeiture in accordance with its determination.

(7) Following the court's disposition of all petitions filed under this subsection, or if no such petitions are filed following the expiration of the period provided in paragraph (2) for the filing of such petitions, the United States shall have clear title to property that is the subject of the order of forfeiture and may warrant good title to any subsequent purchaser or transferee.

(o) Construction

The provisions of this section shall be liberally construed to effectuate its remedial purposes.

(p) Forfeiture of substitute property

(1) In general

Paragraph (2) of this subsection shall apply, if any property described in subsection (a), as a result of any act or omission of the defendant—

(A) cannot be located upon the exercise of due diligence;

(B) has been transferred or sold to, or deposited with, a third party;

(C) has been placed beyond the jurisdiction of the court;

(D) has been substantially diminished in value; or

(E) has been commingled with other property which cannot be divided without difficulty.

(2) Substitute property

In any case described in any of subparagraphs (A) through (E) of paragraph (1), the court shall order the forfeiture of any other property of the defendant, up to the value of any property described in subparagraphs (A) through (E) of paragraph (1), as applicable.

(3) Return of property to jurisdiction

In the case of property described in paragraph (1)(C), the court may, in addition to any other action authorized by this subsection, order the defendant to return the property to the jurisdiction of the court so that the property may be seized and forfeited.

(q) Restitution for cleanup of clandestine laboratory sites

The court, when sentencing a defendant convicted of an offense under this subchapter or subchapter II of this chapter involving the manufacture, possession, or the possession with intent to distribute, of amphetamine or methamphetamine, shall—

(1) order restitution as provided in sections 3612 and 3664 of Title 18;

(2) order the defendant to reimburse the United States, the State or local government concerned, or both the United States and the State or local government concerned for the costs incurred by the United States or the State or local government concerned, as the case may be, for the cleanup associated with the manufacture of amphetamine or methamphetamine by the defendant, or on premises or in property that the defendant owns, resides, or does business in; and

(3) order restitution to any person injured as a result of the offense as provided in section 3663A of Title 18.

18 U.S.C. 1963. Criminal Forfeiture (RICO) (text)

(a) Whoever violates any provision of section 1962 of this chapter shall be fined under this title or imprisoned not more than 20 years (or for life if the violation is based on a racketeering activity for which the maximum penalty includes life imprisonment), or both, and shall forfeit to the United States, irrespective of any provision of State law—

(1) any interest the person has acquired or maintained in violation of section 1962;

(2) any—

(A) interest in;

(B) security of;

(C) claim against; or

(D) property or contractual right of any kind affording a source of influence over; any enterprise which the person has established, operated, controlled, conducted, or participated in the conduct of, in violation of section 1962; and

(3) any property constituting, or derived from, any proceeds which the person obtained, directly or indirectly, from racketeering activity or unlawful debt collection in violation of section 1962. The court, in imposing sentence on such person shall order, in addition to any other sentence imposed pursuant to this section, that the person forfeit to the United States all property described in this subsection. In lieu of a fine otherwise authorized by this section, a defendant who derives profits or other proceeds from an offense may be fined not more than twice the gross profits or other proceeds.

(b) Property subject to criminal forfeiture under this section includes—

(1) real property, including things growing on, affixed to, and found in land; and

(2) tangible and intangible personal property, including rights, privileges, interests, claims, and securities.

(c) All right, title, and interest in property described in subsection (a) vests in the United States upon the commission of the act giving rise to forfeiture under this section. Any such property that is subsequently transferred to a person other than the defendant may be the subject of a special verdict of forfeiture and thereafter shall be ordered forfeited to the United States, unless the transferee establishes in a hearing pursuant to subsection (l) that he is a bona fide purchaser for value of such property who at the time of purchase was reasonably without cause to believe that the property was subject to forfeiture under this section.

(d)(1) Upon application of the United States, the court may enter a restraining order or injunction, require the execution of a satisfactory performance bond, or take any other action to preserve the availability of property described in subsection (a) for forfeiture under this section—

(A) upon the filing of an indictment or information charging a violation of section 1962 of this chapter and alleging that the property with respect to which the order is sought would, in the event of conviction, be subject to forfeiture under this section; or

(B) prior to the filing of such an indictment or information, if, after notice to persons appearing to have an interest in the property and opportunity for a hearing, the court determines that—

(i) there is a substantial probability that the United States will prevail on the issue of forfeiture and that failure to enter the order will result in the property being destroyed, removed from the jurisdiction of the court, or otherwise made unavailable for forfeiture; and

(ii) the need to preserve the availability of the property through the entry of the requested order outweighs the hardship on any party against whom the order is to be entered:

Provided, however, That an order entered pursuant to subparagraph (B) shall be effective for not more than ninety days, unless extended by the court for good cause shown or unless an indictment or information described in subparagraph (A) has been filed.

(2) A temporary restraining order under this subsection may be entered upon application of the United States without notice or opportunity for a hearing when an information or indictment has not yet been filed with respect to the property, if the United States demonstrates that there is probable cause to believe that the property with respect to which the order is sought would, in the event of conviction, be subject to forfeiture under this section and that provision of notice will jeopardize the availability of the property for forfeiture. Such a temporary order shall expire not more than fourteen days after the date on which it is entered, unless extended for good cause shown or unless the party against whom it is entered consents to an extension for a longer period. A hearing requested concerning an order entered under this paragraph shall be held at the earliest possible time, and prior to the expiration of the temporary order.

(3) The court may receive and consider, at a hearing held pursuant to this subsection, evidence and information that would be inadmissible under the Federal Rules of Evidence.

(e) Upon conviction of a person under this section, the court shall enter a judgment of forfeiture of the property to the United States and shall also authorize the Attorney General to seize all property ordered forfeited upon such terms and conditions as the court shall deem proper. Following the entry of an order declaring the property forfeited, the court may, upon application of the United States, enter such appropriate restraining orders or injunctions, require the execution of satisfactory performance bonds, appoint receivers, conservators, appraisers, accountants, or trustees, or take any other action to protect the interest of the United States in the property ordered forfeited. Any income accruing to, or derived from, an enterprise or an interest in an enterprise which has been ordered forfeited under this section may be used to offset ordinary and necessary expenses to the enterprise which are required by law, or which are necessary to protect the interests of the United States or third parties.

(f) Following the seizure of property ordered forfeited under this section, the Attorney General shall direct the disposition of the property by sale or any other commercially feasible means, making due provision for the rights of any innocent persons. Any property right or interest not exercisable by, or transferable for value to, the United States shall expire and shall not revert to the defendant, nor shall the defendant or any person acting in concert with or on behalf of the defendant be eligible to purchase forfeited property at any sale held by the United States. Upon application of a person, other than the defendant or a person acting in concert with or on behalf of the defendant, the court may restrain or stay the sale or disposition of the property pending the conclusion of any appeal of the criminal case giving rise to the forfeiture, if the applicant demonstrates that proceeding with the sale or disposition of the property will result in irreparable injury, harm or loss to him. Notwithstanding 31 U.S.C. 3302(b), the proceeds of any sale or other disposition of property forfeited under this section and any moneys forfeited shall be used to pay all proper expenses for the forfeiture and the sale, including expenses of seizure, maintenance and custody of the property pending its disposition, advertising and court costs. The Attorney General shall deposit in the Treasury any amounts of such proceeds or moneys remaining after the payment of such expenses.

(g) With respect to property ordered forfeited under this section, the Attorney General is authorized to—

(1) grant petitions for mitigation or remission of forfeiture, restore forfeited property to victims of a violation of this chapter, or take any other action to protect the rights of innocent persons which is in the interest of justice and which is not inconsistent with the provisions of this chapter;

(2) compromise claims arising under this section;

(3) award compensation to persons providing information resulting in a forfeiture under this section;

(4) direct the disposition by the United States of all property ordered forfeited under this section by public sale or any other commercially feasible means, making due provision for the rights of innocent persons; and

(5) take appropriate measures necessary to safeguard and maintain property ordered forfeited under this section pending its disposition.

(h) The Attorney General may promulgate regulations with respect to—

(1) making reasonable efforts to provide notice to persons who may have an interest in property ordered forfeited under this section;

(2) granting petitions for remission or mitigation of forfeiture;

(3) the restitution of property to victims of an offense petitioning for remission or mitigation of forfeiture under this chapter;

(4) the disposition by the United States of forfeited property by public sale or other commercially feasible means;

(5) the maintenance and safekeeping of any property forfeited under this section pending its disposition; and

(6) the compromise of claims arising under this chapter.

Pending the promulgation of such regulations, all provisions of law relating to the disposition of property, or the proceeds from the sale thereof, or the remission or mitigation of forfeitures for violation of the customs laws, and the compromise of claims and the award of compensation to informers in respect of such forfeitures shall apply to forfeitures incurred, or alleged to have been incurred, under the provisions of this section, insofar as applicable and not inconsistent with the provisions hereof. Such duties as are imposed upon the Customs Service or any person with respect to the disposition of property under the customs law shall be performed under this chapter by the Attorney General.

(*i*) Except as provided in subsection (l), no party claiming an interest in property subject to forfeiture under this section may—

(1) intervene in a trial or appeal of a criminal case involving the forfeiture of such property under this section; or

(2) commence an action at law or equity against the United States concerning the validity of his alleged interest in the property subsequent to the filing of an indictment or information alleging that the property is subject to forfeiture under this section.

(j) The district courts of the United States shall have jurisdiction to enter orders as provided in this section without regard to the location of any property which may be subject to forfeiture under this section or which has been ordered forfeited under this section.

(k) In order to facilitate the identification or location of property declared forfeited and to facilitate the disposition of petitions for remission or mitigation of forfeiture, after the entry of an order declaring property forfeited to the United States the court may, upon application of the United States, order that the testimony of any witness relating to the property forfeited be taken by deposition and that any designated book, paper, document, record, recording, or other material not privileged be produced at the same time and place, in the same manner as provided for the taking of depositions under Rule 15 of the Federal Rules of Criminal Procedure.

(*l*)(1) Following the entry of an order of forfeiture under this section, the United States shall publish notice of the order and of its intent to dispose of the property in such manner as the Attorney General may direct. The Government may also, to the extent practicable, provide direct written notice to any person known to have alleged an interest in the property that is the subject of the order of forfeiture as a substitute for published notice as to those persons so notified.

(2) Any person, other than the defendant, asserting a legal interest in property which has been ordered forfeited to the United States pursuant to this section may, within thirty days of the final publication of notice or his receipt of notice under paragraph (1), whichever is earlier, petition the court for a hearing to adjudicate the validity of his alleged interest in the property. The hearing shall be held before the court alone, without a jury.

(3) The petition shall be signed by the petitioner under penalty of perjury and shall set forth the nature and extent of the petitioner's right, title, or interest in the property, the time and circumstances of the petitioner's acquisition of the right, title, or interest in the property, any additional facts supporting the petitioner's claim, and the relief sought.

(4) The hearing on the petition shall, to the extent practicable and consistent with the interests of justice, be held within thirty days of the filing of the petition. The court may consolidate the hearing on the petition with a hearing on any other petition filed by a person other than the defendant under this subsection.

(5) At the hearing, the petitioner may testify and present evidence and witnesses on his own behalf, and cross-examine witnesses who appear at the hearing. The United States may present evidence and witnesses in rebuttal and in defense of its claim to the property and cross-examine witnesses who appear at the hearing. In addition to testimony and evidence presented at the hearing, the court shall consider the relevant portions of the record of the criminal case which resulted in the order of forfeiture.

(6) If, after the hearing, the court determines that the petitioner has established by a preponderance of the evidence that—

(A) the petitioner has a legal right, title, or interest in the property, and such right, title, or interest renders the order of forfeiture invalid in whole or in part because the right, title, or interest was vested in the petitioner rather than the defendant or was superior to any right, title, or interest of the defendant at the time of the commission of the acts which gave rise to the forfeiture of the property under this section; or

(B) the petitioner is a bona fide purchaser for value of the right, title, or interest in the property and was at the time of purchase reasonably without cause to believe that the property was subject to forfeiture under this section;

the court shall amend the order of forfeiture in accordance with its determination.

(7) Following the court's disposition of all petitions filed under this subsection, or if no such petitions are filed following the expiration of the period provided in paragraph (2) for the filing of such petitions, the United States shall have clear title to property that is the subject of the order of forfeiture and may warrant good title to any subsequent purchaser or transferee.

(m) If any of the property described in subsection (a), as a result of any act or omission of the defendant—

(1) cannot be located upon the exercise of due diligence;

(2) has been transferred or sold to, or deposited with, a third party;

(3) has been placed beyond the jurisdiction of the court;

(4) has been substantially diminished in value; or

(5) has been commingled with other property which cannot be divided without difficulty; the court shall order the forfeiture of any other property of the defendant up to the value of any property described in paragraphs (1) through (5).

F.R.Crim.P. 32.2. Criminal Forfeiture (text)

(a) *Notice to the Defendant.* A court must not enter a judgment of forfeiture in a criminal proceeding unless the indictment or information contains notice to the defendant that the government will seek the forfeiture of property as part of any sentence in accordance with the applicable statute. The notice should not be designated as a count of the indictment or information. The indictment or information need not identify the property subject to forfeiture or specify the amount of any forfeiture money judgment that the government seeks.

(b) *Entering a Preliminary Order of Forfeiture.*

(1) *Forfeiture Phase of the Trial.*

(A) *Forfeiture Determinations.* As soon as practical after a verdict or finding of guilty, or after a plea of guilty or nolo contendere is accepted, on any count in an indictment or information regarding which criminal forfeiture is sought, the court must determine what property is subject to forfeiture under the applicable statute. If the government seeks forfeiture of specific property, the court must determine whether the government has established the requisite nexus between the property and the offense. If the government seeks a personal money judgment, the court must determine the amount of money that the defendant will be ordered to pay.

(B) Evidence and Hearing. The court's determination may be based on evidence already in the record, including any written plea agreement, and on any additional evidence or information submitted by the parties and accepted by the court as relevant and reliable. If the forfeiture is contested, on either party's request the court must conduct a hearing after the verdict or finding of guilty.

(2) *Preliminary Order.*

(A) Contents of a Specific Order. If the court finds that property is subject to forfeiture, it must promptly enter a preliminary order of forfeiture setting forth the amount of any money judgment, directing the forfeiture of specific property, and directing the forfeiture of any substitute property if the government has met the statutory criteria. The court must enter the order without regard to any third party's interest in the property. Determining whether a third party has such an interest must be deferred until any third party files a claim in an ancillary proceeding under Rule 32.2(c).

(B) Timing. Unless doing so is impractical, the court must enter the preliminary order sufficiently in advance of sentencing to allow the parties to suggest revisions or modifications before the order becomes final as to the defendant under Rule 32.2(b)(4).

(C) General Order. If, before sentencing, the court cannot identify all the specific property subject to forfeiture or calculate the total amount of the money judgment, the court may enter a forfeiture order that:

(i) lists any identified property;

(ii) describes other property in general terms; and

(iii) states that the order will be amended under Rule 32.2(e)(1) when additional specific property is identified or the amount of the money judgment has been calculated.

(3) *Seizing Property.* The entry of a preliminary order of forfeiture authorizes the Attorney

General (or a designee) to seize the specific property subject to forfeiture; to conduct any discovery the court considers proper in identifying, locating, or disposing of the property; and to commence proceedings that comply with any statutes governing third-party rights. The court may include in the order of forfeiture conditions reasonably necessary to preserve the property's value pending any appeal.

(4) *Sentence and Judgment.*

(A) When Final. At sentencing - or at any time before sentencing if the defendant consents - the preliminary forfeiture order becomes final as to the defendant. If the order directs the defendant to forfeit specific property, it remains preliminary as to third parties until the ancillary proceeding is concluded under Rule 32.2(c).

(B) Notice and Inclusion in the Judgment. The court must include the forfeiture when orally announcing the sentence or must otherwise ensure that the defendant knows of the forfeiture at sentencing. The court must also include the forfeiture order, directly or by reference, in the judgment, but the court's failure to do so may be corrected at any time under Rule 36.

(C) Time to Appeal. The time for the defendant or the government to file an appeal from the forfeiture order, or from the court's failure to enter an order, begins to run when judgment is entered. If the court later amends or declines to amend a forfeiture order to include additional property under Rule 32.2(e), the defendant or the government may file an appeal regarding that property under Federal Rule of Appellate Procedure 4(b). The time for that appeal runs from the date when the order granting or denying the amendment becomes final.

(5) *Jury Determination.*

(A) Retaining the Jury. In any case tried before a jury, if the indictment or information states that the government is seeking forfeiture, the court must determine before the jury begins deliberating whether either party requests that the jury be retained to determine the forfeitability of specific property if it returns a guilty verdict.

(B) Special Verdict Form. If a party timely requests to have the jury determine forfeiture, the government must submit a proposed Special Verdict Form listing each property subject to forfeiture and asking the jury to determine whether the government has established the requisite nexus between the property and the offense committed by the defendant.

(6) *Notice of the Forfeiture Order.*

(A) Publishing and Sending Notice. If the court orders the forfeiture of specific property, the government must publish notice of the order and send notice to any person who reasonably appears to be a potential claimant with standing to contest the forfeiture in the ancillary proceeding.

(B) Content of the Notice. The notice must describe the forfeited property, state the times under the applicable statute when a petition contesting the forfeiture must be filed, and state the name and contact information for the government attorney to be served with the petition.

(C) Means of Publication; Exceptions to Publication Requirement. Publication must take place as described in Supplemental Rule G(4)(a)(iii) of the Federal Rules of Civil Procedure, and may be by any means described in Supplemental Rule G(4)(a)(iv). Publication is unnecessary if any exception in Supplemental Rule G(4)(a)(i) applies.

(D) Means of Sending the Notice. The notice may be sent in accordance with Supplemental Rules G(4)(b)(iii)-(v) of the Federal Rules of Civil Procedure.

(7) *Interlocutory Sale*. At any time before entry of a final forfeiture order, the court, in accordance with Supplemental Rule G(7) of the Federal Rules of Civil Procedure, may order the interlocutory sale of property alleged to be forfeitable.

(c) *Ancillary Proceeding; Entering a Final Order of Forfeiture.*

(1) *In General*. If, as prescribed by statute, a third party files a petition asserting an interest in the property to be forfeited, the court must conduct an ancillary proceeding, but no ancillary proceeding is required to the extent that the forfeiture consists of a money judgment.

(A) In the ancillary proceeding, the court may, on motion, dismiss the petition for lack of standing, for failure to state a claim, or for any other lawful reason. For purposes of the motion, the facts set forth in the petition are assumed to be true.

(B) After disposing of any motion filed under Rule 32.2(c)(1)(A) and before conducting a hearing on the petition, the court may permit the parties to conduct discovery in accordance with the Federal Rules of Civil Procedure if the court determines that discovery is necessary or desirable to resolve factual issues. When discovery ends, a party may move for summary judgment under Federal Rule of Civil Procedure 56.

(2) *Entering a Final Order*. When the ancillary proceeding ends, the court must enter a final order of forfeiture by amending the preliminary order as necessary to account for any third-party rights. If no third party files a timely petition, the preliminary order becomes the final order of forfeiture if the court finds that the defendant (or any combination of defendants convicted in the case) had an interest in the property that is forfeitable under the applicable statute. The defendant may not object to the entry of the final order on the ground that the property belongs, in whole or in part, to a codefendant or third party; nor may a third party object to the final order on the ground that the third party had an interest in the property.

(3) *Multiple Petitions*. If multiple third-party petitions are filed in the same case, an order dismissing or granting one petition is not appealable until

rulings are made on all the petitions, unless the court determines that there is no just reason for delay.

(4) *Ancillary Proceeding Not Part of Sentencing.* An ancillary proceeding is not part of sentencing.

(d) *Stay Pending Appeal.* If a defendant appeals from a conviction or an order of forfeiture, the court may stay the order of forfeiture on terms appropriate to ensure that the property remains available pending appellate review. A stay does not delay the ancillary proceeding or the determination of a third party's rights or interests. If the court rules in favor of any third party while an appeal is pending, the court may amend the order of forfeiture but must not transfer any property interest to a third party until the decision on appeal becomes final, unless the defendant consents in writing or on the record.

(e) *Subsequently Located Property; Substitute Property.*

(1) *In General.* On the government's motion, the court may at any time enter an order of forfeiture or amend an existing order of forfeiture to include property that:

(A) is subject to forfeiture under an existing order of forfeiture but was located and identified after that order was entered; or

(B) is substitute property that qualifies for forfeiture under an applicable statute.

(2) *Procedure.* If the government shows that the property is subject to forfeiture under Rule 32.2(e)(1), the court must:

(A) enter an order forfeiting that property, or amend an existing preliminary or final order to include it; and

(B) if a third party files a petition claiming an interest in the property, conduct an ancillary proceeding under Rule 32.2(c).

(3) *Jury Trial Limited.* There is no right to a jury trial under Rule 32.2(e).

28 U.S.C. 524(c). Department of Justice Asset Forfeiture Fund (text)

(c)(1) There is established in the United States Treasury a special fund to be known as the Department of Justice Assets Forfeiture Fund (hereafter in this subsection referred to as the "Fund") which shall be available to the Attorney General without fiscal year limitation for the following law enforcement purposes—

(A) the payment, at the discretion of the Attorney General, of any expenses necessary to seize, detain, inventory, safeguard, maintain, advertise, sell, or dispose of property under seizure, detention, or forfeited pursuant to any law enforced or administered by the Department of Justice, or of any other necessary expense incident to the seizure, detention, forfeiture, or disposal of such property including—

(i) payments for—

(I) contract services;

(II) the employment of outside contractors to operate and manage properties or provide other specialized services necessary to dispose of such properties in an effort to maximize the return from such properties; and

(III) reimbursement of any Federal, State, or local agency for any expenditures made to perform the functions described in this clause;

(ii) payments to reimburse any Federal agency participating in the Fund for investigative costs leading to seizures;

(iii) payments for contracting for the services of experts and consultants needed by the Department of Justice to assist in carrying out duties related to asset seizure and forfeiture; and

(iv) payments made pursuant to guidelines promulgated by the Attorney General if such payments are necessary and directly related to seizure and forfeiture program expenses for—

(I) the purchase or lease of automatic data processing systems (not less than a majority of which use will be related to such program);

(II) training;

(III) printing;

(IV) the storage, protection, and destruction of controlled substances; and

(V) contracting for services directly related to the identification of forfeitable assets, and the processing of and accounting for forfeitures;

(B) the payment of awards for information or assistance directly relating to violations of the criminal drug laws of the United States or of sections 1956 and 1957 of title 18, sections 5313 and 5324 of title 31, and section 6050I of the Internal Revenue Code of 1986;

(C) at the discretion of the Attorney General, the payment of awards for information or assistance leading to a civil or criminal forfeiture involving any Federal agency participating in the Fund;

(D) the compromise and payment of valid liens and mortgages against property that has been forfeited pursuant to any law enforced or administered by the Department of Justice, subject to the discretion of the Attorney General to determine the validity of any such lien or mortgage and the amount of payment to be made, and the employment of attorneys and other personnel skilled in State real estate law as necessary;

(E)(i) for disbursements authorized in connection with remission or mitigation procedures relating to property forfeited under any law enforced or administered by the Department of Justice; and

(ii) for payment for—

(I) costs incurred by or on behalf of the Department of Justice in connection with the removal, for purposes of Federal forfeiture and disposition, of any hazardous substance or pollutant or contaminant associated with the illegal manufacture of amphetamine or methamphetamine; and

(II) costs incurred by or on behalf of a State or local government in connection with such removal in any case in which such State or local government has assisted in a Federal prosecution relating to amphetamine or methamphetamine, to the extent such costs exceed equitable sharing payments made to such State or local government in such case;

(F)(i) for equipping for law enforcement functions of any Government-owned or leased vessel, vehicle, or aircraft available for official use by any Federal agency participating in the Fund;

(ii) for equipping any vessel, vehicle, or aircraft available for official use by a State or local law enforcement agency to enable the vessel, vehicle, or aircraft to assist law enforcement functions if the vessel, vehicle, or aircraft will be used in a joint law enforcement operation with a Federal agency participating in the Fund; and

(iii) payments for other equipment directly related to seizure or forfeiture, including laboratory equipment, protective equipment, communications equipment, and the operation and maintenance costs of such equipment;

(G) for purchase of evidence of any violation of the Controlled Substances Act, the Controlled Substances Import and Export Act, chapter 96 of title 18, or sections 1956 and 1957 of title 18;

(H) the payment of State and local property taxes on forfeited real property that accrued between the date of the violation giving rise to the forfeiture and the date of the forfeiture order; and

(I) payment of overtime salaries, travel, fuel, training, equipment, and other similar costs of State or local law enforcement officers that are incurred in a joint law enforcement operation with a Federal law enforcement agency participating in the Fund.

Amounts for paying the expenses authorized by subparagraphs (B), (F), and (G) shall be specified in appropriations Acts and may be used under authorities available to the organization receiving the funds. Amounts for other authorized expenditures and payments from the Fund, including equitable sharing payments, are not required to be specified in appropriations acts. The Attorney General may exempt the procurement of contract services under subparagraph (A) under the Fund from division C (except sections 3302, 3501(b), 3509, 3906, 4710, and 4711) of subtitle I of title 41, section 6101(b) to (d) of title 41, and other provisions of law as may be necessary to maintain the security and confidentiality of related criminal investigations.

(2) Any award paid from the Fund, as provided in paragraph (1)(B) or (C), shall be paid at the discretion of the Attorney General or his delegate, under existing departmental delegation policies for the payment of awards, except that the authority to pay an award of $250,000 or more shall not be delegated to any person other than the Deputy Attorney General, the Associate Attorney General, the Director of the Federal Bureau of Investigation, or the Administrator of the Drug Enforcement Administration. Any award pursuant to paragraph (1)(B) shall not exceed $500,000. Any award pursuant to paragraph (1)(C) shall not exceed the lesser of $500,000 or one-fourth of the amount realized by the United States from the property forfeited, without both the personal approval of the Attorney General and written notice within 30 days thereof to the Chairmen and ranking minority members of the Committees on Appropriations and the Judiciary of the Senate and of the House of Representatives.

(3) Any amount under subparagraph (G) of paragraph (1) shall be paid at the discretion of the Attorney General or his delegate, except that the authority to pay $100,000 or more may be delegated only to the respective head of the agency involved.

(4) There shall be deposited in the Fund—

(A) all amounts from the forfeiture of property under any law enforced or administered by the Department of Justice, except all proceeds of forfeitures available for use by the Secretary of the Treasury or the Secretary of the Interior pursuant to section 11(d) of the Endangered Species Act (16 U.S.C. 1540(d)) or section 6(d) of the Lacey Act Amendments of 1981 (16 U.S.C. 3375(d)), or the Postmaster General of the United States pursuant to 39 U.S.C. 2003(b)(7);

(B) all amounts representing the Federal equitable share from the forfeiture of property under any Federal, State, local or foreign law, for any Federal agency participating in the Fund;

(C) all amounts transferred by the Secretary of the Treasury pursuant to section 9703(g)(4)(A)(ii) of title 31; and

(D) all amounts collected—

(i) by the United States pursuant to a reimbursement order under paragraph (2) of section 413(q) of the Controlled Substances Act (21 U.S.C. 853(q)); and

(ii) pursuant to a restitution order under paragraph (1) or (3) of section 413(q) of the Controlled Substances Act [21 U.S.C. 853(q)] for injuries to the United States.

(5) Amounts in the Fund, and in any holding accounts associated with the Fund, that are not currently needed for the purpose of this section shall be kept on deposit or invested in obligations of, or guaranteed by, the United States and all earnings on such investments shall be deposited in the Fund.

(6)(A) The Attorney General shall transmit to Congress and make available to the public, not later than 4 months after the end of each fiscal year, detailed reports for the prior fiscal year as follows:

(i) A report on total deposits to the Fund by State of deposit.

(ii) A report on total expenses paid from the Fund, by category of expense and recipient agency, including equitable sharing payments.

(iii) A report describing the number, value, and types of properties placed into official use by Federal agencies, by recipient agency.

(iv) A report describing the number, value, and types of properties transferred to State and local law enforcement agencies, by recipient agency.

(v) A report, by type of disposition, describing the number, value, and types of forfeited property disposed of during the year.

(vi) A report on the year-end inventory of property under seizure, but not yet forfeited, that reflects the type of property, its estimated value, and the estimated value of liens and mortgages outstanding on the property.

(vii) A report listing each property in the year-end inventory, not yet forfeited, with an outstanding equity of not less than $1,000,000.

(B) The Attorney General shall transmit to Congress and make available to the public, not later than 2 months after final issuance, the audited financial statements for each fiscal year for the Fund.

(C) Reports under subparagraph (A) shall include information with respect to all forfeitures under any law enforced or administered by the Department of Justice.

(D) The transmittal and publication requirements in subparagraphs (A) and (B) may be satisfied by—

(i) posting the reports on an Internet website maintained by the Department of Justice for a period of not less than 2 years; and

(ii) notifying the Committees on the Judiciary of the House of Representatives and the Senate when the reports are available electronically.

(7) The provisions of this subsection relating to deposits in the Fund shall apply to all property in the custody of the Department of Justice on or after the effective date of the Comprehensive Forfeiture Act of 1983.

(8)(A) There are authorized to be appropriated such sums as necessary for the purposes described in subparagraphs (B), (F), and (G) of paragraph (1).

(B) Subject to subparagraphs (C) and (D), at the end of each of fiscal years 1994, 1995, and 1996, the Attorney General shall transfer from the Fund not more than $100,000,000 to the Special Forfeiture Fund established by section 6073 of the Anti-Drug Abuse Act of 1988.

(C) Transfers under subparagraph (B) may be made only from the excess unobligated balance and may not exceed one-half of the excess unobligated balance for any year. In addition, transfers under subparagraph (B) may be made only to the extent that the sum of the transfers in a fiscal year and one-half of the unobligated balance at the beginning of that fiscal year for the Special Forfeiture Fund does not exceed $100,000,000.

(D) For the purpose of determining amounts available for distribution at year end for any fiscal year, "excess unobligated balance" means the unobligated balance of the Fund generated by that fiscal year's operations, less any amounts that are required to be retained in the Fund to ensure the availability of amounts in the subsequent fiscal year for purposes authorized under paragraph (1).

(E) Subject to the notification procedures contained in section 605 of P.L. 103-121, and after satisfying the transfer requirement in subparagraph (B) of this paragraph, any excess unobligated balance remaining in the Fund on September 30, 1997 and thereafter shall be available to the Attorney General, without fiscal year limitation, for any Federal law enforcement, litigative/prosecutive, and correctional activities, or any other authorized purpose of the Department of Justice. Any amounts provided pursuant to this subparagraph may be used under authorities available to the organization receiving the funds.

(9)(A) Following the completion of procedures for the forfeiture of property pursuant to any law enforced or administered by the Department, the Attorney General is authorized, in her discretion, to warrant clear title to any subsequent purchaser or transferee of such property.

(B) For fiscal years 2002 and 2003, the Attorney General is authorized to transfer, under such terms and conditions as the Attorney General shall specify, real or personal property of limited or marginal value, to a State or local government agency, or its designated contractor or transferee, for use to support drug abuse treatment, drug and crime prevention and education, housing, job skills, and other community-based public health and safety programs. Each such transfer shall be subject to satisfaction by the recipient involved of any outstanding lien against the property transferred, but no such transfer shall create or confer any private right of action in any person against the United States.

(10) The Attorney General shall transfer from the Fund to the Secretary of the Treasury for deposit in the Department of the Treasury Forfeiture Fund amounts appropriate to reflect the degree of participation of the Department of the Treasury law enforcement organizations (described in section 9703(p) of title 31) in the law enforcement effort resulting in the forfeiture pursuant to laws enforced or administered by the Department of Justice.

(11) For purposes of this subsection and notwithstanding section 9703 of title 31 or any other law, property is forfeited pursuant to a law enforced or administered by the Department of Justice if it is forfeited pursuant to—

(A) a judicial forfeiture proceeding when the underlying seizure was made by an officer of a Federal law enforcement agency participating in the Department of Justice Assets Forfeiture Fund or the property was maintained by the United States Marshals Service; or

(B) a civil administrative forfeiture proceeding conducted by a Department of Justice law enforcement component or pursuant to the authority of the Secretary of Commerce. [(12) Redesignated (11)]

28 U.S.C. 2461. Mode of Recovery (text)

(a) Whenever a civil fine, penalty or pecuniary forfeiture is prescribed for the violation of an Act of Congress without specifying the mode of recovery or enforcement thereof, it may be recovered in a civil action.

(b) Unless otherwise provided by Act of Congress, whenever a forfeiture of property is prescribed as a penalty for violation of an Act of Congress and the seizure takes place on the high seas or on navigable waters within the admiralty and maritime jurisdiction of the United States, such forfeiture may be enforced by libel in admiralty but in cases of seizures on land the forfeiture may be enforced by a proceeding by libel which shall conform as near as may be to proceedings in admiralty.

(c) If a person is charged in a criminal case with a violation of an Act of Congress for which the civil or criminal forfeiture of property is authorized, the Government may include notice of the forfeiture in the indictment or information pursuant to the Federal Rules of Criminal Procedure. If the defendant is convicted of the offense giving rise to the forfeiture, the court shall order the forfeiture of the property as part of the sentence in the criminal case pursuant to the Federal Rules of Criminal Procedure and section 3554 of title 18, United States Code. The procedures in section 413 of the Controlled Substances Act (21 U.S.C. 853) apply to all stages of a criminal forfeiture proceeding, except that subsection (d) of such section applies only in cases in which the defendant is convicted of a violation of such Act.

28 U.S.C. 2465. Successful Claims; Interest and Attorneys Fees (text)

(a) Upon the entry of a judgment for the claimant in any proceeding to condemn or forfeit property seized or arrested under any provision of Federal law—

(1) such property shall be returned forthwith to the claimant or his agent; and

(2) if it appears that there was reasonable cause for the seizure or arrest, the court shall cause a proper certificate thereof to be entered and, in such case, neither the person who made the seizure or arrest nor the prosecutor shall be liable to suit or judgment on account of such suit or prosecution, nor shall the claimant be entitled to costs, except as provided in subsection (b).

(b)(1) Except as provided in paragraph (2), in any civil proceeding to forfeit property under any provision of Federal law in which the claimant substantially prevails, the United States shall be liable for—

(A) reasonable attorney fees and other litigation costs reasonably incurred by the claimant;

(B) post-judgment interest, as set forth in section 1961 of this title; and

(C) in cases involving currency, other negotiable instruments, or the proceeds of an interlocutory sale —(i) interest actually paid to the United States from the date of seizure or arrest of the property that resulted from the investment of the property in an interest-bearing account or instrument; and (ii) an imputed amount of interest that such currency, instruments, or proceeds would have earned at the rate applicable to the 30-day Treasury Bill, for any period during which no interest was paid (not including any period when the property reasonably was in use as evidence in an official proceeding or in conducting scientific tests for the purpose of collecting evidence), commencing 15 days after the property was seized by a Federal law enforcement agency, or was turned over to a Federal law enforcement agency by a State or local law enforcement agency.

(2)(A) The United States shall not be required to disgorge the value of any intangible benefits nor make any other payments to the claimant not specifically authorized by this subsection.

(B) The provisions of paragraph (1) shall not apply if the claimant is convicted of a crime for which the interest of the claimant in the property was subject to forfeiture under a Federal criminal forfeiture law.

(C) If there are multiple claims to the same property, the United States shall not be liable for costs and attorneys fees associated with any such claim if the United States— (i) promptly recognizes such claim;

(ii) promptly returns the interest of the claimant in the property to the claimant, if the property can be divided without difficulty and there are no competing claims to that portion of the property;

(iii) does not cause the claimant to incur additional, reasonable costs or fees; and

(iv) prevails in obtaining forfeiture with respect to one or more of the other claims. (D) If the court enters judgment in part for the claimant and in part for the Government, the court shall reduce the award of costs and attorney fees accordingly.

31 U.S.C. 9703 Department of the Treasury Forfeiture Fund (text)

(a) *In general.*—There is established in the Treasury of the United States a fund to be known as the "Department of the Treasury Forfeiture Fund" (referred to in this section as the "Fund"). The Fund shall be available to the Secretary, without fiscal year limitation, with respect to seizures and forfeitures made pursuant to any law (other than section 7301 or 7302 of the Internal Revenue Code of 1986) enforced or administered by the Department of the Treasury or the United States Coast Guard for the following law enforcement purposes:

(1)(A) Payment of all proper expenses of seizure (including investigative costs incurred by a Department of the Treasury law enforcement organization leading to seizure) or the proceedings of forfeiture and sale, including the expenses of detention, inventory, security, maintenance, advertisement, or disposal of the property, and if condemned by a court and a bond for such costs was not given, the costs as taxed by the court.

(B) Payment for—

(i) contract services;

(ii) the employment of outside contractors to operate and manage properties or to provide other specialized services necessary to dispose of such properties in an effort to maximize the return from such properties; and

(iii) reimbursing any Federal, State, or local agency for any expenditures made to perform the functions described in this subparagraph.

(C) Awards of compensation to informers under section 619 of the Tariff Act of 1930 (19 U.S.C. 1619).

(D) Satisfaction of—

(i) liens for freight, charges, and contributions in general average, notice of which has been filed with the appropriate Customs officer according to law; and

(ii) subject to the discretion of the Secretary, other valid liens and mortgages against property that has been forfeited pursuant to any law enforced or administered by a Department of the Treasury law enforcement organization. To determine the validity of any such lien or mortgage, the amount of payment to be made, and to carry out the functions described in this subparagraph, the Secretary may employ and compensate attorneys and other personnel skilled in State real estate law.

(E) Payment of amounts authorized by law with respect to remission and mitigation.

(F) Payment of claims of parties in interest to property disposed of under section 612(b) of the Tariff Act of 1930 (19 U.S.C. 1612(b)), in the amounts applicable to such claims at the time of seizure.

(G) Equitable sharing payments made to other Federal agencies, State and local law enforcement agencies, and foreign countries pursuant to section 616(c) of the Tariff Act of 1930 (19 U.S.C. 1616a(c)), section 981 of title 18, or subsection (h) of this section, and all costs related thereto.

(H) Payment for services of experts and consultants needed by a Department of the Treasury law enforcement organization to carry out the organization's duties relating to seizure and forfeiture.

(I) payment of overtime salaries, travel, fuel, training, equipment, and other similar costs of State or local law enforcement officers that are incurred in joint law enforcement operations with a Department of the Treasury law enforcement organization;

(J) payment made pursuant to guidelines promulgated by the Secretary, if such payment is necessary and directly related to seizure and forfeiture program expenses for—

(i) the purchase or lease of automatic data processing systems (not less than a majority of which use will be related to such program);

(ii) training;

(iii) printing; and

(iv) contracting for services directly related to— (I) the identification of forfeitable assets;

(ii) the processing of and accounting for forfeitures; and

(iii) the storage, maintenance, protection, and destruction of controlled substances. (2) At the discretion of the Secretary—

(A) payment of awards for information or assistance leading to a civil or criminal forfeiture involving any Department of the Treasury law enforcement organization participating in the Fund;

(B) purchases of evidence or information by—

(i) a Department of the Treasury law enforcement organization with respect to—

(I) a violation of section 1956 or 1957 of title 18 (relating to money laundering); or

(II) a law, the violation of which may subject property to forfeiture under section 981 or 982 of title 18;

(ii) the United States Customs Service with respect to drug smuggling or a violation of section 542 or 545 of title 18 (relating to fraudulent customs invoices or smuggling);

(iii) the United States Secret Service with respect to a violation of—

(I) section 1028, 1029, or 1030 or title 18;

(II) any law of the United States relating to coins, obligations, or securities of the United States or of a foreign government; or

(III) any law of the United States which the United States Secret Service is authorized to enforce relating to fraud or other criminal or unlawful activity in or against any federally insured financial institution, the Resolution Trust Corporation, or the Federal Deposit Insurance Corporation; and

(iv) the United States Customs Service or the Internal Revenue Service with respect to a violation of chapter 53 of this title (relating to the Bank Secrecy Act).

(C) payment of costs for publicizing awards available under section 619 of the Tariff Act of 1930 (19 U.S.C. 1619);

(D) payment for equipment for any vessel, vehicle, or aircraft available for official use by a Department of the Treasury law enforcement organization to enable the vessel, vehicle, or aircraft to assist in law enforcement functions, and for other equipment directly related to seizure or forfeiture, including laboratory equipment, protective equipment, communications equipment, and the operation and maintenance costs of such equipment;

(E) the payment of claims against employees of the Customs Service settled by the Secretary under section 630 of the Tariff Act of 1930;

(F) payment for equipment for any vessel, vehicle, or aircraft available for official use by a State or local law enforcement agency to enable the vessel, vehicle, or aircraft to assist in law enforcement functions if the vessel, vehicle, or aircraft will be used in joint law enforcement operations with a Department of the Treasury law enforcement organization;

(G) reimbursement of private persons for expenses incurred by such persons in cooperating with a Department of the Treasury law enforcement organization in investigations and undercover law enforcement operations;

(H) payment for training foreign law enforcement personnel with respect to seizure or forfeiture activities of the Department of the Treasury; and (b) *Limitations*

(1) Any payment made under subparagraph (D) or (E) of subsection (a)(1) with respect to a seizure or a forfeiture of property shall not exceed the value of the property at the time of the seizure.

(2) Any payment made under subsection (a)(1)(G) with respect to a seizure or forfeiture of property shall not exceed the value of the property at the time of disposition.

(3) The Secretary may exempt the procurement of contract services under the Fund from division C (except sections 3302, 3501(b), 3509, 3906, 4710, and 4711) of subtitle I of title 41, section 6101(b) to (d) of title 41, and other provisions of law as may be necessary to maintain the security and confidentiality of related criminal investigations.

(4) The Secretary shall assure that any equitable sharing payment made to a State or local law enforcement agency pursuant to subsection (a)(1)(G) and any property transferred to a State or local law enforcement agency pursuant to subsection (h)—

(A) has a value that bears a reasonable relationship to the degree of participation of the State or local agency in the law enforcement effort resulting in the forfeiture, taking into account the total value of all property forfeited and the total law enforcement effort with respect to the violation of law on which the forfeiture is based; and

(B) will serve to encourage further cooperation between the recipient State or local agency and Federal law enforcement agencies.

(5) Amounts transferred by the Attorney General pursuant to section 524(c)(1) of title 28, or by the Postmaster General pursuant to section 2003 of

title 39, and deposited into the Fund pursuant to subsection (d), shall be available for Federal law enforcement related purposes of the Department of the Treasury law enforcement organizations.

(c) *Funds available to United States Coast Guard*

(1) The Secretary shall make available to the United States Coast Guard, from funds appropriated under subsection (g)(2) in excess of $10,000,000 for a fiscal year, an amount equal to the net proceeds in the Fund derived from seizures by the Coast Guard.

(2) Funds made available under this subsection may be used to—

(A) pay for equipment for any vessel, vehicle, or aircraft available for official use by the United States Coast Guard to enable the vessel, vehicle, or aircraft to assist in law enforcement functions;

(B) pay for equipment for any vessel, vehicle, equipment, or aircraft available for official use by a State or local law enforcement agency to enable the vessel, vehicle, or aircraft to assist in law enforcement functions if the vessel, vehicle, or aircraft will be used in joint law enforcement operations with the United States Coast Guard;

(C) pay for overtime salaries, travel, fuel, training, equipment, and other similar costs of State and local law enforcement officers that are incurred in joint law enforcement operations with the United States Coast Guard;

(D) pay for expenses incurred in bringing vessels into compliance with applicable environmental laws prior to disposal by sinking.

(d) *Deposits and credits*

(1) With respect to fiscal year 1993, there shall be deposited into or credited to the Fund—

(A) all currency forfeited during fiscal year 1993, and all proceeds from forfeitures during fiscal year 1993, under any law enforced or administered by the United States Customs Service or the United States Coast Guard;

(B) all income from investments made under subsection (e); and

(C) all amounts representing the equitable share of the United States Customs Service or the United States Coast Guard from the forfeiture of property under any Federal, State, local, or foreign law.

(2) With respect to fiscal years beginning after fiscal year 1993, there shall be deposited into or credited to the Fund—

(A) all currency forfeited after fiscal year 1993, and all proceeds from forfeitures after fiscal year 1993, under any law (other than sections 7301 and 7302 of the Internal Revenue Code of 1986) enforced or administered by a Department of the Treasury law enforcement organization or the United States Coast Guard;

(B) all income from investments made under subsection (e); and

(C) all amounts representing the equitable share of a Department of the Treasury law enforcement organization or the United States Coast Guard from the forfeiture of property under any Federal, State, local, or foreign law.

(e) *Investments.*—Amounts in the Fund, and in any holding accounts associated with the Fund, which are not currently needed for the purposes of this section may be kept on deposit or invested in obligations of, or guaranteed by, the United States and all earnings on such investments shall be deposited in the Fund.

(f) *Reports to Congress.*—The Secretary shall transmit to the Congress, not later than February 1 of each year—

(1) a report on—

(A) the estimated total value of property forfeited with respect to which funds were not deposited in the Fund during the preceding fiscal year—

(i) under any law enforced or administered by the United States Customs Service or the United States Coast Guard, in the case of fiscal year 1993; and

(ii) under any law enforced or administered by the Department of the Treasury law enforcement organizations or the United States Coast Guard, in the case of fiscal years beginning after 1993; and

(B) the estimated total value of all such property transferred to any State or local law enforcement agency; and

(2) a report on—

(A) the balance of the Fund at the beginning of the preceding fiscal year;

(B) liens and mortgages paid and the amount of money shared with Federal, State, local, and foreign law enforcement agencies during the preceding fiscal year;

(C) the net amount realized from the operations of the Fund during the preceding fiscal year, the amount of seized cash being held as evidence, and the amount of money that has been carried over into the current fiscal year;

(D) any defendant's property, not forfeited at the end of the preceding fiscal year, if the equity in such property is valued at $1,000,000 or more;

(E) the total dollar value of uncontested seizures of monetary instruments having a value of over $100,000 which, or the proceeds of which, have not been deposited into the Fund pursuant to subsection (d) within 120 days after seizure, as of the end of the preceding fiscal year;

(F) the balance of the Fund at the end of the preceding fiscal year;

(G) the net amount, if any, of the excess unobligated amounts remaining in the Fund at the end of the preceding fiscal year and available to the Secretary for Federal law enforcement related purposes;

(H) a complete set of audited financial statements (including a balance sheet, income statement, and cash flow analysis) prepared in a manner consistent with the requirements of the Chief Financial Officers Act of 1990 (P.L. 101-576); and

(I) an analysis of income and expenses showing the revenue received or lost—

(i) by property category (such as general property, vehicles, vessels, aircraft, cash, and real property); and

(ii) by type of disposition (such as sale, remission, cancellation, placement into official use, sharing with State and local agencies, and destruction).

The Fund shall be subject to annual financial audits as authorized in the Chief Financial Officers Act of 1990 (P.L. 101-576).

(g) *Appropriations*

(1) There are hereby appropriated from the Fund such sums as may be necessary to carry out the purposes described in subsection (a)(1).

(2) There are authorized to be appropriated from the Fund to carry out the purposes set forth in subsections (a)(2) and (c) not to exceed—

(A) $25,000,000 for fiscal year 1993; and

(B) $50,000,000 for each fiscal year after fiscal year 1993.

(3)(A) Subject to subparagraphs (B) and (C), at the end of each of fiscal years 1994, 1995, 1996, and 1997, the Secretary shall transfer from the Fund not more than $100,000,000 to the Special Forfeiture Fund established by section 6073 of the Anti-Drug Abuse Act of 1988.

(B) Transfers pursuant to subparagraph (A) shall be made only from excess unobligated amounts and only to the extent that, as determined by the Secretary, such transfers will not impair the future availability of amounts for the purposes described in subsection (a). Further, transfers under subparagraph (A) may not exceed one-half of the excess unobligated balance for a year. In addition, transfers under subparagraph (A) may be made only to the extent that the sum of the transfers in a fiscal year and one-half of the unobligated balance at the beginning of that fiscal year for the Special Forfeiture Fund does not exceed $100,000,000.

(C) The Secretary of the Treasury shall reserve an amount not to exceed $30,000,000 from the unobligated balances remaining in the Customs Forfeiture Fund on September 30, 1992, and such amount shall be transferred to the Fund on October 1, 1992, or, if later, the date that is 15 days after the date of the enactment of this section. Such amount shall be available for any expenses or activities authorized under this section. At the end of fiscal year 1993, 1994, 1995, and 1996, the Secretary shall reserve in the Fund an amount not to exceed $50,000,000 of the unobligated balances in the Fund, or, if the Secretary determines that a greater amount is necessary for asset specific expenses, an amount equal to not more than 10 percent of the total obligations from the Fund in the preceding fiscal year. At the end of fiscal year 1997, and at the end of each fiscal year thereafter, the Secretary shall reserve any amounts that are required to be retained in the Fund to ensure the availability of amounts in the subsequent fiscal year for purposes authorized under subsection (a). Unobligated balances remaining pursuant to section 4(B) of 9703(g) shall also be carried forward.

(4)(A) After reserving any amount authorized by paragraph (3)(C), any unobligated balances remaining in the Fund on September 30, 1993, shall be deposited into the general fund of the Treasury of the United States.

After reserving any amount authorized by paragraph (3)(C) and after transferring any amount authorized by paragraph (3)(A), any unobligated balances remaining in the Fund on September 30, 1994, and on September 30 of each fiscal year thereafter, shall be available to the Secretary, without fiscal year limitation, for transfers pursuant to subparagraph (A)(ii) and for obligation or expenditure in connection with the law enforcement activities of any Federal agency or of a Department of the Treasury law enforcement organization.

(C) Any obligation or expenditure in excess of $500,000 with respect to an unobligated balance described in subparagraph (B) may not be made by the Secretary unless the Appropriations Committees of both Houses of Congress are notified at least 15 days in advance of such obligation or expenditure.

(h) *Retention or transfer of property.*—

(1) The Secretary may, with respect to any property forfeited under any law (other than section 7301 or 7302 of the Internal Revenue Code of 1986) enforced or administered by the Department of the Treasury—

(A) retain any of the property for official use; or

(B) transfer any of the property to—

(i) any other Federal agency; or

(ii) any State or local law enforcement agency that participated directly or indirectly in the seizure or forfeiture of the property.

(2) The Secretary may transfer any forfeited personal property or the proceeds of the sale of any forfeited personal or real property to any foreign country which participated directly or indirectly in the seizure of forfeiture of the property, if such a transfer—

(A) is one with which the Secretary of State has agreed;

(B) is authorized in an international agreement between the United States and the foreign country; and

(C) is made to a country which, if applicable, has been certified under section 481(h) of the Foreign Assistance Act of 1961 (22 U.S.C. 2291(h)).

(3) Nothing in this section shall affect the authority of the Secretary under section 981 of title 18 or section 616 of the Tariff Act of 1930 (19 U.S.C. 1616a).

(i) *Regulations.*—The Secretary may prescribe such rules and regulations as may be necessary to carry out this section.

(j) *Customs forfeiture fund.*—Notwithstanding any other provision of law—

(1) during any period when forfeited currency and proceeds from forfeitures under any law (other than section 7301 or 7302 of the Internal Revenue Code of 1986) enforced or administered by the Department of the Treasury or the United States Coast Guard, are required to be deposited in the Fund pursuant to this section—

(A) all moneys required to be deposited in the Customs Forfeiture Fund pursuant to section 613A of the Tariff Act of 1930 (19 U.S.C. 1613b) shall instead be deposited in the Fund; and

(B) no deposits or withdrawals may be made to or from the Customs Forfeiture Fund pursuant to section 613A of the Tariff Act of 1930 (19 U.S.C. 1613b); and

(2) any funds in the Customs Forfeiture Fund and any obligations of the Customs Forfeiture Fund on the effective date of the Treasury Forfeiture Act of 1992, shall be transferred to the Fund and all administrative costs of such transfer shall be paid for out of the Fund.

(k) Limitation of liability.—The United States shall not be liable in any action relating to property transferred under this section or under section 616 of the Tariff Act of 1930 (19 U.S.C. 1616a) if such action is based on an act or omission occurring after the transfer.

(l) *Authority to warrant title.*—Following the completion of procedures for the forfeiture of property pursuant to any law enforced or administered by the Department of the Treasury, the Secretary is authorized, at the Secretary's discretion, to warrant clear title to any subsequent purchaser or transferee of such forfeited property.

(m) *Forfeited property.*—For purposes of this section and notwithstanding section 524(c)(11) of title 28 or any other law—

(1) during fiscal year 1993, property and currency shall be deemed to be forfeited pursuant to a law enforced or administered by the United States Customs Service if it is forfeited pursuant to—

(A) a judicial forfeiture proceeding when the underlying seizure was made by an officer of the United States Customs Service or the property was maintained by the United States Customs Service; or

(B) a civil administrative forfeiture proceeding conducted by the United States Customs Service; and (2) after fiscal year 1993, property and currency shall be deemed to be forfeited pursuant to a law enforced or administered by a Department of the Treasury law enforcement organization if it is forfeited pursuant to—

(A) a judicial forfeiture proceeding when the underlying seizure was made by an officer of a Department of the Treasury law enforcement organization or the property was maintained by a Department of the Treasury law enforcement organization; or

(B) a civil administrative forfeiture proceeding conducted by a Department of the Treasury law enforcement organization.

(n) *Transfers to Attorney General and Postmaster General*

(1) The Secretary shall transfer from the Fund to the Attorney General for deposit in the Department of Justice Assets Forfeiture Fund amounts appropriate to reflect the degree of participation of participating Federal agencies in the law enforcement effort resulting in the forfeiture pursuant to laws enforced or administered by a Department of the Treasury law enforcement organization. For purposes of the preceding sentence, a "participating Federal agency" is an agency that participates in the Department of Justice Assets Forfeiture Fund.

(2) The Secretary shall transfer from the Fund to the Postmaster General for deposit in the Postal Service Fund amounts appropriate to reflect the degree of participation of the United States Postal Service in the law enforcement effort resulting in the forfeiture pursuant to laws enforced or administered by a Department of the Treasury law enforcement organization.

(o) *Definitions.*—For purposes of this section—

(1) Department of the Treasury law enforcement organization.—The term "Department of the Treasury law enforcement organization" means the United States Customs Service, the United States Secret Service, the Tax and Trade Bureau, the Internal Revenue Service, the Federal Law Enforcement Training Center, the Financial Crimes Enforcement Network, and any other law enforcement component of the Department of the Treasury so designated by the Secretary.

(2) Secretary.—The term "Secretary" means the Secretary of the Treasury.

42 U.S.C. 10601 Crime Victims Fund (text)

(a) Establishment

There is created in the Treasury a separate account to be known as the Crime Victims Fund (hereinafter in this chapter referred to as the "Fund").

Fines deposited in Fund; penalties; forfeited appearance bonds

Except as limited by subsection (c) of this section, there shall be deposited in the Fund—

(1) all fines that are collected from persons convicted of offenses against the United States except—

(A) fines available for use by the Secretary of the Treasury pursuant to—

(i) section 11(d) of the Endangered Species Act (16 U.S.C. 1540(d)); and

(ii) section 6(d) of the Lacey Act Amendments of 1981 (16 U.S.C. 3375(d)); and

(B) fines to be paid into—

(i) the railroad unemployment insurance account pursuant to the Railroad Unemployment Insurance Act (45 U.S.C. 351 et seq.);

(ii) the Postal Service Fund pursuant to sections 2601(a)(2) and 2003 of Title 39 and for the purposes set forth in section 404(a)(7) of Title 39;

(iii) the navigable waters revolving fund pursuant to section 311 of the Federal Water Pollution Control Act (33 U.S.C. 1321); and

(iv) county public school funds pursuant to section 3613 of Title 18;

(2) penalty assessments collected under section 3013 of Title 18;

(3) the proceeds of forfeited appearance bonds, bail bonds, and collateral collected under section 3146 of Title 18;

(4) any money ordered to be paid into the Fund under section 3671(c)(2) of Title 18; and

(5) any gifts, bequests, or donations to the Fund from private entities or individuals, which the Director is hereby authorized to accept for deposit into the Fund, except that the Director is not hereby authorized to accept any such gift, bequest, or donation that—

(A) attaches conditions inconsistent with applicable laws or regulations; or

(B) is conditioned upon or would require the expenditure of appropriated funds that are not available to the Office for Victims of Crime.

(c) *Retention of sums in Fund; availability for expenditure without fiscal year limitation*

Sums deposited in the Fund shall remain in the Fund and be available for expenditure under this chapter for grants under this chapter without fiscal year limitation. Notwithstanding subsection (d)(5), all sums deposited in the Fund in any fiscal year that are not made available for obligation by Congress in the subsequent fiscal year shall remain in the Fund for obligation in future fiscal years, without fiscal year limitation.

(d) *Availability for judicial branch administrative costs; grant program percentages*

The Fund shall be available as follows:

(1) Repealed. P.L. 105-119, Title I, §109(a)(1), Nov. 26, 1997, 111 Stat. 2457

(2)(A) Except as provided in subparagraph (B), the first $10,000,000 deposited in the Fund shall be available for grants under section 10603a of this title.

(B)(i) For any fiscal year for which the amount deposited in the Fund is greater than the amount deposited in the Fund for fiscal year 1998, the $10,000,000 referred to in subparagraph (A) plus an amount equal to 50 percent of the increase in the amount from fiscal year 1998 shall be available for grants under section 10603a of this title.

(ii) Amounts available under this subparagraph for any fiscal year shall not exceed $20,000,000.

(3) Of the sums remaining in the Fund in any particular fiscal year after compliance with paragraph (2), such sums as may be necessary shall be available for the United States Attorneys Offices and the Federal Bureau of Investigation to improve services for the benefit of crime victims in the Federal criminal justice system, and for a Victim Notification System.

(4) Of the remaining amount to be distributed from the Fund in a particular fiscal year—

(A) 47.5 percent shall be available for grants under section 10602 of this title;

(B) 47.5 percent shall be available for grants under section 10603(a) of this title; and

(C) 5 percent shall be available for grants under section 10603(c) of this title.

(5)(A) In addition to the amounts distributed under paragraphs (2), (3), and (4), the Director may set aside up to $50,000,000 from the amounts transferred to the Fund in response to the airplane hijackings and terrorist acts that occurred on September 11, 2001, as an antiterrorism emergency reserve. The Director may replenish any amounts obligated from such reserve in subsequent fiscal years by setting aside up to 5 percent of the amounts remaining in the Fund in any fiscal year after distributing amounts under paragraphs (2), (3) and (4). Such reserve shall not exceed $50,000,000.

(B) The antiterrorism emergency reserve referred to in subparagraph (A) may be used for supplemental grants under section 10603b of this title and to provide compensation to victims of international terrorism under section 10603c of this title.

(C) Amounts in the antiterrorism emergency reserve established pursuant to subparagraph (A) may be carried over from fiscal year to fiscal year. Notwithstanding subsection (c) and section 619 of the Departments of Commerce, Justice, and State, the Judiciary, and Related Agencies Appropriations Act, 2001 (and any similar limitation on Fund obligations in any future Act, unless the same should expressly refer to this section), any such amounts carried over shall not be subject to any limitation on obligations from amounts deposited to or available in the Fund.

(e) *Amounts awarded and unspent*

Any amount awarded as part of a grant under this chapter that remains unspent at the end of a fiscal year in which the grant is made may be expended for the purpose for which the grant is made at any time during the 3 succeeding fiscal years, at the end of which period, any remaining unobligated sums shall be available for deposit into the emergency reserve fund referred to in subsection (d)(5) at the discretion of the Director. Any remaining unobligated sums shall be returned to the Fund.

(f) *"Offenses against the United States" as excluding*

As used in this section, the term "offenses against the United States" does not include—

(1) a criminal violation of the Uniform Code of Military Justice (10 U.S.C. 801 et seq.);

(2) an offense against the laws of the District of Columbia; and

(3) an offense triable by an Indian tribal court or Court of Indian Offenses.

(g) *Grants for Indian tribes; child abuse cases*

(1) The Attorney General shall use 15 percent of the funds available under subsection (d)(2) of this section to make grants for the purpose of assisting Native American Indian tribes in developing, establishing, and operating programs designed to improve—

(A) the handling of child abuse cases, particularly cases of child sexual abuse, in a manner which limits additional trauma to the child victim; and

(B) the investigation and prosecution of cases of child abuse, particularly child sexual abuse.

(2) The Attorney General may use 5 percent of the funds available under subsection (d)(2) of this section (prior to distribution) for grants to Indian tribes to establish child victim assistance programs, as appropriate.

(3) As used in this subsection, the term "tribe" has the meaning given that term in section 450b(b) of Title 25.

Federal Forfeiture Statutes (citations)[242]

7 U.S.C. 1595 violation of the Federal Seed Act (seed)
7 U.S.C. 2024 Food Stamp Act felonies (property traceable to proceeds)*
7 U.S.C. 2024(e) misuse of food stamp coupons or authorization cards (nonfood items, money, negotiable instruments, securities, things of value furnished in exchange of coupons)
7 U.S.C. 2024(f) Food Stamp Act felonies (property traceable to proceeds and property used to facilitate)*
7 U.S.C. 2156 animal fighting violations (animals)
8 U.S.C. 1324 bringing in and harboring aliens for profit (property traceable to proceeds)*
8 U.S.C. 1324(b) bringing in or harboring aliens (conveyances)
8 U.S.C. 1327 aiding or assisting aliens to enter the U.S. for profit (property traceable to proceeds)*
8 U.S.C. 1328 importing aliens for immoral purpose for profit (property traceable to proceeds)*
11 U.S.C. 1 et seq. bankruptcy fraud (except 11 U.S.C. 157 cases)(property traceable to proceeds)*
15 U.S.C. 6 restraint of interstate or foreign trade (property in transit and involved in restraint)
15 U.S.C. 11 restraint of trade (property in transit)
15 U.S.C. 77 unauthorized departure of vessel detained in time of war in the interests of American neutrality (vessel)
15 U.S.C. 77q fraud in the sale of securities (property traceable to proceeds)*
15 U.S.C. 78dd-2 Foreign Corrupt Practices Act felonies (property traceable to proceeds)*
15 U.S.C. 292 falsely stamped gold or silver (gold, silver, gold goods, silver goods in transit)
15 U.S.C. 715f hot oil (illegally transported contraband oil)
15 U.S.C. 1177 illegally transporting gambling devices (gambling devices)

15 U.S.C. 1195 making, moving or dealing in materials without complying with the Flammable Fabrics Act (material)

15 U.S.C. 1265 Federal Hazardous Substances Act violations (misbranded and banned substances)

15 U.S.C. 2071(b) consumer product safety violations (prohibited products and those which fail to comply with an applicable consumer product safety rule)

15 U.S.C. 2104 political or numismatic items violations (imported products)

16 U.S.C. 26 hunting or fishing in Yellowstone National Park (guns, traps, beasts of burden, means of transportation)

16 U.S.C. 65 hunting or fishing in Sequoia or Yosemite National Parks (guns, teams, horses, means of transportation, and traps)

16 U.S.C. 99 hunting or fishing in Mt. Rainier National Park (guns, traps, beasts of burden, means of transportation)

16 U.S.C. 117d hunting or fishing in Mesa Verde National Park (guns, traps, beasts of burden, means of transportation)

16 U.S.C. 128 hunting or fishing in Crater Lake National Park (guns, traps, beasts of burden, means of transportation)

16 U.S.C. 171 hunting or fishing in Glacier National Park (guns, traps, beasts of burden, means of transportation)

16 U.S.C. 198d hunting or fishing in Rocky Mountain National Park (guns, traps, beasts of burden, means of transportation)

16 U.S.C. 204d hunting or fishing in Lassen Volcanic National Park (guns, traps, beasts of burden, means of transportation)

16 U.S.C. 256c hunting or fishing in Olympic Volcanic National Park (guns, bows, traps, nets, seines, fishing tackle, clothing, beasts of burden, machinery, logging equipment, motor vehicles, aircraft, boats or means of transportation)

16 U.S.C. 395d hunting or fishing in Hawaii National Park (guns, traps, beasts of burden, means of transportation)

16 U.S.C. 403c-4 hunting or fishing in the Shenandoah National Park (guns, traps, nets, seines, teams, horses, means of transportation)

16 U.S.C. 403h-4 hunting or fishing in Great Smoky Mountains National Park (guns, traps, nets, seines, fishing tackle, beasts of burden, means of transportation)

16 U.S.C. 404c-4 hunting or fishing in Mammoth Cave National Park (guns, traps, nets, seines, fishing tackle, beasts of burden, means of transportation)

16 U.S.C. 408l hunting or fishing in Isle Royale National Park (guns, traps, nets, seines, fishing tackle, beasts of burden, means of transportation)

16 U.S.C. 470gg(b) excavation of and dealing in archaeological resources (archaeological resources, vehicles and equipment used)

16 U.S.C. 470aaa-7 unlawfully acquired paleontological resources (paleontological resources)

16 U.S.C. 668b Bald and Golden Eagle protection violations (products, guns, traps, nets, equipment, vessels, vehicles, aircraft, means of transportation)

16 U.S.C. 668dd endangered species violations (species members)

16 U.S.C. 670j hunting or fishing on wetlands (guns, traps, nets, equipment, vessels, vehicles and other means of transportation)

16 U.S.C. 690e hunting in Bear River Migratory Bird Refuge (game)

16 U.S.C. 707 migratory bird hunting violations (guns, traps, nets, equipment, vessels, vehicles, means of transportation)

16 U.S.C. 727 hunting and fishing in Upper Mississippi River Wild Life and Fish Refuge (fish, game, guns, fishing equipment, boats, other paraphernalia)

16 U.S.C. 742j-1 hunting or harassing game from a plane (game, guns, plane, equipment)

16 U.S.C. 773h Northern Pacific Halibut Act violations (vessel, fishing gear, furniture, appurtenances, stores, cargo, fish of fishing boat)

16 U.S.C. 916f Whaling Convention violations (whales, whale products)

16 U.S.C. 957 violations of the Tuna conventions (fish)

16 U.S.C. 959 Tuna Convention violations (fish)

16 U.S.C. 971e Atlantic Tuna Convention violations (fish)

16 U.S.C. 972f Eastern Pacific Tuna Convention violations (fish)

16 U.S.C. 1171 North Pacific Fur Seal violations (vessel, gear, furniture, appurtenances, stores, cargo, furs) *16 U.S.C. 1376* marine mammal violations (vessel's unlawful cargo)

16 U.S.C. 1417 sell or transport tuna not taken in compliance with an International Dolphin Conservation program (vessel, equipment and fish)

16 U.S.C. 1437 marine sanctuary violations (vessel, equipment, stores, cargo, item used in violation, sanctuary resources)

16 U.S.C. 1540 endangered species violations (species, guns, traps, nets, equipment, vessels, vehicles, aircraft, means of transportation)

16 U.S.C. 1860 Fishery Conservation and Management Act violations (fishing vessels, their gear, furniture, appurtenances, stores, cargo, and fish)

16 U.S.C. 2409 Antarctic conservation violations (game, guns, traps, nets, equipment, vessels, vehicles, aircraft, other means of transportation)

16 U.S.C. 2439 Antarctic Marine Living Resources Convention violations (guns, traps, nets, other equipment, vessels, their gear, furniture, appurtenances, stoves, and cargo, vessels, vehicles, aircraft, and other means of transportation)

16 U.S.C. 3374 transporting fish, wildlife or plants contrary to law (fish, wildlife, plants, vessels, vehicles, aircraft, and other means of transportation)

16 U.S.C. 3606 North Atlantic salmon violations (vessels and fish)

16 U.S.C. 3637 Pacific salmon violations (fish and vessels, their gear, furniture, appurtenances, stores, and cargo)

16 U.S.C. 5010 North Pacific anadromous fish violations (fish and vessels including fishing gear, furniture, appurtenances, stores and cargo)

16 U.S.C. 5106 Atlantic coastal fisheries moratorium violations (fish, vessels, gear, equipment, appurtenances, stores and cargo)

16 U.S.C. 5305a rhinoceros and tiger conservation violations (derivative products)

16 U.S.C. 5154 violations of Atlantic striped bass moratorium (vessel, equipment, cargo, fish)

16 U.S.C. 5158 violations relating to striped bass in the exclusive economic zone (vessel, equipment, cargo, fish)

16 U.S.C. 5509 high seas fish conservation offenses (fish, vessels, gear, equipment, furniture, appurtenances, stores, and cargo)

16 U.S.C. 5606 Northwest Atlantic Fisheries Convention offenses (fishing vessels, their gear, furniture, appurtenances, stores, cargo, and fish)

17 U.S.C. 506 copyright infringement (copies, and copying implements, devices, and equipment)

17 U.S.C. 603 importation of items infringing on copyright (copies)

17 U.S.C. 1328 infringement on copyrighted original design (articles imported)

18 U.S.C. 32 destruction of aircraft (property traceable to proceeds)*

18 U.S.C. 37 violence at international airports (property traceable to proceeds)*

18 U.S.C. 38 fraud involving aircraft or spacecraft parts (proceeds and property used to facilitate offenses) *18 U.S.C. 81* arson within U.S. special maritime and territorial jurisdiction (property traceable to proceeds)*

18 U.S.C. 115 influencing, impeding, or retaliating against a Federal official by threatening or injuring a family member (property traceable to proceeds)*

18 U.S.C. 152 concealment of assets; false oaths and claims; bribery (property traceable to proceeds)*

18 U.S.C. 175 biological weapons offenses (property traceable to proceeds)*

18 U.S.C. 175b unlawful possession of biological materials (property traceable to proceeds)* *18 U.S.C. 175c* unlawful possession of smallpox materials (property traceable to proceeds)* *18 U.S.C. 176* Biological Weapons Act violations (biological agent, toxin and delivery system) *18 U.S.C. 201* bribery of U.S. officials (property traceable to proceeds)*

18 U.S.C. 215 commissions or gifts for procuring loans (property traceable to proceeds)*

18 U.S.C. 224 sports bribery (property traceable to proceeds)*

18 U.S.C. 229 chemical weapons offenses (property traceable to proceeds)*

18 U.S.C. 229B Chemical Weapons Act offenses (property used in, constituting the proceeds from, or facilitating offenses)

18 U.S.C. 287 false claims involving health care benefits (property traceable to proceeds)*

18 U.S.C. 351 congressional or Cabinet officer assassination (property traceable to proceeds)* *18 U.S.C. 371* conspiracy to defraud health care programs (property traceable to proceeds)* *18 U.S.C. 471* counterfeiting obligations or securities of the United States (property traceable to proceeds)* *18 U.S.C. 472* uttering counterfeit obligations or securities (property traceable to proceeds)*

18 U.S.C. 473 dealing in counterfeit obligations or securities (property traceable to proceeds)*

18 U.S.C. 474 possession of plates or stones for counterfeit obligations or securities (property traceable to proceeds)*

18 U.S.C. 476 taking impressions of tools used for obligations or securities (property traceable to proceeds)*

18 U.S.C. 477 sale or possession of impressions of tools used for obligations or securities (property traceable to proceeds)*

18 U.S.C. 478 counterfeiting foreign obligations or securities (property traceable to proceeds)* *18 U.S.C. 479* uttering counterfeit foreign obligations or securities (property traceable to proceeds)* *18 U.S.C. 480* possessing counterfeit foreign obligations or securities (property traceable to proceeds)* *18 U.S.C. 481* possession of plates or stones for counterfeit foreign obligations or securities (property traceable to proceeds)*

18 U.S.C. 485 counterfeiting U.S. coins (property traceable to proceeds)*

18 U.S.C. 486 uttering counterfeit coins (property traceable to proceeds)*

18 U.S.C. 487 possession of counterfeit dies for U.S. coins (property traceable to proceeds)*
18 U.S.C. 488 possession of counterfeit dies for foreign coins (property traceable to proceeds)*
18 U.S.C. 492 counterfeiting U.S. or foreign government coins, obligations or securities (counterfeits, and any articles, devices, and things used to counterfeit)
18 U.S.C. 500 counterfeiting U.S. postal money orders (property traceable to proceeds)*
18 U.S.C. 501 counterfeiting U.S. postage stamps (property traceable to proceeds)*
18 U.S.C. 502 counterfeiting foreign postage stamps (property traceable to proceeds)*
18 U.S.C. 503 counterfeiting U.S. postmarking stamps (property traceable to proceeds)*
18 U.S.C. 510 forging U.S. checks, bonds or securities (property traceable to proceeds)*
18 U.S.C. 511 altering motor vehicle identification numbers (property traceable to proceeds)*
18 U.S.C. 512 removing or changing motor vehicle identifications numbers (vehicle or part with altered or removed id. number)
18 U.S.C. 513 counterfeiting securities of States and private entities (property traceable to proceeds)*
18 U.S.C. 541 entry of falsely classified goods (property traceable to proceeds)*
18 U.S.C. 542 entry of goods by means of false statements (property traceable to proceeds)*
18 U.S.C. 544 relanding goods(goods)
18 U.S.C. 545 smuggling (goods smuggled)
18 U.S.C. 545 smuggling goods into the United States (property traceable to proceeds)* *18 U.S.C. 548* removing or repacking goods stored in customs warehouses (goods) *18 U.S.C. 549* removing goods from Customs custody (property traceable to proceeds)* *18 U.S.C. 550* false claims for refund of duties (merchandise)
18 U.S.C. 553 importing/exporting stolen motor vehicles (property traceable to proceeds)*
18 U.S.C. 554 smuggling goods from the United States (property traceable to proceeds)*
18 U.S.C. 555 border tunnels (property traceable to proceeds)*

18 U.S.C. 641 theft of public money, property, or records (property traceable to proceeds)*
18 U.S.C. 656 theft, embezzlement, or misapplication by bank officer or employee (property traceable to proceeds)*
18 U.S.C. 657 theft from lending, credit, and insurance institutions (property traceable to proceeds)*
18 U.S.C. 658 property mortgaged or pledged to farm credit agencies (property traceable to proceeds)*
18 U.S.C. 659 felonious theft from interstate shipments (property traceable to proceeds)*
18 U.S.C. 664 pension fund embezzlement (property traceable to proceeds)*
18 U.S.C. 666 theft or bribery concerning programs receiving Federal funds (property traceable to proceeds)*
18 U.S.C. 669 health care theft or embezzlement (property traceable to proceeds)*
18 U.S.C. 670 theft of medical products (property traceable to proceeds)*
18 U.S.C. 793 espionage (property derived from payments from foreign sources)
18 U.S.C. 793 espionage (property traceable to proceeds)*
18 U.S.C. 794 serious espionage (property derived from or used in commission of violation)
18 U.S.C. 794 serious espionage (property traceable to proceeds)*
18 U.S.C. 798 disclosure of classified information (property derived from or used in violation)*
18 U.S.C. 798 disclosure of classified information (property traceable to proceeds)*
18 U.S.C. 831 transactions involving nuclear materials (property traceable to proceeds)*
18 U.S.C. 832 participation in foreign terrorist production of weapons of mass destruction (property traceable to proceeds)*
18 U.S.C. 842 explosives offenses (property traceable to proceeds)*
18 U.S.C. 844 explosives offenses (property traceable to proceeds)*
18 U.S.C. 844 explosives violations (explosives)
18 U.S.C. 875 threats in interstate communications (property traceable to proceeds)*
18 U.S.C. 892 loansharking (property traceable to proceeds)*
18 U.S.C. 893 financing a loansharking operation (property traceable to proceeds)*
18 U.S.C. 894 collecting extortionate loans (property traceable to proceeds)*

18 U.S.C. 922(l) unlawfully importing firearms (property traceable to proceeds)*

18 U.S.C. 924(d) firearms violations (guns and ammunition)

18 U.S.C. 924(n) gun running (property traceable to proceeds)*

18 U.S.C. 930(c) armed violence at federal facility (property traceable to proceeds)*

18 U.S.C. 956 conspiracy to kill, kidnap, maim, or injure certain property in a foreign country (property traceable to proceeds)*

18 U.S.C. 962 arming vessel against friendly nation (vessel, its tackle, apparel, furniture, arms, materials, ammunition and stores)

18 U.S.C. 963 departure of detained vessel in violation of neutrality (vessel, its tackle, apparel, furniture, equipment and cargo)

18 U.S.C. 964 delivery of armed vessel to belligerent (vessel, its tackle, apparel, furniture, equipment and cargo)

18 U.S.C. 965 departure without filing verification statements (vessel, its tackle, apparel, furniture, equipment and cargo)

18 U.S.C. 966 departure after filing falsified statements (vessel, its tackle, apparel, furniture, equipment and cargo)

18 U.S.C. 967 departure without clearance (vessel, its tackle, apparel, furniture, equipment and cargo)

18 U.S.C. 981 money laundering, civil forfeiture (all property, real or personal, constituting, derived from, or traceable to a violation)

18 U.S.C. 982 money laundering, criminal forfeiture (all property, real or personal involved in or traceable to a violation)

18 U.S.C. 984 fungible property involved in money laundering (fungible property)

18 U.S.C. 1001 false statements in a matter with the jurisdiction of a federal agency with respect to health care benefits (property traceable to proceeds)*

18 U.S.C. 1005 fraudulent bank entries (property traceable to proceeds)*

18 U.S.C. 1006 fraudulent Federal credit institution entries (property traceable to proceeds)*

18 U.S.C. 1007 fraudulent Federal Deposit Insurance transactions) (property traceable to proceeds)*

18 U.S.C. 1014 fraudulent loan or credit applications (property traceable to proceeds)*

18 U.S.C. 1027 ERISA fraud involving health care benefits (property traceable to proceeds)*

18 U.S.C. 1028 identification fraud (property traceable to proceeds)*

18 U.S.C. 1028 fraud with respect to identification documents (property used)
18 U.S.C. 1029 access device fraud (property traceable to proceeds)*
18 U.S.C. 1029 fraud with respect to access devices (property used)
18 U.S.C. 1030 computer fraud and abuse (property traceable to proceeds)*
18 U.S.C. 1031 major fraud against the U.S. involving the assets of a financial institution (property traceable to proceeds)*
18 U.S.C. 1032 concealment of assets from conservator, receiver, or liquidating agent of financial institution) (property traceable to proceeds)*
18 U.S.C. 1035 false statements in health care matters (property traceable to proceeds)*
18 U.S.C. 1037 fraud relating to electronic mail (property traceable to or used to facilitate the offense) *18 U.S.C. 1082* gambling ships (vessel, its tackle, apparel, and furniture)
18 U.S.C. 1084 interstate transmission of gambling information (property traceable to proceeds)*
18 U.S.C. 1111 murder in the special maritime and territorial jurisdiction of the United States (property traceable to proceeds)*
18 U.S.C. 1114 federal officers or employees (property traceable to proceeds)*
18 U.S.C. 1116 murder of foreign officials, official guests, or internationally protected persons (property traceable to proceeds)*
18 U.S.C. 1165 hunting, trapping or fishing on Indian land (game, pelts, and fish)
18 U.S.C. 1201 kidnaping (property traceable to proceeds)*
18 U.S.C. 1203 hostage taking (property traceable to proceeds)*
18 U.S.C. 1341 mail fraud (property traceable to proceeds)*
18 U.S.C. 1343 wire fraud (property traceable to proceeds)*
18 U.S.C. 1344 bank fraud (property traceable to proceeds)*
18 U.S.C. 1347 health care fraud (property traceable to proceeds)*
18 U.S.C. 1351 fraud in foreign labor contracts (property traceable to proceeds)*
18 U.S.C. 1361 willful injury of Government property (property traceable to proceeds)*
18 U.S.C. 1362 destruction of communications facilities (property traceable to proceeds)*
18 U.S.C. 1363 destruction of property within U.S. special maritime and territorial jurisdiction (property traceable to proceeds)*
18 U.S.C. 1366 destruction of energy facilities (property traceable to proceeds)*

18 U.S.C. 1425 procuring citizenship unlawfully (property traceable to proceeds)*
18 U.S.C. 1426 reproducing of citizenship papers (property traceable to proceeds)*
18 U.S.C. 1427 sale of citizenship papers (property traceable to proceeds)*
18 U.S.C. 1461 mailing obscene material (property traceable to proceeds)*
18 U.S.C. 1462 importing/exporting obscene material (property traceable to proceeds)*
18 U.S.C. 1463 mailing indecent material (property traceable to proceeds)*
18 U.S.C. 1464 broadcasting obscene language (property traceable to proceeds)*
18 U.S.C. 1465 transporting obscene material for sale (property traceable to proceeds)*
18 U.S.C. 1467 obscene material (material, real and personal property derived from, traceable to, or used to commit a violation)
18 U.S.C. 1503 obstruction of justice (property traceable to proceeds)*
18 U.S.C. 1510 obstructing criminal investigations (property traceable to proceeds)*
18 U.S.C. 1511 obstructing state law enforcement (property traceable to proceeds)*
18 U.S.C. 1512 tampering with federal witnesses (property traceable to proceeds)*
18 U.S.C. 1513 retaliating against federal witnesses (property traceable to proceeds)*
18 U.S.C. 1518 obstruction of health care crime investigations (property traceable to proceeds)*
18 U.S.C. 1542 false statement in a passport application (property traceable to proceeds)*
18 U.S.C. 1543 passport forgery (property traceable to proceeds)*
18 U.S.C. 1544 passport misuse (property traceable to proceeds)*
18 U.S.C. 1546 visa fraud (property traceable to proceeds)*
18 U.S.C. 1581 peonage (property traceable to proceeds)*
18 U.S.C. 1582 vessels in the slave trade (property traceable to proceeds)* *18 U.S.C. 1583* enticing another into slavery (property traceable to proceeds)* *18 U.S.C. 1584* selling another into slavery (property traceable to proceeds)* *18 U.S.C. 1585* slave trading (property traceable to proceeds)*
18 U.S.C. 1586 service on a slave ship (property traceable to proceeds)*

18 U.S.C. 1587 possession of slaves aboard ship (property traceable to proceeds)*

18 U.S.C. 1588 transportation of slaves to the United States (property traceable to proceeds)*

18 U.S.C. 1589 forced labor (property traceable to proceeds)*

18 U.S.C. 1590 trafficking relating to peonage, slavery, involuntary servitude or forced labor (property traceable to proceeds)*

18 U.S.C. 1591 sex trafficking in children (property traceable to proceeds)*

18 U.S.C. 1592 false statements relating to peonage (property traceable to proceeds)*

18 U.S.C. 1594 peonage, slavery, and forced labor violations (property derived from or used to facilitate the offense)

18 U.S.C. 1708 theft from the mail (property traceable to proceeds)*

18 U.S.C. 1751 Presidential assassination (property traceable to proceeds)*

18 U.S.C. 1762 illicit transportation of prisoner-made goods (goods)

18 U.S.C. 1834 trade secret offenses (proceeds and property used to facilitate offenses)

18 U.S.C. 1951 robbery or violence affecting interstate commerce (Hobbs Act) (property traceable to proceeds)*

18 U.S.C. 1952 use of interstate commerce to facilitate unlawful activity (Travel Act) (property traceable to proceeds)*

18 U.S.C. 1953 interstate transportation of wagering paraphernalia (property traceable to proceeds)*

18 U.S.C. 1954 corruption of employee benefit plans (property traceable to proceeds)*

18 U.S.C. 1955 illegal gambling business (property traceable to proceeds)*

18 U.S.C. 1955 illegal gambling business (any property including money used in violation)

18 U.S.C. 1956 money laundering (property traceable to proceeds)*

18 U.S.C. 1957 unlawful monetary transactions (property traceable to proceeds)*

18 U.S.C. 1958 interstate murder for hire (property traceable to proceeds)*

18 U.S.C. 1960 unlawful money transmission business (property involved or traceable to proceeds)* *18 U.S.C. 1963* Racketeer Influenced and Corrupt Organizations (RICO) (property derived from and interest acquired and maintained in violation)

18 U.S.C. 1992 terrorist attacks on mass transit (property traceable to proceeds)* *18 U.S.C. 2113* bank robbery (property traceable to proceeds)*

18 U.S.C. 2114 postal robbery and theft (property traceable to proceeds)*

18 U.S.C. 2119 carjacking (property traceable to proceeds)*

18 U.S.C. 2155 destruction of national defense material (property traceable to proceeds)*

18 U.S.C. 2156 product of defective national defense material (property traceable to proceeds)*

18 U.S.C. 2241(c), 2253, 2254 aggravated sexual abuse (property traceable to proceeds or used to commit or promote)

18 U.S.C. 2242, 2253, 2254 sexual abuse (property traceable to proceeds or used to commit or promote)

18 U.S.C. 2243, 2253, 2254 sexual abuse of a minor or ward (property traceable to proceeds or used to commit or promote)

18 U.S.C. 2244, 2253, 2254 abusive sexual contact (property traceable to proceeds or used to commit or promote)

18 U.S.C. 2251, 2253, 2254 sexual exploitation of children (property traceable to proceeds or used to commit or promote)

18 U.S.C. 2251 sexual exploitation of children (property traceable to proceeds)*

18 U.S.C. 2251A, 2253, 2254 selling children (property traceable to proceeds or used to commit or promote)

18 U.S.C. 2251A selling children (property traceable to proceeds)*

18 U.S.C. 2252, 2253, 2254 material involving sexual exploitation of children (property traceable to proceeds or used to commit or promote)

18 U.S.C. 2252 material involving sexual exploitation of children (property traceable to proceeds)*

18 U.S.C. 2252A, 2253, 2254 activities relating to child pornography (property traceable to proceeds or used to commit or promote)

18 U.S.C. 2252B, 2253, 2254 misleading Internet domain names (property traceable to proceeds or used to commit or promote)

18 U.S.C. 2260, 2253, 2254 production of sexual exploitative material for importation (property traceable to proceeds or used to commit or promote)

18 U.S.C. 2260 production of sexual exploitative material for importation (property traceable to proceeds)*

18 U.S.C. 2274 destruction or misuse of vessel by owner (vessel, its tackle, apparel, furniture and equipment)

18 U.S.C. 2280 violence against maritime navigation (property traceable to proceeds)*

18 U.S.C. 2281 violence against maritime fixed platforms (property traceable to proceeds)*

18 U.S.C. 2312 interstate transportation of stolen motor vehicles (property traceable to proceeds)*
18 U.S.C. 2313 receipt of a stolen motor vehicle transported interstate (property traceable to proceeds)*
18 U.S.C. 2314 interstate transportation of stolen property (property traceable to proceeds)*
18 U.S.C. 2315 receipt of a stolen property transported interstate (property traceable to proceeds)*
18 U.S.C. 2318 trafficking in counterfeit labels affixed or to be affixed to phonograph records, motion pictures or other audiovisual works (counterfeit labels and articles to which they are affixed)
18 U.S.C. 2318 same (property traceable to proceeds)*
18 U.S.C. 2319 copyright infringement (property traceable to proceeds)*
18 U.S.C. 2319A unauthorized commercial exploitation of sound recordings (property traceable to proceeds)*
18 U.S.C. 2319A same (recordings and phonorecords)
18 U.S.C. 2320 trafficking in counterfeit goods and services (property traceable to proceeds)*
18 U.S.C. 2321 chop shop offenses (property traceable to proceeds)*
18 U.S.C. 2332 terrorist acts abroad against United States nationals (property traceable to proceeds)*
18 U.S.C. 2332a weapons of mass destruction (property traceable to proceeds)*
18 U.S.C. 2332b international terrorist acts transcending national boundaries (property traceable to proceeds)*
18 U.S.C. 2332f bombing public places and facilities (property traceable to proceeds)*
18 U.S.C. 2332g anti-aircraft missile offenses (property traceable to proceeds)*
18 U.S.C. 2332h radiological dispersal device offenses (property traceable to proceeds)*
18 U.S.C. 2339 harboring terrorists (property traceable to proceeds)*
18 U.S.C. 2339A providing material support to terrorists (property traceable to proceeds)*
18 U.S.C. 2339B providing material support to terrorist organizations (property traceable to proceeds)* *18 U.S.C. 2339C* financing terrorism (property traceable to proceeds)*
18 U.S.C. 2339D receipt of military training from a foreign terrorist organization (property traceable to proceeds)*

18 U.S.C. 2340A torture (property traceable to proceeds)*

18 U.S.C. 2342 trafficking in untaxed cigarettes (property traceable to proceeds)*

18 U.S.C. 2344 same (cigarettes)

18 U.S.C. 2421 interstate transportation for sexual purposes (property traceable to proceeds)*

18 U.S.C. 2422 coercing or enticing another to travel interstate for sexual purposes (property traceable to proceeds)*

18 U.S.C. 2423 interstate transportation of minors for sexual purposes (property traceable to proceeds)*

18 U.S.C. 2424 keeping a house of alien prostitution without registering with immigration officials (property traceable to proceeds)*

18 U.S.C. 2513 interception of wire, oral or electronic communications (wiretapping and bugging devices)

18 U.S.C. 3113 liquor violations in Indian country (unlawful liquor and the conveyances and packages in which it is found)

18 U.S.C. 3665 interstate transportation of a stolen vehicle or commission of a violent federal crime while armed with a firearm (firearms and ammunition)

18 U.S.C. 3667 liquors involved in violations of 18 U.S.C. 1261-1265 relating to tax and transportation of liquor (liquor and conveyances)

18 U.S.C. 3669 using conveyances to unlawful transport liquor into Indian country (conveyances)

18 U.S.C. 4012 prison contraband (contraband)

19 U.S.C. 467 unstamped imported distilled spirits (spirits)

19 U.S.C. 469 dealing in empty stamped imported liquor containers (containers)

19 U.S.C. 1305 importation of immoral materials (contents of packages in which immoral materials are found)

19 U.S.C. 1322 rescue and relief equipment imported contrary to regulations for admission pursuant to treaty with Mexico (equipment)

19 U.S.C. 1338 foreign discrimination against American commerce (articles imported in violation)

19 U.S.C. 1436 failure to comply with Customs entry requirements (goods)

19 U.S.C. 1453 unloading without meeting Customs requirements (goods and, if their value exceeds $500, the importing vessel)

19 U.S.C. 1462 refusal to allow customs inspection of container or vehicle (container or vehicle and its contents)

19 U.S.C. 1464 failure to comply with Customs requirements for sealed conveyances (conveyances and contents)
19 U.S.C. 1466 avoiding duty on repairs made overseas (vessel)
19 U.S.C. 1497 failure to declare goods upon entry (goods)
19 U.S.C. 1526 import of foreign made goods with American labels (goods)
19 U.S.C. 1527 import of animals and birds contrary to foreign law (animals and birds)
19 U.S.C. 1584 failure to describe goods in a manifest (goods and importing vessels of less than 500 tons)
19 U.S.C. 1586 unlawful unloading or shipment (vessel and cargo)
19 U.S.C. 1587 smuggled goods discovered on inspection (vessel and cargo)
19 U.S.C. 1588 transportation of goods between U.S. ports via foreign ports (goods)
19 U.S.C. 1590 aviation smuggling (plane or vessel)
19 U.S.C. 1590 same (property traceable to proceeds)*
19 U.S.C. 1592 false or incomplete statements to customs (goods)
19 U.S.C. 1594 smuggling (conveyances)
19 U.S.C. 1595a use of conveyances for smuggling (conveyances and merchandise)
19 U.S.C. 1627a importing or exporting stolen conveyances (conveyances)
19 U.S.C. 1703 smuggling (vessel and cargo)
19 U.S.C. 1706 importation in unlicensed planes and small boats (planes, small boats and goods)
19 U.S.C. 2093 unlawfully imported pre-Columbian art (art)
19 U.S.C. 2609 theft or unlawfully importing archaeological or ethnological material or articles (material or articles)
21 U.S.C. 334 misbranded or adulterated foods, drugs and cosmetics (products, counterfeit drugs, their containers, manufacturing equipment)
21 U.S.C. 467b processing, transporting or distributing diseased poultry and poultry products (poultry and poultry products)
21 U.S.C. 673 processing, transporting or distributing diseased meat (meat)
21 U.S.C. 841 controlled substance trafficking (property traceable to proceeds)*
21 U.S.C. 842 controlled substance regulatory offenses (property traceable to proceeds)*
21 U.S.C. 843 unlawful conduct relating to controlled substance (property traceable to proceeds)*
21 U.S.C. 846 attempt or conspiracy to a commit controlled substance offense (property traceable to proceeds)*

21 U.S.C. 848 drug kingpin offenses (property traceable to proceeds)*

21 U.S.C. 853 controlled substance violations, criminal forfeiture (property derived from, traceable to, used to facilitate violation)

21 U.S.C. 854 investment of controlled substance offense proceeds (property traceable to proceeds)* *21 U.S.C. 856* maintaining drug-involved premises (property traceable to proceeds)*

21 U.S.C. 858 endangerment in the illicit production of controlled substances (property traceable to proceeds)*

21 U.S.C. 859 drug trafficking to minors (property traceable to proceeds)*

21 U.S.C. 860 drug trafficking near schools and similar facilities (property traceable to proceeds)*

21 U.S.C. 861 drug trafficking using minors (property traceable to proceeds)*

21 U.S.C. 863 transportation of drug paraphernalia (property traceable to proceeds)*

21 U.S.C. 863 same (property traceable to proceeds)*

21 U.S.C. 881 controlled substance violations, civil forfeiture (substance, raw materials, precursor chemicals, records, containers, conveyances, property including real property traceable to, derived from or used to facilitate violations)

21 U.S.C. 952 unlawfully importing controlled substances (property traceable to proceeds)*

21 U.S.C. 953 unlawfully exporting controlled substances (property traceable to proceeds)*

21 U.S.C. 957 unlicensed exporting or importing controlled substances (property traceable to proceeds)*

21 U.S.C. 959 overseas controlled substance offenses (property traceable to proceeds)*

21 U.S.C. 960 violations of 21 U.S.C. 952, 953, 957, 959 (property traceable to proceeds)*

21 U.S.C. 960A narcoterrorism (property traceable to proceeds)*

21 U.S.C. 961 regulatory import/export offenses (property traceable to proceeds)*

21 U.S.C. 963 attempt or conspiracy to commit controlled substance import/export offenses (property traceable to proceeds)*

21 U.S.C. 970 controlled substance importing and exporting violations (property derived from, traceable to, used to facilitate violation)

21 U.S.C. 1049 processing, transporting or distributing contaminated eggs (eggs)

22 U.S.C. 401 illegal exportation of war materials (arms, munitions of war and other articles, vessels, vehicles, and aircraft)

22 U.S.C. 611 et seq. felonious violations of the Foreign Agents Registration Act (property traceable to proceeds)*

22 U.S.C. 1978 importing fish and wildlife from countries threatening endangered species (fish and wildlife)

22 U.S.C. 2778 Arms Export Control Act offenses (property traceable to proceeds)*

22 U.S.C. 6744 disclosure trade secrets acquired through Chemical Weapons Convention implementation (property used in, constituting the proceeds from, or facilitating offenses)

25 U.S.C. 264 trading in Indian country without a license (merchandise)

26 U.S.C. 5607 unlawful use, recovery or concealment of denatured distilled spirits (all personal property used, buildings and grounds constituting business premises on which violations occurred)

26 U.S.C. 5608 smuggling liquor (liquor, vessels, vehicles and planes)

26 U.S.C. 5612 mingling taxed and untaxed liquor in distilling plants (liquor)

26 U.S.C. 5613 improperly marked liquor (liquor)

26 U.S.C. 5615 bootlegging (unregistered stills, distilling apparatus, products, land used or facilitating, personal property proximate)

26 U.S.C. 5661 wine tax evasion (property used)

26 U.S.C. 5671 beer tax evasion (beer, vessels, utensils, and apparatus)

26 U.S.C. 5673 evading beer tax (lands and buildings holding brewery)

26 U.S.C. 5681 transporting liquor or raw materials to plants or warehouses with insufficient signs (vehicles, planes, and vessels used)

26 U.S.C. 5683 transporting liquor under improper brands (liquor)

26 U.S.C. 5685 possession of illegal firearms (firearms)

26 U.S.C. 5763 tobacco tax violations (all property, real and personal, used in violation, property of illicit operators used to defraud, tobacco and tobacco products)

26 U.S.C. 5872 firearms tax violations (firearms)

26 U.S.C. 7301 tax avoidance (property subject to taxation, and associated raw material, equipment, containers, conveyances)

26 U.S.C. 7302 possession of property to be used to violate the tax laws (property intended to such use) *26 U.S.C. 7303* use of counterfeit tax stamps and documents (counterfeit stamps, falsely stamped containers and their contents, fraudulent permits and like documents)

27 U.S.C. 206 violation of bulk intoxicating liquor sales regulations (liquor)

29 U.S.C. 186 restrictions on payments and loans to labor organizations (property traceable to proceeds)*
29 U.S.C. 501(c) embezzlement from union funds (property traceable to proceeds)*
30 U.S.C. 1466 Deep Seabed Hard Mineral Resource Act violations (minerals, vessel and its gear, furniture, appurtenances, stores and cargo)
31 U.S.C. 5111 U.S. coins exported, melted or treated contrary to regulation (coins)
31 U.S.C. 5317 crossing a U.S. border with more than $10,000 in unreported cash (cash)
31 U.S.C. 5311 et seq. currency and foreign transaction reporting violations (property traceable to proceeds)*
33 U.S.C. 384 piracy (vessels)
33 U.S.C. 1251 et seq. Federal Water Pollution Control Act felonies (property traceable to proceeds)*
33 U.S.C. 1401 et seq. Ocean Dumping Act felonies (property traceable to proceeds)*
33 U.S.C. 1415 ocean dumping (proceeds of, property used in, property facilitate violation)
33 U.S.C. 1901 et seq. Act to Prevent Pollution from Ships felonies (property traceable to proceeds)*
33 U.S.C. 2236 failure pay harbor dues (cargo)
33 U.S.C. 2716 oil tankers failure to maintain evidence of financial responsibility (vessel)
42 U.S.C. 300f et seq. Safe Drinking Water Act felonies (property traceable to proceeds)*
42 U.S.C. 1490s equity skimming (property traceable to proceeds)*
42 U.S.C. 2122 atom weapons offenses (property traceable to proceeds)*
42 U.S.C. 2284 sabotage of nuclear facilities (property traceable to proceeds)*
42 U.S.C. 6901 et seq. Resources Conservation and Recovery Act felonies (property traceable to proceeds)*
46 U.S.C. 12118 unlawful foreign shipping in domestic commerce (vessel and merchandise)
46 U.S.C. 12151 failure to report foreign rebuilding (vessel, tackle, apparel, equipment and furniture)
46 U.S.C. 12507 vessel identification offenses (vessel and its equipment)
46 U.S.C. 31330 violation of restrictions on sale of mortgaged vessels (vessel)
46 U.S.C. 55109 use of unlicensed foreign built dredges (dredge)
46 U.S.C. 55118 unlawful salvage operations by foreign vessels (vessel)

46 U.S.C. 56101 improper transfer of a U.S. registered vessel to foreign registry (vessel)
46 U.S.C. 56102 violation of restrictions on transfer of shipping facilities (vessel, shipyard, drydock, ship building or repairing facilities, or interest therein)
46 U.S.C. 60505 retaliatory suspension of commercial privileges to foreign vessels (vessel and goods)
46 U.S.C. 70507 manufacture, distribution or possession of controlled substances in violation of the Maritime Drug Enforcement Act (controlled substances and other property used or intended for use in violation of Act)
46 U.S.C. 80103 carrying property from ship wrecks to foreign ports (vessel, its tackle, apparel and furniture)
47 U.S.C. 510 broadcasting without a license (radio equipment)
49 U.S.C. 46306 aircraft registration violations (plane)
49 U.S.C. 46502 chemical trafficking offenses (property traceable to proceeds)*
49 U.S.C. 46504 assault of aircraft flight crew with a dangerous weapons (property traceable to proceeds)*
49 U.S.C. 46505 placing explosives aboard an aircraft (property traceable to proceeds)*
49 U.S.C. 46506 homicide or attempted homicide aboard an aircraft (property traceable to proceeds)*
49 U.S.C. 80303 contraband in the Guam and the North Marianas (conveyances)
49 U.S.C. 60123 destruction of interstate gas pipeline facilities (property traceable to proceeds)*
50 U.S.C. 192 failure to comply with regulations during a national emergency (vessel, tackle, apparel, furniture and equipment)
50 U.S.C. 205 suspension of commercial intercourse with State in insurrection (goods, vessels or vehicles entering or departing after suspension)
50 U.S.C. 212 property employed in aid of insurrection (property used)
50 U.S.C. 216 transportation of goods in aid of insurrection (goods)
50 U.S.C. 221 entering ports of entry closed due to insurrection (vessel and its tackle, apparel, furniture and cargo)
50 U.S.C. 223 states in insurrection (vessels)
50 U.S.C. 224 unauthorized departure during time of insurrection (vessel and its tackle, apparel, furniture and cargo)
50 U.S.C. 783 unlawful communication of classified information (proceeds from, property used, or property facilitating offense)

50 U.S.C. 1705 International Emergency Economic Powers Act offenses (property traceable to proceeds)* *50 U.S.C. App. 16* Trading With the Enemy Act violations (property and vessels that is the subject of a violation)

50 U.S.C. App. 16 Trading With the Enemy Act offenses (property traceable to proceeds)* *50 U.S.C. App. 2410* export regulation violations (resulting property interests and proceeds)

State Forfeiture Statutes (citations)

State Drug Forfeiture Acts

Alabama: Ala.Code §20-2-93;	**Nebraska:** Neb.Rev.Stat. §28-431;
Alaska: Alaska Stat. §§17.30.100 to 17.30.126;	**Nevada:** Nev.Rev.Stat. §§453.301 to 453. 311;
Arizona: Ariz.Rev.Stat.Ann. §§13-4301 to 13-4315;	**New Hampshire:** N.H.Rev.Stat.Ann. §§318-B:17 to 318-B:17-f;
Arkansas: Ark.Code §§5-64-505 to 5-64-510;	**New Jersey:** N.J.Stat.Ann. §§2C:64-1 to 2C:64-9;
California: Cal.Health & Safety Code §§ 11469 to 11495;	**New Mexico:** N.M.Stat.Ann. §§30-31-34 to 30-31-36;
Colorado: Colo.Rev.Stat. §§16-13-501 to 16-13-702;	**New York:** N.Y.Pub.Health Law §§3387, 3388; N.Y.Civil Practice Law §§1310 to 1352;
Connecticut: Conn.Gen.Stat.Ann. §§54-36a to 54-36p;	**North Carolina:** N.C.Gen.Stat. §§90-112, 112.1;
Delaware: Del.Code tit.16 §4784;	**North Dakota**: N.D.Cent.Code §§19-03.1-36 to 19-03.1-36.7;
Florida: Fla.Stat.Ann. §§893.12, 932.701 to 932.706;	**Ohio:** Ohio Rev.Code §§2981.01 to 2981.14;
Georgia: Ga.Code Ann. §16-13-49;	**Oklahoma:** Okla.Stat.Ann. tit.63 §§2-501 to 2-508;
Hawaii: Hawaii Rev.Stat. §329-55;	**Oregon:** Ore.Rev.Stat. §§131A.005 to 131A.460;
Idaho: Idaho Code §§37-2744 to 37-2744B, 37-2801 to 37-2815;	**Pennsylvania:** Pa.Stat.Ann. tit.42 §§6801, 6802;

(Continued)

Illinois: Ill.Stat.Ann. ch.720 §§550/12, 570/505; ch.725 §§150/1 to 150/14;	**Rhode Island:** R.I.Gen.Laws §§21-28-5.0 to 21-28-5.07.5;
Indiana: Ind.Code Ann. §§34-24-1-1 to 34-24-1-8;	**South Carolina:** S.C.Code §§44-53-520 to 44-53-590;
Iowa: Iowa Code Ann. §§809A.1 to 809A.25;	**South Dakota:** S.D.Comp.Laws §§34-20B-70 to 34-20B 101;
Kansas: Kan.Stat.Ann. §§60-4101 to 60-4126;	**Tennessee:** Tenn.Code Ann. §§53-11-201 to 53-11-204; 53-11-451, 53-11-452;
Kentucky: Ky.Rev.Stat. §§218A.405 to 218A.460;	**Texas:** Tex.Code of Crim.Pro. Arts. 59.01 to 59.14;
Louisiana: La.Rev.Stat.Ann. §§40:2601 to 40:2622;	**Utah:** Utah Code Ann. §§58-37-13 to 58-37-20;
Maine: Me.Rev.Stat.Ann. ch.15 §§5821 to 5827;	**Vermont:** Vt.Stat.Ann. tit.18 §§4241 to 4248;
Maryland: Md.Crim.Pro.Code §§12-101 to 13-206;	**Virginia:** Va.Code §19.2-386.1 to 19.2-386.34;
Massachusetts: Mass.Gen.Laws Ann. ch. 94C §§47, 47A;	**Washington:** Wash.Rev.Code Ann. §§69.50.505 to 69.50.509;
Michigan: Mich.Comp.Laws Ann. §§333.7521 to 333.7524a;	**West Virginia**: W.Va.Code §§60A-7-701 to 60A-7-707;
Minnesota: Minn.Stat.Ann. 609.531 to 609.5319;	**Wisconsin:** Wis.Stat.Ann. §§961.55, 961.555;
Mississippi: Miss.Code §41-29-176 to 41-29-187;	**Wyoming:** Wyo.Stat. §35-7-1049.
Missouri: Mo.Ann.Stat. §§195.130 to 195.146;	
Montana: Mont.Code Ann. §§44-12-101 to 44-12-206;	

State RICO Forfeiture Acts

Arizona: Ariz.Rev.Stat.Ann. §§13-2314 to 13-2314.04;	**New Mexico:** N.M.Stat.Ann. §§30-42-1 to 30-42-6;
California: Cal.Penal Code §§186 to 186.8;	**New York:** N.Y.Penal Law §§460.00 to 460.80;
Colorado: Colo.Rev.Stat. §§18-17-101 to 18-17-109;	**North Carolina:** N.C.Gen.Stat. §§75D-1 to 75D-14;

Connecticut: Conn.Gen.Stat.Ann. §§53-393 to 53-403;	**North Dakota:** N.D.Cent.Code §§12.1-06.1-01 to 12.1-06.1-08;
Delaware: Del.Code tit.11 §§1501 to 1511;	**Ohio:** Ohio Rev.Code §§2923.31 to 2923.36;
Florida: Fla.Stat.Ann. §§895.01 to 895.09;	**Oklahoma:** Okla.Stat.Ann. tit.22 §§1401 to 1419;
Georgia: Ga.Code Ann. §§16-14-1 to 16-14-15;	**Oregon:** Ore.Rev.Stat. §§166.715 to 166.735;
Hawaii: Haw.Rev.Stat. §§842-1 to 842-12;	**Pennsylvania:** Pa.Stat.Ann. tit.18 §911;
Idaho: Idaho Code §§18-7801 to 18-7805;	**Rhode Island:** R.I.Gen.Laws §§7-15-1 to 7-15-11;
Indiana: Ind.Code Ann. §§34-24-2-1 to 34-24-2-8;	**Tennessee:** Tenn.Code Ann. §§39-12-201 to 39-12-210;
Iowa: Iowa Code Ann. §706A.3;	**Texas:** Tex.Penal Code §§71.01 to 71.05;
Louisiana: La.Rev.Stat.Ann. §§15:1351 to 15:1356;	**Utah:** Utah Code Ann. §§76-10-1601 to 76-10-1610;
Massachusetts: Mass.Gen.Laws.Ann. ch.271 §§1 to 3;	
Michigan: Mich.Comp.Laws Ann. §§750.159f to 750.159x;	**Virginia:** Va.Code §§18.2-512 to 18.2-517;
Minnesota: Minn.Stat.Ann. §§609.901 to 609.912;	**Washington:** Wash.Rev.Code Ann. §§9A.82.010 to 9A.82.170;
Mississippi: Miss.Code §§97-43-1 to 97-43-11;	**West Virginia:** W.Va. Code §§61-13-1 to 61-13-6;
Missouri: Mo.Ann.Stat. §§513.600 to 513.653;	**Wisconsin:** Wis.Stat.Ann. §§946.80 to 946.88.
Nevada: Nev.Rev.Stat. §§207.350 to 207.520;	
New Jersey: N.J.Stat.Ann. §§2C:41-1 to 2C:41-6.2;	

End Notes

[1] Forfeiture is the loss of any right—ordinarily a property right—as a consequence of a breach of some legal obligation, BLACK'S LAW DICTIONARY, 667 (8th ed. 2004). Discussion in this report is limited to forfeitures associated with criminal conduct, other than the forfeiture of bail. Throughout this report, the terms "forfeiture" and "confiscation" will be used interchangeably.

[2] *Austin v. United States*, 509 U.S. 602, 611-13 (1993); *Calero-Toledo v. Pearson Yacht Leasing Co.*, 416 U.S. 663, 680-82 (1974); *Bane of American Forfeiture Law—Banished at Last?* 62 CORNELL LAW REVIEW 768, 770 (1977).

[3] *Goldsmith-Grant Co. v. United States*, 254 U.S. 505 (1921); 1 HALE, HISTORY OF THE PLEAS OF THE CROWN 419 (1778); 2 POLLOCK & MAITLAND, THE HISTORY OF ENGLISH LAW 473 (2d ed. 1923); Finklestein, *The Goring Ox: Some Historical Perspective on Deodands, Forfeiture, Wrongful Death and the Western Notion of Sovereignty*, 46 TEMPLE LAW QUARTERLY 169 (1973).

[4] 1 HALE, HISTORY OF THE PLEAS OF THE CROWN, 419 (1778); 1 BLACKSTONE, COMMENTARIES, 290 (1765-69). The value of the offending object or animal had to be determined because the owner was permitted to recover his property as long as he paid the Crown its value, *id.*

[5] *Id.* Originally, the proceeds were used to pay for a Mass to be said for the repose of the soul of the deceased, hence the name—giving ("dand") to God ("deo").

[6] GOEBEL, LAW ENFORCEMENT IN COLONIAL NEW YORK 717 (1944); SEMMES, CRIME AND PUNISHMENT IN EARLY MARYLAND 136 (1938); SCOTT, CRIMINAL LAW IN COLONIAL VIRGINIA 52 (1930).

[7] BISHOP, COMMENTARIES ON THE CRIMINAL LAW §827 (7th ed. 1882); N.J. Const. Art.XVII (1776); Vt. Const. ch.2, §35 (1777); N.H. Const. pt.2, Art.89 (1783); Del. Const. Art.I, §15 (1792).

[8] *United States v. United States Coin & Currency*, 401 U.S. 715, 720-21 (1971); *Calero-Toledo v. Pearson Yacht Leasing Co.*, 416 U.S. at 680-81; *Goldsmith-Grant Co. v. United States*, 254 U.S. at 510-11.

[9] 1 HALE, HISTORY OF THE PLEAS OF THE CROWN 354-67 (1778); 1 CHITTY, A PRACTICAL TREATISE ON CRIMINAL LAW 727-39 (1816); 1 STEPHENS, A HISTORY OF THE CRIMINAL LAW OF ENGLAND 468-88 (1883); 4 BLACKSTONE, COMMENTARIES 376-81 (1765-69).

[10] *Id.* at 373-74. Attainder not only resulted in forfeiture but in corruption of the blood as well, "so that an attained person can neither inherit lands or hereditaments from his ancestors, nor retain those he is already in possession of, nor transmit them by descent to any heir; but the same shall escheat to the lord of the fee, subject to the king's superior right of forfeiture; and the person attained shall also obstruct all descents of his posterity, wherever they are obliged to derive a title through him to a remoter ancestor." *Id.* at 381.

[11] SEMMES, CRIME AND PUNISHMENT IN EARLY MARYLAND 107-10 (1938); GOEBEL, LAW ENFORCEMENT IN COLONIAL NEW YORK 717 (1944). During the Revolution, some of the states enacted provisions forfeiting the land and goods of those considered sympathetic to the Crown, *see, e.g.*, 5 Mass. Acts & Resolves 1769-1780, 966-67 (1779); 9 Hening's (Va.) Stat. at Large 1775-1778, ch.9 (1777); 1 N.H. Laws 22 (1778).

[12] "The Congress shall have power to declare the punishment of treason, but no attainder of treason shall work corruption of blood, or forfeiture except during the life of the person attainted." U.S.Const. Art.III, §3.

"[N]o conviction or judgment for any of the offenses aforesaid, shall work corruption of blood, or any forfeiture of estate." 1 Stat. 177 (1790). This provision and its successors remained in force until 1984, Rev. Stat. §5326; 35 Stat. 1151 (1909); 62 Stat. 837 (1948); 18 U.S.C. 3563 (1982 ed.); 98 Stat. 1987 (1984).

[13] 1 MADDOX, HISTORY AND ANTIQUITIES OF THE EXCHEQUER 781-82 (1769); HARPER, THE ENGLISH NAVIGATION LAWS 109-10 (1964); Currency, *The Courts in the American Colonies* 11 AMERICAN JOURNAL OF LEGAL HISTORY 253, 357

(1967). Admiralty jurisdiction extended to piracy, spoils of war, and ship registration offenses, all of which called for confiscation, 1 HOLDSWORTH, HISTORY OF ENGLISH LAW 328 (1903 ed.); ii SELDON SOCIETY, SELECT PLEAS OF THE COURT OF ADMIRALTY, A.D.1517-1602 (Vol.II) xvi-xxii (Marsden ed. 1897). The Exchequer dealt with customs duties and other revenue matters.

[14] HARPER, THE ENGLISH NAVIGATION LAWS 109-11 (1964); Currency, *The Courts in the American Colonies*, 11 AMERICAN JOURNAL OF LEGAL HISTORY 253, 357 (1967).

[15] *E.g.*, 18 Stat. 186, 188 (1874) (smuggling); 41 Stat. 305, 315 (1919) (prohibition); 18 U.S.C. 3665 (unlawful firearms possession).

[16] The Supreme Court in *Calero-Toledo* summarized the relative contributions of the three English procedures with the observation that:

Deodands did not become part of the common law tradition of this country. Nor has forfeiture of estate as a consequence of a federal criminal conviction been permitted. Forfeiture of estate resulting from a conviction for treason has been constitutionally proscribed by Art.III, §3 though forfeitures of estate for the lifetime of a traitor have been sanctioned. But "[l]ong before the adoption of the Constitution the common law courts in the Colonies—and later in the states during the period of Confederation—were exercising jurisdiction *in rem* in the enforcement of [English and local] forfeiture statutes" which provided for the forfeiture of commodities and vessels used in violation of the customs and revenue laws. And almost immediately after adoption of the Constitution, ships and cargoes involved in customs offenses were made subject to forfeiture under federal law, as were vessels used to deliver slaves to foreign countries, and somewhat later those used to deliver slaves to this country. The enactment of forfeiture statutes has not abated; contemporary federal and state forfeiture statutes reach virtually any type of property that might be used in the conduct of a criminal enterprise. 416 U.S. at 682-83 (citations and footnotes omitted).

Calero-Toledo, however, was written prior to legislation apparently authorizing forfeiture of the estates of certain terrorists, 18 U.S.C. 981(a)(1)(G)(i)("The following property is subject to forfeiture to the United States ... (G) All assets, foreign or domestic—(i) of any individual ... engaged in planning or perpetrating any Federal crime of terrorism (as defined in section 2332b(g)(5)) against the United States, citizens or residents of the United States, or their property ... "); see also 50 U.S.C. 1702(a)(1)(C). At least to date, this authority has rarely been used, but see *United States v. Saade*, 2013 WL 6847034, *2 (S.D.N.Y. Dec. 30, 2013)("18 U.S.C. §981(a)(1)(G)(i) ... requires no connection between the property forfeited and defendant's crimes"), rejecting an excessive fines argument; Saade raised no forfeiture of estate challenge.

[17] A list of federal forfeiture laws, along with the type of property whose confiscation they permit or require, is attached, as are the citations to state RICO and drug forfeiture statutes.

[fv] *E.g.*, 21 U.S.C. 853(b); 18 U.S.C. 1963(b)("[p]roperty subject to criminal forfeiture under this section includes—(1) real property, including things growing on, affixed to, and found in land; and (2) tangible and intangible personal property, including rights, privileges, interests, claims and securities");*United States v. Dicter*, 198 F.3d 1284, 1290 (11th Cir. 1999) (a physician's license to practice medicine is forfeitable under section 853); the text of 18 U.S.C. 1963 is attached.

[19] *E.g.*, 18 U.S.C. 2513 (wiretapping equipment), 18 U.S.C. 844 (unlawful explosives); 19 U.S.C. 467 (distilled spirits without a tax stamp).

[20] *E.g.*, 19 U.S.C. 1595a (conveyances used for smuggling); 18 U.S.C. 492 (counterfeiting paraphernalia); 16 U.S.C. 128 (guns and traps used in violation of hunting and trapping

restrictions); 18 U.S.C. 229B("any person convicted under section 229A(a)[relating to chemical weapons] shall forfeit to the United States ... any of the property used in any manner or part, to commit, or to facilitate the commission of such violation").

[21] *E.g.*, 18 U.S.C. 1963(a)(3) (racketeer influenced and corrupt organizations (RICO)); 21 U.S.C. 881(a)(6) (drug trafficking).

[22] "If the property described in subsection (a) [listing the types of property forfeitable], as a result of any act or omission of the defendant—(1) cannot be located upon the exercise of due diligence; (2) has been transferred or sold to, or deposited with, a third party; (3) has been placed beyond the jurisdiction of the court; (4) has been substantially diminished in value; or (5) has been commingled with other property which cannot be divided without difficulty; the court shall order the forfeiture of any other property of the defendant up to the value of any property described in paragraphs (1) through (5)." 18 U.S.C. 1963(m); 21 U.S.C. 853(p); see also 18 U.S.C. 984(a)(1)("In any forfeiture action in rem in which the subject property is cash, monetary instruments in bearer form, funds deposited in an account in a financial institution (as defined in section 20 of this title), or precious metals—(A) it shall not be necessary for the Government to identify the specific property involved in the offense that is the basis for the forfeiture; and (B) it shall not be a defense that the property involved in such an offense has been removed and replaced by identical property").

[23] 18 U.S.C. 981, 982 (money laundering); 18 U.S.C. 1963 (RICO).

[24] P.L. 106-185, 114 Stat. 202 (2000).

[25] 18 U.S.C. 981(a)(1)(C)("the following property is subject to forfeiture to the United States ... (C) Any property, real or personal, which constitutes or is derived from proceeds traceable to ... any offense constituting 'specified unlawful activity' (as defined in section 1956(c)(7) of this title)[*i.e.*, the list of predicate offenses form money laundering (18 U.S.C. 1956) which list includes by cross reference all the predicate offenses for a RICO prosecution)], or a conspiracy to commit such offense").

As one court noted, this trend could have unfortunate consequences, *United States v. Funds Held in the Name or for the Benefit of Wetterer*, 210 F.3d 96, 110 (2d Cir. 2000)("We have previously observed the government's virtually unchecked use of the civil forfeiture statutes and the disregard for due process that is buried in those statutes. Another source of potential abuse is that the forfeited funds are kept by the Department of Justice as a supplement to its budget. Thus the agency that conceives the jurisdiction and ground for seizures, and executes them, also absorbs their proceeds. This arrangement creates incentives that evidently require a more-than-human judgment and restraint. The Supreme Court has politely remarked on the Department of Justice's direct pecuniary interest in maximizing drug forfeitures to meet the Department's budget target. *See United States v. James Daniel Good Real Property*, 510 U.S. 43, 56 n.2 (1993)(quoting 1990 memo of the Attorney General: 'We must significantly increase production to reach our budget target.... Every effort must be made to increase forfeiture income during the remaining three months of fiscal year 1990.'). The bare financial facts of this case shine a light on the corrupting incentives of this arrangement: we see aggressive but marginal claims asserted on dubious jurisdiction to seize charitable funds raised for the relief of abject orphans in an impoverished country, so that the money can be diverted for expenditure by the Department of Justice"). Sensitive to such criticism, CAFRA sought to balance increased procedural efficiency with additional procedural safeguards.

[26] 50 U.S.C. 1702(a)(1)(C)(" ... the President may ... when the United States is engaged in armed hostilities or has been attacked by a foreign country or foreign nationals, confiscate any property, subject to the jurisdiction of the United States, of any foreign person, foreign

organization, or foreign country that he determines has planned, authorized, aided, or engaged in such hostilities or attacks against the United States ... "); see also 18 U.S.C. 981(a)(1)(G)(i). At first glance, the two seem to resemble common law forfeiture of estate, but as noted earlier, these provisions are rarely involved.

[27] 18 U.S.C. 981(a)(1)(B)("(a)(1) The following property is subject to forfeiture to the United States ... (B) Any property, real or personal, within the jurisdiction of the United States, constituting, derived from, or traceable to, any proceeds obtained directly or indirectly from an offense against a foreign nation, or any property used to facilitate such an offense, if the offense—(i) involves trafficking in nuclear, chemical, biological, or radiological weapons technology or material, or the manufacture, importation, sale, or distribution of a controlled substance (as that term is defined for purposes of the Controlled Substances Act), or any other conduct described in section 1956(c)(7)(B); (ii) would be punishable within the jurisdiction of the foreign nation by death or imprisonment for a term exceeding 1 year; and (iii) would be punishable under the laws of the United States by imprisonment for a term exceeding 1 year, if the act or activity constituting the offense had occurred within the jurisdiction of the United States"); *see, e.g., United States v. $125,938.62 (Cardenal)*, 537 F.3d 1287, 1288 (11th Cir. 2008).

[28] More precisely, " ... an offense against a foreign nation involving—(i) the manufacture, importation, sale, or distribution of a controlled substance (as such term is defined for the purposes of the Controlled Substances Act); (ii) murder, kidnapping, robbery, extortion, destruction of property by means of explosive or fire, or a crime of violence (as defined in section 16); (iii) fraud, or any scheme or attempt to defraud, by or against a foreign bank (as defined in paragraph 7 of section 1(b) of the International Banking Act of 1978); (iv) bribery of a public official, or the misappropriation, theft, or embezzlement of public funds by or for the benefit of a public official; (v) smuggling or export control violations involving—(I) an item controlled on the United States Munitions List established under section 38 of the Arms Export Control Act (22 U.S.C. 2778); or (II) an item controlled under regulations under the Export Administration Regulations (15 C.F.R. Parts 730-774); (vi) an offense with respect to which the United States would be obligated by a multilateral treaty, either to extradite the alleged offender or to submit the case for prosecution, if the offender were found within the territory of the United States; or (vii) trafficking in persons, selling or buying children, sexual exploitation of children, or transporting, recruiting or harboring a person, including a child, for commercial sex acts, " 18 U.S.C. 1956(c)(7)(B).

[29] *United States v. Smith*, 770 F.3d 628, 637 (7th Cir. 2014)("Criminal forfeiture is considered to be punishment and therefore is part of the sentencing process"); *United States v. Lazarenko*, 476 F.3d 642, 647 (9th Cir. 2007); *United States v. Totaro*, 345 F.3d 989, 993 (8th Cir. 2003); *cf., United States v. Ferrario-Pozzi*, 368 F.3d 5, 8 (1st Cir. 2004).

[30] *E.g.*, 21 U.S.C. 853(a); 18 U.S.C. 982, 1963(a); *United States v. Nava*, 404 F.3d 1119, 1124 (9th Cir. 2005).

[31] "This [civil] 'forfeiture proceeding ... is in rem. It is the property which is proceeded against, and by resort to a legal fiction, held guilty and condemned as though it were conscious instead of inanimate and insentient,'" *United States v. Ursery*, 518 U.S. 267, 275 (1996), quoting, *Various Items of Personal Property v. United States*, 282 U.S. 577, 584 (1931); see also *United States v. Timley*, 443 F.3d 615, 627-28 (8th Cir. 2006); *United States v. Fleet*, 498 F.3d 1225, 1231 (11th Cir. 2007); *United States v. Liquidators of European Federal Credit Bank*, 630 F.3d 1139, 1149-150 (9th Cir. 2011); *United States v. $196,969.00 United States Currency (Johnson)*, 719 F.3d 644, 646 (7th Cir. 2013); *United States v. The Federative Republic of Brazil*, 748 F.3d 86, 95 (2d Cir. 2014).

[32] *Bennis v. Michigan*, 516 U.S. 442, 453 (1996); *United States v. One "Piper" Aztec "F" DeLuxe Model 250 PA 23 Aircraft*, 321 F.3d 355, 360 (3d Cir. 2003); *United States v. Funds in the Amount of Thirty Thousand Six Hundred Seventy Dollars (Calhoun)*, 403 F.3d 448, 469 (7th Cir. 2005); *United States v. Contorinis*, 692 F.3d 136, 146 (2d Cir. 2012); *United States v. Liquidators of European Federal Credit Bank*, 630 F.3d at 1150 ("The government may pursue civil forfeiture even after a failed criminal prosecution").

[33] 18 U.S.C. 981(d); 21 U.S.C. 881(d).

[34] 18 U.S.C. 983; the new procedural framework, however, does not apply to forfeitures that originate under the customs laws, the tax laws, and several others, 18 U.S.C. 983(i)("In this section, the term 'civil forfeiture statute'—(1) means any provision of Federal law providing for the forfeiture of property other than as a sentence imposed upon conviction of a criminal offense; and (2) does not include—(A) the Tariff Act of 1930 or any other provision of law codified in title 19 [(the customs laws)]; (B) the Internal Revenue Code of 1986 [(federal tax laws)]; (C) the Federal Food, Drug, and Cosmetic Act (21 U.S.C. 301 et seq.)[(relating to misbranded, adulterated and other unhealthy or unsafe food, drugs, or cosmetics)]; (D) the Trading with the Enemy Act (50 U.S.C. App. 1 et seq.) or the International Emergency Economic Powers Act (IEEPA)(50 U.S.C. 1701 et seq.); or (E) section 1 of title VI of the Act of June 15, 1917 (40 Stat. 233; 22 U.S.C. 401)[relating to the export of war materials in violation of the Neutrality Act]; see also 18 U.S.C. 985 (civil forfeiture of real property), 986 (subpoena of bank records) which contain additional provisions applicable to "all civil forfeitures" and to "any civil forfeiture," respectively.

[35] *United States v. Ursery*, 518 U.S. 267, 289 (1996)("'In contrast to the in personam nature of criminal actions, [forfeiture] actions in rem have traditionally been viewed as civil proceedings, with jurisdiction dependent upon seizure of a physical object'")(quoting *United States v. One Assortment of 89 Firearms*, 465 U.S. 354, 363 (1984); *CaleroToledo v. Pearson Yacht Leasing Co.*, 416 U.S. 663, 684 (1974)); see also *Dobbin's Distillery v. United States*, 96 U.S. 395, 396 (1877); *United States v. $506,231 (Lombardo)*, 125 F.3d 442, 447-49 (7th Cir. 1997); *United States v. All Funds Distributed to Weiss*, 345 F.3d 49, 55 (2d Cir. 2003); *United States v. All Funds in Account Banco Espanol de Credito, Spain*, 295 F.3d 23, 27 n* (D.C. Cir. 2002); *United States v. Real Property Located at 475 Martin Lane*, 545 F.3d 1134, 1144 (9th Cir. 2008); but see *Contents of Account Number 03001288 (Jalal) v. United States*, 344 F.3d 399, 404-405 (3d Cir. 2003); *United States v. Vazquez-Alvarez*, 760 F.3d 193, 197 (2d Cir. 2014)("[E]xecution of the arrest warrant [to begin civil forfeiture proceedings] is specifically excused by the Forfeiture Rules when the property is already in the government's possession, custody or control").

In fact, until the Supreme Court's decision in *Republic National Bank v. United States*, 506 U.S. 80 (1992), confirmed that initial rather than continued control was ordinarily sufficient to support jurisdiction, some believed that a court's continued jurisdiction depended upon its continued control over the res, and that its power to proceed disappeared if the property were released other than by accident, fraud or some other improper or inequitable means, *United States v. $1,322,242.58 (Road Atlanta, Inc.)*, 938 F.2d 433, 437 (3d Cir. 1991); *United States v. $84,740.00 (Potter)*, 900 F.2d 1402, 1404 (9th Cir. 1990); *United States v. Four Parcels of Real Property*, 941 F.2d 1428, 1435-436 (11th Cir. 1991); *Appellate Jurisdiction for Civil Forfeiture: The Case for the Continuation of Jurisdiction Beyond the Release of the Res*, 65 FORDHAM LAW REVIEW 679 (1991).

When the property is located overseas, three of the circuits have concluded that as long as the court has subject matter jurisdiction, in person jurisdiction over the res is only necessary after the fact, if at all, *United States v. Approximately $1.67 Million (US) in Cash, Stock,* *and Other Valuable Assets (Hartog)*, 513 F.3d 991, 997 (9th Cir. 2008)("Spain's compliance and cooperation determines only the effectiveness of the forfeiture orders of the district courts, not their jurisdiction to issue those orders"), quoting *United States v. All Funds in Accounts Nos. 747.034/278 (Banco Espanol de Credito)*, 295 F.3d 23, 27 (D.C.Cir. 2002); accord, *Contents of Account Number 03001288 (Jalal) v. United States*, 344 F.3d 399, 405 (3d Cir. 2003); contra, *United States v. All Funds on Deposit in Any Accounts Maintained in the Names of Meza*, 63 F.3d 148, 151-54 (2d Cir. 1995). Congress provided an alternative mechanism in 18 U.S.C. 981(k) which permits the confiscation of funds in interbank accounts of a foreign bank held in this country when the foreign banks holds forfeitable assets on account overseas, *United States v. Union Bank for Savings & Investment (Jordan)*, 487 F.3d 8, 15-6 (1st Cir. 2007); *United States v. $6,976,934.65, Plus Interest Deposited into Royal Bank of Scotland (Soulbury Limited)*, 554 F.3d 123, 125 (D.C.Cir. 2009).

[36] 18 U.S.C. 981(b)(2); *United States v. $29,828 in United States Currency (Braddy)*, 536 F.3d 1234, 1237 (11th Cir. 2008). The court may permit the pretrial sale of property seized under the Supplemental Rules with an eye to preservation of the property's value and the parties' interests, *United States v. Real Property and Residence Located at 4816 Chaffey Lane (Coffman)*, 699 F.3d 956, 959-62 (6th Cir. 2012), but it may refuse to do so for reasons of public safety, *United States v. Approximately 81,454 Cans of Baby Formula*, 560 F.3d 638, 641-42 (7th Cir. 2009).

[37] *United States v. James Daniel Good Real Property*, 510 U.S. 43, 48 (1993).

[38] 18 U.S.C. 985.

[39] 18 U.S.C. 983(f)("(1) A claimant under subsection (a) is entitled to immediate release of seized property if—(A) the claimant has a possessory interest in the property; (B) the claimant has sufficient ties to the community to provide assurance that the property will be available at the time of the trial; (C) the continued possession by the Government pending the final disposition of forfeiture proceedings will cause substantial hardship to the claimant, such as preventing the functioning of a business, preventing an individual from working, or leaving an individual homeless; (D) the claimant's likely hardship from the continued possession by the Government of the seized property outweighs the risk that the property will be destroyed, damaged, lost, concealed, or transferred if it is returned to the claimant during the pendency of the proceeding; and (E) none of the conditions set forth in paragraph (8) applies.... (8) This subsection shall not apply if the seized property—(A) is contraband, currency, or other monetary instrument, or electronic funds unless such currency or other monetary instrument or electronic funds constitutes the assets of a legitimate business which has been seized; (B) is to be used as evidence of a violation of the law; (C) by reason of design or other characteristic, is particularly suited for use in illegal activities; or (D) is likely to be used to commit additional criminal acts if returned to the claimant"); see also *United States v. Contents of Accounts (Chavez)*, 629 F.3d 601, 606-609 (6th Cir. 2011)(when §983(f) precludes release, recourse may not be had to injunctive relief for release of the property under Rule 65 of the Federal Rules of Civil Procedure); *United States v. Undetermined Amount of U.S. Currency (Warren)*, 376 F.3d 260, 263-69 (4th Cir. 2004)(petition for release seized funds in order to pay attorneys' fees without incurring undue hardship denied on the grounds the funds would likely be dissipated before the completion of forfeiture proceedings).

In a similar vein, the customs laws authorize the release of seized property upon the posting of an amount equal to its value, perhaps conscious of the fact that the seizure of vessel may cause economic hardship greater than its market value, 19 U.S.C. 1614.

[40] 18 U.S.C. 983(j); *Gang Luan v. United States*, 722 F.3d 388, 394 (D.C.Cir. 2013); *United States v. Melrose East Subdivision*, 357 F.3d 493, 498-500 (5th Cir. 2004)(recognizing the government's right to seek a restraining order, but acknowledging that in such cases due process may require a post-restraint, pretrial hearing on the forfeitability of the encumbered property).

[41] Under CAFRA and the customs laws, administrative forfeiture may be used if the property to be forfeited is cash; or if the property is worth less than $500,000; or is a boat, plane or car used to carry or store drugs, 19 U.S.C. 1607; 21 U.S.C. 881(d); 18 U.S.C. 981(d). Under the tax laws, the procedure is available with respect to personal property valued at $100,000 or less, 26 U.S.C. 7325. Commentators have estimated that administrative forfeitures account for over 80 percent of federal civil forfeitures, McCaw, *Assets Forfeiture as a Form of Punishment: A Case for Integrating Asset Forfeiture into Criminal Sentencing*, 38 AMERICAN JOURNAL OF CRIMINAL LAW 181, 190 (2011); Rabiej, *Proposed Supplemental Rule G Governing Pretrial Procedures in Forfeiture in Rem Actions*, 51 FEDERAL LAWYER 41,

[42] (Sept. 2004).

[42] 18 U.S.C. 981(b)(2).

[43] 18 U.S.C. 983(a); 19 U.S.C. 1607, 1608; *Dusenbery v. United States*, 534 U.S. 161, 167 (2002); *United States v. James Daniel Good Real Property*, 510 U.S. 43, 48 (1993).

At any point after seizure, an owner or anyone else with a property interest in the res may petition for remission or mitigation. Remission is a petition for return of all of the property seized or its entire value; mitigation for return of only a portion, *see, e.g.*, 28 C.F.R. pt. 9; *Malladi Drugs & Pharmaceuticals, Ltd. v. Tandy*, 552 F.3d 885, 887-88 (D.C.Cir. 2009). The authority to grant remission or mitigation is ordinarily a matter of discretion vested in the executive official whose agency is responsible for enforcement of the law under which the property was confiscated and is subject to only limited review. Courts will not review a decision to grant or withhold remission or mitigation, although they will grant relief upon a showing of refusal to consider a remission petition, *In re $67,470.00 (Averhart)*, 901 F.2d 1540, 1543-545 (11th Cir. 1990); *Yskamp v. DEA*, 163 F.3d 767, 770 (3d Cir. 1998); *Vereda, Ltda v. United States*, 271 F.3d 1367, 1371 (Fed. Cir. 2001); Congress, of course, may provide otherwise, *e.g.*, 18 U.S.C. 3668 (permitting judicial remission or mitigation for forfeitures under federal liquor laws).

[44] *United States v. One Star Class Sloop Sailboat (Flash II)*, 458 F.3d 16, 22 (1st Cir. 2006).

[45] 18 U.S.C. 983(a)(4); Rule G of the F.R. Civ.P. Supp. (Rule G). Rule G(5)(a)("(i) A person who asserts an interest in the defendant property may contest the forfeiture by filing a claim in the court where the action is pending. The claim must: (A) identify the specific property claimed; (B) identify the claimant and state the claimant's interest in the property; (C) be signed by the claimant under penalty of perjury; and (D) be served on the government attorney designated under Rule G(4)(b).... (iii) A claim filed by a person asserting an interest as a bailee must identify the bailor, and if filed on the bailor's behalf must state the authority to do so").

[46] 18 U.S.C. 983(a)(4)(A); 20 days in customs cases, F.R.Civ.P.Supp.Rule C(6).

[47] 18 U.S.C. 983(a)(4)(B); F.R.Civ.P.Supp. Rule C(6).

[48] *United States v. Clark*, 84 F.3d 378, 380 (10th Cir. 1996)("Due process thus requires 'notice reasonably calculated, under all the circumstances, to apprise interested parties of the pendency of the action and afford them an opportunity to present their objections'")(quoting *Mennonite Bd. of Missions v. Adams*, 462 U.S. 791, 800 (1983)); *ArmendarizMata v. U.S. Dept. of Justice*, 82 F.3d 679, 683 (5th Cir. 1996); *United States v. Marolf*, 173 F.3d 1213,

1216 (9th Cir. 1999); *Clymore v. United States*, 164 F.3d 569, 572-74 (10th Cir. 1999); *Ikelionwu v. United States*, 150 F.3d 233, 238- 39 (2d Cir. 1998).

[49] *E.g., United States v. DEA*, 92 F.3d 648, 654 (8th Cir. 1996)("Should the citizen prove inept, the government may keep the property, without having to explain its actions"); *United States v. Lot 65 Pine Meadow*, 976 F.2d 1155, 1156- 157 (8th Cir. 1992)(upholding a decree of forfeiture by default for filing a verified claim and answer on August 26, 1991, instead of on August 13, when the claim should have been filed, and on August 20, when the answer was due); *Sarit v. U.S. Drug Enforcement Administration*, 987 F.2d 10, 15-7 (1st Cir. 1993); *United States v. Commodity Account No. 549 54930 (Lindstrom)*, 219 F.3d 595, 597-98 (7th Cir. 2000); *United States v. Shigemura*, 664 F.3d 310, 312 (10th Cir. 2011)("[B]ecause Defendant failed to file an administrative claim to contest the forfeiture of the $44,853.39 in cash, the court lacked jurisdiction to hear his 41(g) motion [for return of the money]"); cf., *Malladi Drugs & Pharmaceuticals, Ltd. v. Tandy*, 552 F.3d 885, 887-88 (D.C.Cir. 2009)("If no interested party files a claim, then the DEA administratively forfeits the property by default and the only option remaining for an interested party is to file a petition for remission or mitigation of the forfeiture with the DEA"); *United States v. Real Properties Located at 7215 Longboat Dr. (Mariani)*, 750 F.3d 968, 972-75 (8th Cir. 2014)(district court dismissal for want of a timely claim, reversed because the government had failed to provide notice).

[50] Rule G(8)(c)(i)(B); *United States v. Technodyne LLC*, 753 F.3d 368, 380 (2d Cir. 2014)(internal citations omitted)("In general, in order to contest a governmental forfeiture action, claimants must have both standing under the statute or statutes governing their claims and standing under Article III of the Constitution as required for any action brought in federal court. Litigants have Article III standing if they have suffered an injury in fact that is fairly ... traceable to the challenged action and likely to be redressed by a favorable decision. Litigants have statute standing to oppose forfeiture in a civil in rem proceeding commenced by the government if they claim an interest in the seized property, ... asserting that interest in the property in the manner set forth in the Supplemental Rules for Certain Admiralty and Maritime Claims"); *United States v. $8,440,190 in U.S. Currency (Van Bommel-Duyzing)*, 719 F.3d 49, 57 n.11 (1st Cir. 2013)("Standing in forfeiture actions has both constitutional and statutory aspects"); *United States v. $154,8563.99 in U.S. Currency, More or Less (Marcus)*, 744 F.3d 559, 564 (8th Cir. 2014)("Marcus also contends the district court abused its discretion in striking his claims.... Yet, Marcus's refusal to answer the special interrogatories on the asserted basis of this Fourth and Fifth Amendment privileges did not preclude the district court from striking his claims. A claimant's decision to invoke the Fifth Amendment's protection against self-incrimination ... does not decrease his burden of establishing standing.").

[51] 19 U.S.C. 1609; 26 U.S.C. 7325.

[52] "(1) Any person entitled to written notice in any nonjudicial civil forfeiture proceeding under a civil forfeiture statute who does not receive such notice may file a motion to set aside a declaration of forfeiture with respect to that person's interest in the property, which motion shall be granted if—(A) the Government knew, or reasonably should have known, of the moving party's interest and failed to take reasonable steps to provide such party with notice; and (B) the moving party did not know or have reason to know of the seizure within sufficient time to file a timely claim. (2)(A) Notwithstanding the expiration of any applicable statute of limitations, if the court grants a motion under paragraph (1), the court shall set aside the declaration of forfeiture as to the interest of the moving party without prejudice to the right of the Government to commence a subsequent forfeiture proceeding as

to the interest of the moving party. (B) Any proceeding described in subparagraph (A) shall be commenced—(i) if nonjudicial, within 60 days of the entry of the order granting the motion; or (ii) if judicial, within 6 months of the entry of the order granting the motion. (3) A motion under paragraph (1) may be filed not later than 5 years after the date of final publication of notice of seizure of the property. (4) If, at the time a motion made under paragraph (1) is granted, the forfeited property has been disposed of by the Government in accordance with law, the Government may institute proceedings against a substitute sum of money equal to the value of the moving party's interest in the property at the time the property was disposed of. (5) A motion filed under this subsection shall be the exclusive remedy for seeking to set aside a declaration of forfeiture under a civil forfeiture statute," 18 U.S.C. 983(e). Otherwise, "[o]nce an administrative forfeiture is complete, a district court may review only whether the forfeiture comported with constitutional due process guarantees," *Taylor v. United States*, 483 F.3d 385, 388 (5th Cir. 2007); *Mesa Valderrama v. United States*, 417 F.3d 1189, 1194 (11th Cir. 2005).

[53] This resolved an earlier conflict among the circuits over whether the statute of limitations barred further forfeiture proceedings in cases where an administrative forfeiture was set aside after the period of limitations had run. *United States v. Dusenbery*, 201 F.3d 763, 768 (6th Cir. 2000); *cf., Boero v. Drug Enforcement Administration*, 111 F.3d 301, 306 (2d Cir. 1997); contra, *United States v. Marolf*, 173 F.3d 1213, 1216-217 (9th Cir. 1999); *Clymore v. United States*, 164 F.3d 569, 572-74 (10th Cir. 1999); *Kadonsky v. United States,* 216 F.3d 499, 505-6 (5th Cir. 2000); *cf., United States v. One Toshiba Color Television (McGlory),* 213 F.3d 147, 158-59 (3d Cir. 2000). A related conflict has arisen, however, *United States v. $11,500.00 in United States Currency (Guerrero),* 710 F.3d 1006, 1016 (9th Cir. 2013) ("Some courts have held that ... when the government has failed to provide timely notice, it must return the seized property to the claimant even though it had already commenced forfeiture proceedings. But others have held that the government need not return the seized property")(internal citations omitted).

[54] 18 U.S.C. 983(a)(1). The timetables of 18 U.S.C. 983 apply to the noncustoms forfeiture statutes that once relied extensively upon customs procedure, *e.g.*, 18 U.S.C. 981 (money laundering) and 21 U.S.C. 881 (controlled substances), they do not apply to forfeitures arising under the customs laws, 18 U.S.C. 983(i).

[55] 18 U.S.C. 983(a)(2)(the deadline is set in the notice but must give the claimant at least 35 days from the mailing of personal notice; 30 days from the final publication notice, if personal notice is not received).

[56] 18 U.S.C. 983(a)(3). The deadline is not jurisdictional. If the party does not claim it, it is waived, *United States v. Wilson*, 699 F.3d 789, 797 (4th Cir. 2012). Moreover, the claimant must meet statutory standing requirements before he may direct the court's attention to the government's tardiness, *United States v. Vazquez-Alvarez*, 760 F.3d 193, 197-98 (2d Cir. 2014).

[57] *United States v. Robinson*, 434 F.3d 357, 364 (5th Cir. 2005); *see discussion infra*, at footnote 208 and accompanying text; *Delay Between Seizure of Personal Property by Federal Government and Institution of Proceedings for Forfeiture Thereof as Violative of Fifth Amendment Due Process Requirements*, 69 ALR Fed. 373.

[58] 18 U.S.C. 983(a)(3); 19 U.S.C. 1608.

[59] 18 U.S.C. 983(c); *United States v. $132,245.00 in U.S. Currency (Cyr)*, 764 F.3d 1055, 1057 (9th Cir. 2014); *United States v. $48,100.00 in United States Currency (Nelson)*, 756 F.3d 650, 653 (8th Cir. 2014); *United States v. The Sum of $185,336.07 United States Currency (Pellegrino)*, 731 F.3d 189, 196 (2d Cir. 2013); *United States v. Funds in the Amount of*

One Hundred Thousand One Hundred and Twenty Dollars ($100,120.00)(Marrocco), 730 F.3d 711, 716 (7th Cir. 2013). The government may not rely on hearsay evidence to meet its burden under section 983(c), *United States v. $92,203 in United States Currency (Garcia-Baeza)*, 537 F.3d 504, 510 (5th Cir. 2008).

[60] 19 U.S.C. 1615; *United States v. 3234 Washington Avenue North*,480 F.3d 841, 843 (8th Cir. 2007); *United States v. One Harrington and Richardson Rifle, Model M-14, 7.62 Caliber*, 378 F.3d 533, 534 (6th Cir. 2004); *United States v. Collado*, 348 F.3d 323, 326-327 (2d Cir. 2003); *United States v. One "Piper" Aztec "F" DeLuxe Model 250 PA 23 Aircraft*, 321 F.3d 355, 359-60 (3d Cir. 2003); *Kadonsky v. United States*, 216 F.3d 499, 503 (5th Cir. 2000); *United States v. United States Currency Deposited for Active Trade Co.*, 176 F.3d 941, 944 (7th Cir. 1999); *United States v. 22249 Dolorosa St.*, 167 F.3d 509, 513 (9th Cir. 1999); *United States v. $141,770 (Moreno-Pena)*, 157 F.3d 600, 603 (8th Cir. 1998). *United States v. One 1978 Piper Cherokee Aircraft*, 91 F.3d 1204, 1207 (9th Cir. 1996)("The standard for probable cause in forfeiture proceedings resembles that required to support a search warrant. The determination of probable cause is based upon a totality of the circumstances test, and the government's evidence must be more than that which gives rise to a mere suspicion, although it need not rise to the level of prima facie proof"); *United States v. $39,873 (Armfield)*, 80 F.3d 317, 318 (8th Cir. 1996); *United States v. United States Currency Deposited for Active Trade Co.*, 176 F.3d 941, 944 (7th Cir. 1999); *United States v. $9,041,598.68 (Massieu)*, 163 F.3d 238, 246 (5th Cir. 1999); *United States v. $141,770 (Moreno-Pena)*, 157 F.3d 600, 603 (8th Cir. 1998).

CAFRA does not apply retroactively; proceedings initiated prior to August 23, 2000 are governed by earlier law, *United States v. $100,348 (Mayzel)*, 354 F.3d 1110, 1116 (9th Cir. 2004); *United States v. Collado*, 348 F.3d 323, 326 (2d Cir. 2003); *United States v. One "Piper" Aztec "F" DeLuxe Model 250 PA 23 Aircraft*, 321 F.3d 355, 357-58 (3d Cir. 2003); *United States v. $174,206 (Ricard)*, 320 F.3d 658, 661-62 (6th Cir. 2003); *United States v. Wagoner County Real Estate*, 278 F.3d 1091, 1097 n.5 (10th Cir. 2002).

[61] *United States v. $39,873*, 80 F.3d 317, 318 (8th Cir. 1996); *United States v. All Assets of G.P.S. Automotive Corp.*, 66 F.3d 483, 487 (2d Cir. 1996); *United States v. 22249 Dolorosa St.*, 167 F.3d 509, 511 (9th Cir. 1999).

[62] 18 U.S.C. 983(c)(3); *United States v. The Sum of $185,336.07 United States Currency (Pellegrino)*, 731 F.3d 189, 196-97 (2d Cir. 2013); *United States v. Funds in the Amount of One Hundred Thousand One Hundred and Twenty Dollars ($100,120.00)(Marrocco)*, 730 F.3d 711, 716 (7th Cir. 2013).

[63] *Austin v. United States*, 509 U.S. 602, 617 (1993). The Supreme Court has observed that due process only precludes forfeiture either (1) where the property has "been taken from [its owner] without his privity or consent" and used in a manner which would ordinarily give rise to confiscation, or (2) where the owner was "not only ... uninvolved in and unaware of the wrongful activity, but also that he had done all that reasonably could be expected to prevent the proscribed use of the property," *Calero-Toledo v. Pearson Yacht Leasing Co.*, 416 U.S. 663, 689 (1974). Although some argue that the splintered nature of the majority in *Bennis v. Michigan*, 516 U.S. 442 (1996), erodes the support for this view, it remains the law until modified or rejected by the Court.

[64] Outside of CAFRA, statutory "innocent owner" defenses in civil forfeiture, more generous than due process requires, are relatively rare. *See, e.g.*, *United States v. Davis*, 648 F.3d 84, 94 (2d Cir. 2011)(noting that the customs forfeiture provisions are not covered by CAFRA or its innocent owner defense).

[65] 18 U.S.C. 983(d); *United States v. One 1990 Beechcraft 1900 C Twin Engine Turbo-Prop Aircraft (International Aviation Inc.)*, 619 F. 3d 1275, 1277 (11th Cir. 2010)(CAFRA's innocent owner bar to confiscation is only available to those who qualify as "owners").

[66] 18 U.S.C. 983(d)(2)(A); *United States v. Ferro*, 681 F.3d 1105, 1109 (9th Cir. 2012); *United States v. $493,850 in U.S. Currency (Bruno)*, 518 F.3d 1159, 1170 (9th Cir. 2008); *von Hofe v. United States*, 492 F.3d 175, 180 (2d Cir. 2007); *United States v. 45 Claremont St.*, 395 F.3d 1, 4-5 (1st Cir. 2004); *United States v. One Lincoln Navigator*, 328 F.3d 1011, 1014 (8th Cir. 2003); *United States v. 16328 South 43rd East Avenue*, 275 F.3d 1281, 1284 n.1 (10th Cir. 2002).

[67] 18 U.S.C. 983(d)(3)(A). The defense may also be available to claimants who acquire an interest in their primary residence through inheritance or divorce rather than by purchase, 18 U.S.C. 983(d)(3)(B); *United States v. 221 Dana Avenue*, 261 F.3d 65, 74 (1st Cir. 2001); *United States v. $125,938.62 (Cardenal)*, 537 F.3d 1287, 1293 n.3 (11th Cir. 2008).

[68] 18 U.S.C. 983(g); *United States v. $132,245.00 In U.S. Currency (Cyr)*,764 F.3d 1055, 1058 (9th Cir. 2014); *United States v. $92,203.00 in United States Currency (Garcia-Baeza)*, 537 F.3d 504, 510 (5th Cir. 2008).

[69] 28 U.S.C. 2465; *Republic National Bank v. United States*, 506 U.S. 80, 95 (1992); *United States v. Seifuddin*, 820 F.2d 1074, 1078-79 (9th Cir. 1987); *cf., Lee v. City of Chicago*, 330 F.3d 456, 466 (7th Cir. 2003)("the government should not, by virtue of its authority to seize, effect *de facto* forfeitures of property by retaining items indefinitely. But we know that due process guarantees would prevent this ... "); but see *Synagogue v. United States*, 482 F.3d 1058, 1064 (9th Cir. 2007)(a property owner is not entitled interest, attorney fees or costs when the government seizes his property but later returns it without initiating forfeiture proceedings).

A property owner may petition the court for return of his property under Rule 41(g) of the Federal Rules of Criminal Procedure, *Jackson v. United States*, 526 F.3d 394, 396-97 (8th Cir. 2008). An owner, however, is not entitled to the return of property that cannot be lawfully possessed, *Boggs v. Rubin*, 161 F.3d 37, 40 (D.C. Cir. 1998); *United States v. Felici*, 208 F.3d 667, 670 (8th Cir. 2000); *United States v. Vanhorn*, 296 F.3d 713, 719 (8th Cir. 2002).

[70] 28 U.S.C. 2680(c)("The provisions of this chapter and section 1346(b) of this title [relating to federal tort claims] shall not apply to ... (c) Any claim arising in respect of the assessment or collection of any tax or customs duty, or the detention of any goods, merchandise, or other property by any officer of customs or excise or any other law enforcement officer, except that the provisions of this chapter and section 1346(b) of this title apply to any claim based on injury or loss of goods, merchandise, or other property, while in the possession of any officer of customs or excise or any other law enforcement officer, if—(1) the property was seized for the purpose of forfeiture under any provision of Federal law providing for the forfeiture of property other than as a sentence imposed upon conviction of a criminal offense; (2) the interest of the claimant was not forfeited; (3) the interest of the claimant was not remitted or mitigated (if the property was subject to forfeiture); and (4) the claimant was not convicted of a crime for which the interest of the claimant in the property was subject to forfeiture under a Federal criminal forfeiture law").

[71] *United States v. $186,416.00 in U.S. Currency (Gabbert)*, 722 F.3d 1173, 1175 (9th Cir. 2013); *United States v. $186,416.00 in U.S. Currency (United Medical Caregivers Clinic, Inc.)*, 642 F.3d 753, 754 (9th Cir. 2011). Attorneys' fees are available for civil forfeiture costs but not for related criminal proceedings, even though the result may permit the government to first press weak criminal charges and thus ensure that the lion's share of the cost of related

civil forfeiture attorneys' services are beyond recovery, *United States v. Certain Real Property, Located at 317 Nick Fitchard Rd, N.W.*, 579 F.3d 1315, 1318-319 (11th Cir. 2009)("The district court added that 'if [it] were to find that fees incurred defending the criminal case were not recoverable under CAFRA, then the government would be allowed to avoid CAFRA, as it has tried to in this case, by moving for a stay in the civil case and prosecuting the criminal case'"), quoting 566 F.Supp.2d 1252, 1261 (N.D.Ala. 2008). Moreover, an award of attorneys' fees may be adjusted to reflect the prevailing party's level of success as well as the reasonableness of the level of litigation effort, although not for failure to overcome lack of notice, *United States v. One Star Class Sloop Sailboat Named Flash II*, 546 F.3d 26, 38-43 (1st Cir. 2008).

72 "(a) Upon the entry of a judgment for the claimant in any proceeding to condemn or forfeit property seized or arrested under any provision of Federal law—(1) such property shall be returned forthwith to the claimant or his agent; and (2) if it appears that there was reasonable cause for the seizure or arrest, the court shall cause a proper certificate thereof to be entered and, in such case, neither the person who made the seizure or arrest nor the prosecutor shall be liable to suit or judgment on account of such suit or prosecution, nor shall the claimant be entitled to costs, except as provided in subsection (b).

"(b)(1) Except as provided in paragraph (2), in any civil proceeding to forfeit property under any provision of Federal law in which the claimant substantially prevails, the United States shall be liable for—(A) reasonable attorney fees and other litigation costs reasonably incurred by the claimant; (B) post-judgment interest, as set forth in section 1961 of this title; and (C) in cases involving currency, other negotiable instruments, or the proceeds of an interlocutory sale—(i) interest actually paid to the United States from the date of seizure or arrest of the property that resulted from the investment of the property in an interest-bearing account or instrument; and (ii) an imputed amount of interest that such currency, instruments, or proceeds would have earned at the rate applicable to the 30-day Treasury Bill, for any period during which no interest was paid (not including any period when the property reasonably was in use as evidence in an official proceeding or in conducting scientific tests for the purpose of collecting evidence), commencing 15 days after the property was seized by a Federal law enforcement agency, or was turned over to a Federal law enforcement agency by a State or local law enforcement agency. (2)(A) The United States shall not be required to disgorge the value of any intangible benefits nor make any other payments to the claimant not specifically authorized by this subsection. (B) The provisions of paragraph (1) shall not apply if the claimant is convicted of a crime for which the interest of the claimant in the property was subject to forfeiture under a Federal criminal forfeiture law. (C) If there are multiple claims to the same property, the United States shall not be liable for costs and attorneys fees associated with any such claim if the United States—(i) promptly recognizes such claim; (ii) promptly returns the interest of the claimant in the property to the claimant, if the property can be divided without difficulty and there are no competing claims to that portion of the property; (iii) does not cause the claimant to incur additional, reasonable costs or fees; and (iv) prevails in obtaining forfeiture with respect to one or more of the other claims. (D) If the court enters judgment in part for the claimant and in part for the Government, the court shall reduce the award of costs and attorney fees accordingly," 28 U.S.C. 2465; see also *United States v. Craig*, 694 F.3d 509, 512-13 (3d Cir. 2012), citing cases on either side of the circuit split over the question of whether, under Rule 41 of the Federal Rules of Criminal Procedure (return of seized property) rather than Section 2465, the United States may be found liable for interest.

[73] The number of criminal forfeiture judgments has surpassed the number of civil forfeiture judgments every year since FY1995, U.S. Department of Justice, Executive Office for United States Attorneys, *United States Attorneys' Annual Statistical Report: Fiscal Year 2005, 2008, 2009, 2010, 2011, 2012*, and *2013*, AF Chart in the older reports; Table 16 in the more recent reports, http://www.justice.gov/usaoresources/annual-statistical-reports. The statistics, however, do not include civil administrative forfeitures. It is not clear where the balance would stand if administrative forfeitures were added to the civil forfeiture side of the equation.

[74] 18 U.S.C. 982(a)(1)("The court, in imposing sentence on a person convicted of an offense in violation of section ... 1960 of this title, shall order that the person forfeit to the United States any property, real or personal, involved in such offense, or any property traceable to such property").

[75] 18 U.S.C. 982(a)(2) ("The court, in imposing sentence on a person convicted of a violation of, or a conspiracy to violate ... (B) section 471, 472, 473, 474, 476, 477, 478, 479, 480, 481, 485, 486, 487, 488, 501, 502, 510, 542, 545, 555, 842, 844 ... of this title, shall order that the person forfeit to the United States any property constituting, or derived from, proceeds the person obtained directly or indirectly, as the result of such violation").

[76] 18 U.S.C. 982(a)(2)("The court, in imposing sentence on a person convicted of a violation of, or a conspiracy to violate ... (B) section ... 1028 ... of this title, shall order that the person forfeit to the United States any property constituting, or derived from, proceeds the person obtained directly or indirectly, as the result of such violation").

[77] 18 U.S.C. 982(a)(2)("The court, in imposing sentence on a person convicted of a violation of, or a conspiracy to violate ... (B) section ... 1029 ... of this title, shall order that the person forfeit to the United States any property constituting, or derived from, proceeds the person obtained directly or indirectly, as the result of such violation").

[78] 18 U.S.C. 982(a)(2)("The court, in imposing sentence on a person convicted of a violation of, or a conspiracy to violate ... (B) section ... 1030 of this title, shall order that the person forfeit to the United States any property constituting, or derived from, proceeds the person obtained directly or indirectly, as the result of such violation").

[79] 18 U.S.C. 982(a)(5)("The court, in imposing sentence on a person convicted of a violation or conspiracy to violate— (A) section 511 (altering or removing motor vehicle identification numbers); (B) section 553 (importing or exporting stolen motor vehicles); (C) section 2119 (armed robbery of automobiles); (D) section 2312 (transporting stolen motor vehicles in interstate commerce); or (E) section 2313 (possessing or selling a stolen motor vehicle that has moved in interstate commerce); shall order that the person forfeit to the United States any property, real or personal, which represents or is traceable to the gross proceeds obtained, directly or indirectly, as a result of such violation").

[80] 18 U.S.C. 982(a)(7)("The court, in imposing sentence on a person convicted of a Federal health care offense, shall order the person to forfeit property, real or personal, that constitutes or is derived, directly or indirectly, from gross proceeds traceable to the commission of the offense").

[81] 18 U.S.C. 982(a)(8)("The court, in sentencing a defendant convicted of an offense under section 1028, 1029, 1341, 1342, 1343, or 1344, or of a conspiracy to commit such an offense, if the offense involves telemarketing (as that term is defined in section 2325), shall order that the defendant forfeit to the United States any real or personal property—(A) used or intended to be used to commit, to facilitate, or to promote the commission of such offense; and (B) constituting, derived from, or traceable to the gross proceeds that the defendant obtained directly or indirectly as a result of the offense").

[82] 18 U.S.C. 982(a)(2), (3), (4)("(2) The court, in imposing sentence on a person convicted of a violation of, or a conspiracy to violate—(A) section 215, 656, 657, 1005, 1006, 1007, 1014, 1341, 1343, or 1344 of this title, affecting a financial institution, ... shall order that the person forfeit to the United States any property constituting, or derived from, proceeds the person obtained directly or indirectly, as the result of such violation.

(3) The court, in imposing a sentence on a person convicted of an offense under—(A) section 666(a)(1) (relating to Federal program fraud); (B) section 1001 (relating to fraud and false statements); (C) section 1031 (relating to major fraud against the United States); (D) section 1032 (relating to concealment of assets from conservator, receiver, or liquidating agent of insured financial institution); (E) section 1341 (relating to mail fraud); or (F) section 1343 (relating to wire fraud), involving the sale of assets acquired or held by the Resolution Trust Corporation, the Federal Deposit Insurance Corporation, as conservator or receiver for a financial institution or any other conservator for a financial institution appointed by the Office of the Comptroller of the Currency, or the National Credit Union Administration, as conservator or liquidating agent for a financial institution, shall order that the person forfeit to the United States any property, real or personal, which represents or is traceable to the gross receipts obtained, directly or indirectly, as a result of such violation.

(4) With respect to an offense listed in subsection (a)(3) committed for the purpose of executing or attempting to execute any scheme or artifice to defraud, or for obtaining money or property by means of false or fraudulent statements, pretenses, representations, or promises, the gross receipts of such an offense shall include any property, real or personal, tangible or intangible, which is obtained, directly or indirectly, as a result of such offense").

[83] 18 U.S.C. 982(a)(6)("The court, in imposing sentence on a person convicted of a violation of, or conspiracy to violate, section 274(a), 274A(a)(1), or 274A(a)(2) of the Immigration and Nationality Act or section 554, 1425, 1426, 1427, 1541, 1542, 1543, 1544, or 1546 of this title, or a violation of, or conspiracy to violate, section 1028 of this title if committed in connection with passport or visa issuance or use, shall order that the person forfeit to the United States, regardless of any provision of State law—(i) any conveyance, including any vessel, vehicle, or aircraft used in the commission of the offense of which the person is convicted; and (ii) any property real or personal—(I) that constitutes, or is derived from or is traceable to the proceeds obtained directly or indirectly from the commission of the offense of which the person is convicted; or (II) that is used to facilitate, or is intended to be used to facilitate, the commission of the offense of which the person is convicted. (B) The court, in imposing sentence on a person described in subparagraph (A), shall order that the person forfeit to the United States all property described in that subparagraph").

[84] "If a person is charged in a criminal case with a violation of an Act of Congress for which the civil or criminal forfeiture of property is authorized, the Government may include notice of the forfeiture in the indictment or information pursuant to the Federal Rules of Criminal Procedure. If the defendant is convicted of the offense giving rise to the forfeiture, the court shall order the forfeiture of the property as part of the sentence in the criminal case pursuant to the Federal Rules of Criminal Procedure and section 3554 of title 18, United States Code. The procedures in section 413 of the Controlled Substances Act (21 U.S.C. 853) apply to all stages of a criminal forfeiture proceeding, except that subsection (d) of such section applies only in cases in which the defendant is convicted of a violation of such Act," 28 U.S.C. 2461(c); e.g., *United States v. Newman*, 659 F.3d 1235 (9th Cir. 2011).

At one time, the bridge statute only applied if "no specific statutory provision is made for criminal forfeiture," 28 U.S.C. 2461(c)(2000 ed.). Some questioned whether the bridge statute might be used in general mail and wire fraud cases. True, tainted property was subject to civil forfeiture in mail and wire fraud cases as a general rule, but it was also subject to criminal forfeiture as long as the fraud was committed against a financial institution, 18 U.S.C. 982(a)(2) (A)(2000 ed.). Nevertheless, federal appellate courts read section 2461 to permit criminal forfeiture in mail and wire fraud cases in which a financial institution was not the victim, *United States v. Day*, 524 F.3d 1361, 1374-377 (D.C.Cir. 2008); *United States v. Schlesinger*, 514 F.3d 277, 278 (2d Cir. 2008); *United States v. Foley*, 508 F.3d 627, 635 (11th Cir. 2007). Congress changed the language to its present form to eliminate any uncertainty.

85 *E.g.*, 18 U.S.C. 982 (money laundering); 18 U.S.C. 1963 (RICO); 21 U.S.C. 853 (drug dealing). Or a creature of several statutes, as demonstrated by the facts underlying the Supreme Court's decision in *Kaley v. United States*, 134 S.C. 1090 (2014). The Kaleys were indicted for interstate transportation of stolen property in violation of 18 U.S.C. 2314. To pay their anticipated legal defense costs, they secured a $500,000 line of credit secured by their home and used the line of credit to purchase a certificate of deposit in that amount. Through a series of cross references, property traceable to the proceeds of a stolen property violation is subject to civil forfeiture. More precisely, the stolen property offense is a RICO predicate offense, that is, one of the crimes upon which a racketeering prosecution might be based, 18 U.S.C. 1961(1). Moreover, any RICO predicate offense is automatically a money laundering predicate offense, 18 U.S.C. 1956(c)(7)(A). Section 981(a)(1)(C) calls for the civil forfeiture of proceeds traceable to any money laundering predicate offense. An offense's status as a predicate offense is all that is required; there is no need to establish the other elements of either a RICO or money laundering offense. In *Kaley*, however, the grand jury subsequently indicted the Kaleys for conspiracy to money launder, 18 U.S.C. 1956(h). Although it is not completely clear, it appears the grand jury believed that in order to conceal the illegal source of their wealth the Kaleys had used the proceeds from the stolen property offense to purchase or pay the mortgage on their home or had engaged in the line of credit and CD transactions for that purpose, cf., 18 U.S.C. 1956(a)(1)(B)(i). Money laundering forfeiture reaches property on both sides of the transaction, i.e., any property "involved" in a prohibited money laundering transaction or traceable to such property, 18 U.S.C. 981(a)(1)(A). This would explain how the forfeiture liability of $140,000 resulting from the Kaleys' alleged stolen property offense grew to over $2 million: $140,000 from the proceeds of the stolen property offense; plus the $500,000 line of credit and the value of the home used to secure the line of credit; plus the $500,000 CD and the value of the $500,000 line of credit used to purchase of the CD. ($140,000 + $500,000 (home) + $500,000 (credit line) + $500,000(credit line) + $500,000(CD)).

86 *United States v. Shakur*, 691 F.3d 979, 984 (8th Cir. 2012)(quoting, *Libretti v. United States*, 516 U.S. 29, 39 (1995))("Criminal forfeiture is an aspect of punishment imposed following conviction of a substantive criminal offense"); 18 U.S.C. 982 (money laundering).

87 *United States v. Smith*, 770 F.3d 628, 637 (7th Cir. 2014); *United States v. Davis*, 706 F.3d 1081, 1083 (9th Cir. 2013); *United States v. McGinty*, 610 F.3d 1242, 1247 (10th Cir. 2010).

88 The federal Racketeer Influenced and Corrupt Organization (RICO) forfeiture statute, for example, is designed not only to sever the offender from the organization he or she has corrupted but to confiscate any property right which affords a source of influence over the enterprise, 18 U.S.C. 1963(a)(2)(D).

89 21 U.S.C. 853(n)(6); *United States v. Contorinis*, 692 F.3d 136, 146 (2d Cir. 2012)(quoting, *United States v. Bajakajian,* 524 U.S. 321, 332 (1998))("Forfeiture in criminal proceedings ... is designed to punish the offender, and cannot be imposed upon innocent owners");

United States v. Fleet, 498 F.3d 1225, 1232 (11th Cir. 2007); *United States v. Vampire Nation*, 451 F.3d 189, 202 (3d Cir. 2006)("criminal forfeiture is a sanction against the individual defendant rather than against the property itself"); *United States v. Saccoccia*, 354 F.3d 9, 15 (1st Cir. 2003)("[T]he government may reach only the defendant's substitute assets and not those of a third party").

[90] *United States v. Bader*, 678 F.3d 858, 895 (10th Cir. 2012)("If the conviction that supported a forfeiture is reversed on appeal, the forfeiture—along with all other aspects of the defendant's sentence for that offense—must be reversed as well"); *United States v. Juluke*, 426 F.3d 323, 327-28 (5th Cir. 2005). When a defendant is convicted of racketeering under RICO, 18 U.S.C. 1961-1963, he need not have personally committed each of the enterprise's predicate offenses and consequently his property derived from those offenses is subject to criminal forfeiture under RICO, *United States v. Hively*, 437 F.3d 752, 765 (11th Cir. 2006).

[91] "(2) In any case described in any of subparagraphs (A) through (E) of paragraph (1) [below], the court shall order the forfeiture of any other property of the defendant, up to the value of any property described in subparagraphs (A) through (E) of paragraph (1), as applicable.
"(1) Paragraph (2) of this subsection shall apply, if any property described in subsection (a), as a result of any act or omission of the defendant—(A) cannot be located upon the exercise of due diligence; (B) has been transferred or sold to, or deposited with, a third party; (C) has been placed beyond the jurisdiction of the court; (D) has been substantially diminished in value; or (E) has been commingled with other property which cannot be divided without difficulty," 21 U.S.C. 853(p)(2),(1); see also 18 U.S.C. 1963(m); *United States v. Smith*, 770 F.3d 628, 641-42 (7th Cir. 2014).

[92] F.R.Crim.P. 7(c), 32.2(a); *United States v. Hampton*, 732 F.3d 687, 690 (6th Cir. 2013); *United States v. Torres*, 703 F.3d 194, 196 n.1 (2d Cir. 2012); *United States v. Marquez*, 685 F.3d 501, 509 (5th Cir. 2012); *United States v. Oregon*, 671 F.3d 484, 487 (4th Cir. 2012).

[93] F.R.Crim.P. 32.2(b)(5); in *Libretti v. United States*, 516 U.S. 29, 49 (1995), the Supreme Court observed that "the nature of criminal forfeiture as an aspect of sentencing compels the conclusion that the right to a jury verdict on forfeitability does not fall within the Sixth Amendment's constitutional protection." Thereafter, however, the Court held in *Apprendi v. New Jersey*, 530 U.S. 466, 490 (2000) that sentencing factors are not beyond the Amendment's reach and that "any crime that increases the penalty for a crime beyond the prescribed statutory maximum must be submitted to a jury." In *Southern Union Co. v. United States*, 132 S.Ct. 2346, 2357 (2012), it held that *Apprendi* applies to fines as well as terms of imprisonment. Criminal forfeiture defendants have sometimes argued, to no avail, that *Apprendi* and *Southern Union*, abrogate *Libretti* notwithstanding their election under Rule 32.2 to forego a jury determination of the forfeitability of their property, *United States v. Sigillito*, 759 F.3d 913, 936 (8th Cir. 2014), citing in accord, *United States v. Wilkes*, 744 F.3d 1101, 1109 (9th Cir. 2014); *United States v. Simpson*, 741 F.3d 539, 560 (5th Cir. 2014); *United States v. Day*, 700 F.3d 713, 733 (4th Cir. 2012).

[94] Rule 32.2 permits the Attorney General to seize the property upon the court's entry of a preliminary forfeiture order, F.R.Crim.P. 32.2(b)(3); *United States v. Davenport*, 668 F.3d 1316, 1320 (11th Cir. 2012).

[95] *E.g.*, 21 U.S.C. 853(e)(1), (2). At least one circuit has held that pretrial restraining orders are not available when the government opts for a criminal forfeiture by merging a civil forfeiture authorization with a criminal prosecution under the auspices of 28 U.S.C. 2461(c), *United States v. Razmilovic*, 419 F.3d 134, 137-41 (2d Cir. 2005). Neither the Sixth Amendment right to counsel nor the Fifth Amendment right to due process afford a

defendant the right to a pre-trial, post-indictment hearing to determine whether the government has probable cause to believe that the restrained property is subject to confiscation, even if the property is the defendant's only means of securing the services of his counsel of choice, *United States v. Kaley*, 134 S.Ct. 1090, 1105 (2014).

[96] Substitute assets may become subject to forfeiture if the tainted property has become unavailable, but most courts have refused to permit pre-trial restraint orders on substitute assets, *United States v. Gordon*, 710 F.3d 1124, 1136 n.14 (10th Cir. 2013); *United States v. Erpenbeck*, 682 F.3d 472, 477 (6th Cir. 2012); *United States v. Patelidis*, 335 F.3d 226, 234 (3d Cir. 2003); *United States v. Gotti*, 155 F.3d 144, 147-49 (2d Cir. 1998); *United States v. Riley*, 78 F.3d 367, 371 (8th Cir. 1996); *In re Assets of Martin*, 1 F.3d 1351, 1359 (3d Cir. 1993); *United States v. Floyd*, 992 F.2d 498, 502 (5th Cir. 1993); *cf., United States v. Farmer*, 274 F.3d 800, 802 (4th Cir. 2001)(emphasis added)("Furthermore, in *Caplin's* companion case, the Court held that the pre-trial restraint of a criminal defendant's assets does not violate the constitution *as long as the assets are restrained based upon a finding of probable cause that they are subject to forfeiture. United States v. Monsanto*, 491 U.S. 600, 615-16 (1989)"). In some instances, the government may reach the same end by recording a notice of *lis pendens* under applicable state law, thereby providing public notice that the property is the subject of pending forfeiture litigation and precluding disposal to a good faith purchaser in the interim, *United States v. Parrett*, 530 F.3d at 431-32; *United States v. Grossman*, 501 F.3d 846, 849-51(7th Cir. 2007).

[97] 28 U.S.C. 2461.

[98] 28 U.S.C. 2461(c)(2000 ed.)("If a forfeiture of property is authorized in connection with a violation of an Act of Congress, and any person is charged in an indictment or information with such violation but no specific statutory provision is made for criminal forfeiture upon conviction, the Government may include the forfeiture in the indictment or information in accordance with the Federal Rules of Criminal Procedure, and upon conviction, the court shall order the forfeiture of the property in accordance with the procedures set forth in section 413 of the Controlled Substances Act (21 U.S.C. 853), other than subsection (d) of that section").

[99] 28 U.S.C. 2461(c) (2000 ed.).

[100] H.Rept. 109-333 at 56. The new language which appears in the act under the caption "uniform procedures for criminal forfeiture," is not mentioned in the report's Joint Explanatory Statement of the Committee of Conference where the act's other sections are briefly described.

[101] "If a person is charged in a criminal case with a violation of an Act of Congress for which the civil or criminal forfeiture of property is authorized, the Government may include notice of the forfeiture in the indictment or information pursuant to the Federal Rules of Criminal Procedure. If the defendant is convicted of the offense giving rise to the forfeiture, the court shall order the forfeiture of the property as part of the sentence in the criminal case pursuant to the Federal Rules of Criminal Procedure and section 3554 of title 18, United States Code. The procedures in section 413 of the Controlled Substances Act (21 U.S.C. 853) apply to all stages of a criminal forfeiture proceeding, except that subsection (d) of such section [(rebuttable presumption of forfeitability)]] applies only in cases in which the defendant is convicted of a violation of such Act," 18 U.S.C. 2461(c)).

[102] *United States v. Bader*, 678 F.3d 858, 895 (10th Cir. 2012)("If the conviction that supported a forfeiture is reversed on appeal, the forfeiture—along with all other aspects of the defendant's sentence for that offense—must be reversed as well"); *United States v. Juluke*, 426 F.3d 323, 327-28 (5th Cir. 2005).

[103] Perhaps the best known of these are found in the RICO and the drug trafficking criminal forfeiture provisions, ".... [a]ny such property that is subsequently transferred to a person other than the defendant may be the subject of a special verdict of forfeiture and thereafter shall be ordered forfeited to the United States, unless the transferee establishes in a hearing pursuant to subsection (*l*) that he is a bona fide purchaser for value of such property who at the time of purchase was reasonably without cause to believe that the property was subject to forfeiture under this section." 18 U.S.C. 1963(c); 21 U.S.C. 853(c).

[104] *United States v. Smith*, 770 F.3d 628, 637 (7th Cir. 2014); *United States v. Smith*, 749 F.3d 465, 448 (6th Cir. 2014); *United States v. Peters*, 732 F.3d 93, 98 (2d Cir. 2013).

[105] F.R.Crim.P. 32.2(b)(1); *United States v. Peters*, 732 F.3d at 98; *United States v. Oregon,* 671 F.3d 484, 487-88 (4th Cir. 2012); *United States v. Zorrilla-Echevarria*, 671 F.3d 1, 6 (1st Cir. 2011); *United States v. Smith*, 656 F.3d 821, 827 (8th Cir. 2011).

[106] F.R.Crim.P. 32.2(b)(1); *United States v. Peters*, 732 F.3d at 98; *United States v. Shakur*, 691 F.3d 979, 988 (8th Cir. 2012); *United States v. Bader*, 678 F.3d 858, 894 (10th Cir. 2012); *United States v. Davenport*, 668 F.3d 1316, 1320 (11th Cir. 2012); *United States v. Martin*, 301, 307 (4th Cir. 2011).

[107] F.R.Crim.P. 32.2(b)(1); *United States v. Peters*, 732 F.3d at 98; *United States v. Marquez*, 685 F.3d 501, 509 (5th Cir. 2012); *United States v. Zorrilla-Echevarria*, 671 F.3d at 6.

[108] F.R.Crim.P. 32.2(b)(2); *United States v. Lazarenko*, 476 F.3d 642, 648 (9th Cir. 2007). There is some disagreement among the circuits over whether a governmental victim may be the beneficiary of both a forfeiture order and an order to make restitution, *United States v. Davis*, 706 F.3d 1081, 1083-84 (9th Cir. 2013)(internal citations omitted)("Other circuits have considered whether an off-set is warranted to avoid double recovery when government entities will receive both forfeiture and restitution. These cases hold or imply that if two entities are related closely enough, restitution or forfeiture should be reduced. We disagree with this approach. Even if the same government entity will receive both forfeiture and restitution, there simply is no double recovery. The two payments represent different types of funds: punitive and compensatory. They are different in nature, kind, and purpose").

[109] 21 U.S.C. 853(n)(1).

[110] F.R.Crim.P. 32.2(c); 21 U.S.C. 853(n); *United States v. Caruthers*, 765 F.3d 843, 845-86 (8th Cir. 2014)("A petitioner must meet the pleading requirements in §853(n)(3): 'The petition shall be signed by the petitioner under penalty of perjury and shall set forth the nature and extent of the petitioner's rights, title, or interest in the property, the tie and circumstances of the petitioner's acquisition of the right, title or interest in the property, any additional facts supporting the petitioner's claim, and the relief sought.' The petitioner must state an interest that is legal, as opposed to equitable.... Unexplained naked possession of a cash hoard ... does not rise to the level of possessory interest requisite for standing to attack the forfeiture proceeding. The district court properly ruled that Matthews did not meet the statutory requirements").

[111] 21 U.S.C. 853(n)(2). The petition must be filed within 30 days or the claimant's interest is lost, 21 U.S.C. 853(n)(7); *United States v. Marion*, 562 F.3d 1330, 1341 (11th Cir. 2009); *United States v. Grossman*, 501 F.3d 846, 848-49 (7th Cir. 2007).

[112] F.R.Crim.P. 32.2(e)(1); *United States v. Duboc*, 694 F.3d 1223, 1228 (11th Cir. 2012)(petition to amend filed 11 years after initial entry).

[113] 18 U.S.C. 982(b)(1); 21 U.S.C. 853(n)(6); 18 U.S.C. 1963(*l*)(6); *United States v. Fabian*, 764 F.3d 636, 638 (6th Cir. 2014); *United States v. Holy Land Foundation for Relief and Development*, 722 F.3d 677, 684-85 (5th Cir. 2013); *United States v. White,* 675 F.3d 1073, 1081 (8th Cir. 2012); *United States v.* Cox, 575 F.3d 352, 355 (4th Cir. 2009); *United States*

v. Soreide, 461 F.3d 1351, 1354-355 (11th Cir. 2006). Under 21 U.S.C. 853(k) third parties are barred from intervening in earlier or other separate proceedings to contest the forfeiture of property in which they have an interest, *United States v. Fabian*, 764 F.3d at 637-38; *United States v. White,* 675 F.3d at 1077-78; *United States v. Cox*, 575 F.3d at 358; *United States v. Porchay*, 533 F.3d 704, 710 (8th Cir. 2008); *DSI Associates LLC v. United States*, 496 F.3d 175, 183 (2d Cir. 2007); *United States v. Lazarenko*, 476 F.3d at 648.

114 *United States v. Cox*, 575 F.3d at 356; *DSI Associates LLC v. United States*, 496 F.3d at 184.

115 *United States v. Shefton*, 548 F.3d 1360, 1364 (11th Cir. 2008); *United States v. Andrews*, 530 F.3d 1232, 1238 (10th Cir. 2008); *United States v. White*, 675 F.3d 1073, 1078 (8th Cir. 2012); *United States v. Huntington National Bank*, 682 F.3d 429, 433 (6th Cir. 2102)(holding that the bank purchased an interest in forfeitable assets when it granted a line of credit secured by those assets)("Federal law controls whether a party qualifies as a BFP [bona fide purchaser] under 21 U.S.C. 853(n)(6)(B). If a court determines the claimant has an interest in the property under the law of the jurisdiction that created the property right, then it must next look to federal law to determine if the claimant will prevail"). The courts are divided over the question of whether a recognized constructive trust for the benefit of a victim is sufficient to establish a superior interest under section 853(n). Compare *Willis Management (Vermont), Ltd. v. United States*, 652 F.3d 236, 241-46 (2d Cir. 2011); *United States v. Shefton*, 548 F.3d at 1364-366; *United States v. $4,224,958.57(Boylan)*, 392 F.3d 1002, 1004-1005 (9th Cir. 2004), with *United States v. Andrews*, 530 F.3d at 1238- 239; *United States v. BCCI Holdings (Luxembourg), S.A.*, 46 F.3d 1185, 1190-191(D.C.Cir. 1995).

116 21 U.S.C. 853(n)(6); *United States v. Oregon*, 671 F.3d 484, 492 (4th Cir. 2012); *United States v. Lazarenko*, 476 F.3d at 648.

117 *United States v. Misla-Aldarondo*, 478 F.3d 52, 73-4 (1st Cir. 2007); *United States v. Casey*, 444 F.3d 1071, 1077 (9th Cir. 2006)("money judgments are appropriate under §853, even in cases of insolvent defendants.... the government is entitled to a money judgment in criminal forfeiture cases, even when a defendant has no assets ... ").

118 *United States v. Hall*, 434 F.3d 42, 59 (1st Cir. 2006)("A money judgment permits the government to collect on the forfeiture order in the same way that a successful plaintiff collects a money judgment from a civil defendant"); *United States v. Newman*, 659 F.3d 1235, 1242-243 (9th Cir. 2011)("Because the government sought a money judgment in the first instance, there was no need to seek substitute property"); contra, *United States v. Vampire Nation*, 451 F.3d 189, 202 (3d Cir. 2006)("The judgment *in personam* here is one in forfeiture and is limited by the provisions of 21 U.S.C. 853(a) to [forfeitable assets]. In the event that property traceable to the crime is not available, the Court may direct forfeiture of substitute property subject to the conditions set out in 21 U.S.C. 853(p)").

119 *E.g.*, 21 U.S.C. 881(f), 853(i).

120 *E.g.*, 21 U.S.C. 881(e), 853(i).

121 *United States v. Carter*, 742 F.3d 440, 446 (9th Cir. 2014)("[D]efendants may be required to pay restitution and forfeit the same amounts.... However, the Government may choose to assign forfeited proceeds to victims.... 18 U.S.C. 981(e)(6); ... 21 U.S.C. 853(i)"), citing in accord the proposition that a defendant may be ordered to pay both restitution and forfeiture, and that a defendant has no right to offset the amount owed under one obligation against the amount owed under the other, *United States v. Kalish*, 626 F.3d 165, 169-70 (2d Cir. 2010); *United States v. Emerson*, 128 F.3d 557, 566-67 (7th Cir. 1997); *United States v. Taylor*, 582 F.3d 558, 567 (5th Cir. 2009); *United States v. Alalade*, 204 F.3d 536, 540-41 (4th Cir. 2000); see also 31 U.S.C. 9703(h)(3)(confirming the authority of the Secretary of

the Treasury under 18 U.S.C. 981(e)(6) to transfer forfeited property to victims as restitution).

[122] "(1) The Secretary of the Treasury may apply property forfeited under this chapter in accordance with subparagraph (A) or (B), or both: (A) Retain any of the property for official use. (B) Transfer any of the property to—(i) any other Federal agency; (ii) any State or local law enforcement agency that participated directly or indirectly in the seizure or forfeiture of the property; or (iii) the Civil Air Patrol.
(2) The Secretary may transfer any forfeited personal property or the proceeds of the sale of any forfeited personal or real property to any foreign country which participated directly or indirectly in the seizure or forfeiture of the property, if such a transfer—A) has been agreed to by the Secretary of State; (B) is authorized in an international agreement between the United States and the foreign country; and (C) is made to a country which, if applicable, has been certified under section 2291j(b) of Title 22.
(3) Aircraft may be transferred to the Civil Air Patrol under paragraph (1)(B)(iii) in support of air search and rescue and other emergency services and, pursuant to a memorandum of understanding entered into with a Federal agency, illegal drug traffic surveillance. Jet-powered aircraft may not be transferred to the Civil Air Patrol under the authority of paragraph (1)(B)(iii)," 19 U.S.C. 1616a(c). The Attorney General enjoys similar authority under 21 U.S.C. 881(e) and 18 U.S.C. 981(e), (*i*).

[123] "The Attorney General shall assure that any property transferred to a State or local law enforcement agency under [21 U.S.C. 881(e)(1)(A)]—(A) has a value that bears a reasonable relationship to the degree of direct participation of the State or local agency in the law enforcement effort resulting in the forfeiture, taking into account the total value of all property forfeited and the total law enforcement effort with respect to the violation of law on which the forfeiture is based; and (B) will serve to encourage further cooperation between the recipient State or local agency and Federal law enforcement agencies," 21 U.S.C. 881(e)(3); see also 31 U.S.C. 9703(b)(4).

[124] 21 U.S.C. 881(e)(3)(B)(1988 ed.).

[125] *In re U.S. Currency, $844,520 (Cole)*, 136 F.3d 581, 582 (8th Cir. 1998)(Loken, J., concurring) ("But the underlying facts of this case should prompt Congress and the Department of Justice to investigate whether federal law enforcement officials are using their extensive forfeiture powers to frustrate the fiscal policy of States such as Missouri"); *United States v. Winston-Salem/Forsyth County Bd. of Education*, 902 F.2d 267, 267(4th Cir. 1990)("Practice of local officials of allowing federal officials to adopt seizures made by the local law enforcement official and to federally forfeit the property, with a portion returned to the local law enforcement agency, does not violate federal law, even though the practice assertedly allows state officials to avoid following [a] state constitutional provision that all forfeited monies be used to maintain the public schools").

[126] Executive Office for Asset Forfeiture, United States Department of the Treasury, *Guide to Equitable Sharing for Foreign Countries and Federal, State, and Local Law Enforcement Agencies*, 16, 22 (April 2009), http://www.treas.gov/offices/enforcement/teoaf /guidelines/greenbook.pdf; United States Department of Justice, *United States Attorneys' Manual*, §9-118.510, http://www.usdoj.gov/usao/eousa/foia_reading. Recipients, however, may use assets acquired through an equitable sharing program for matching purposes with respect to any COPS (Community Policing) grants they receive, 42 U.S.C. 3796dd-3(b)(1).
In FY2015, the Department of Justice expected to share $314.6 million with state and local law enforcement agencies and an additional $154.7 million for joint operations with state and local law enforcement agencies. Department of Justice, *Asset Forfeiture Program: FY*

2015 Performance Budget, at 9 (2014), http://www.justice.gov/sites/default/files/jmd/legacy/2013/03/17/aff-justification.pdf. The Treasury Department made equitable sharing payments of $64.477 million in FY2014, *United States Department of the Treasury, Treasury Forfeiture Fund: Accountability Report: Fiscal Year 2014*, 23 (2014), http://www.treasury.gov/resource-center/terrorist-illicit-finance/Asset-Forfeiture/Documents/FY%202012%20Annual%20Report.pdf.

[127] "Federal adoption of property seized by state or local law enforcement under state law is prohibited, except for property that directly relates to public safety concerns, including firearms, ammunition, explosives, and property associated with child pornography. To the extent that seizures of property other than these four specified categories of property are being considered for federal adoption under this public safety exception, such seizures may not be adopted without the approval of the Assistant Attorney General for the Criminal Division.... This order does not apply to (1) seizures by state and local authorities working together with federal authorities in a joint task force; (2) seizures by state and local authorities that are the result of joint federal-state investigations or that are coordinated with federal authorities as part of ongoing federal investigations; or (3) seizures pursuant to federal seizure warrants, obtained from federal courts to take custody of assets originally seized under state laws," Eric H. Holder, Jr., Office of the Attorney General, *Order No. ___, Prohibition on Certain Federal Adoptions of Seizures by State and Local Law Enforcement Agencies* (Jan. 16, 2015), available at http://www.justice.gov/sites/default/files/opa/press-releases/attachments/2015/01/ 16/attorney_general_order_prohibiting_adoptions.pdf.

[128] 28 U.S.C. 524(c).

[129] 31 U.S.C. 9703.

[130] Creation of the forfeiture funds and other forfeiture adjustments can be traced to criticisms, beginning in the 96th Congress, that the drug and racketeering forfeiture provisions enacted in 1970 were being underutilized, were difficult to enforce, and that the proceeds from such confiscations should be used more directly for law enforcement purposes. *E.g., Forfeiture of Narcotics Proceeds: Hearings Before the Subcomm. on Criminal Justice of the Senate Comm. on the Judiciary*, 96th Cong., 2d Sess. (1980); *Forfeiture in Drug Cases: Hearings Before the Subcomm. on Crime of the House Comm. on the Judiciary*, 97th Cong., 1st & 2d Sess. (1982); *DEA Oversight and Budget Authority: Hearing Before the Subcomm. on Security and Terrorism of the Senate Comm. on the Judiciary*, 97th Cong., 2d Sess. (1982); General Accounting Office, *Asset Forfeiture—A Seldom Used Tool in Combating Drug Trafficking*, GGD 81-5 (April 10, 1981).

[131] The Constitution requires that "[n]o money shall be drawn from the Treasury, but in consequence of appropriations made by law," U.S. Const. Art. I, §9, cl.7, and so "no money can be paid out of the Treasury unless it has been appropriated by an act of Congress," *OPM v. Richmond*, 496 U.S. 414, 424 (1990). Congress ordinarily authorizes an appropriation before it makes an appropriation. An authorization of appropriation is little more than a prediction of future appropriations; it is not an appropriation nor is Congress bound by it. Most appropriations are made on an annual basis, but Congress may enact an appropriation measure covering several years or making a "permanent" appropriation. Sometimes Congress requires that money appropriated be spent within a particular time period such as during a particular fiscal year; other times such as here it gives its permission "without fiscal year limitation." *See generally*, General Accounting Office [Government Accountability Office], I *Principles of Federal Appropriations Law*, 2-13 to 2-14, 2-40 to 2-42 (2004), http://www.gao.gov/special.pubs/d04261sp.pdf.

[132] Forfeiture receipts can fluctuate considerably, making hazardous estimates of future returns. The Department of Justice (DOJ) anticipated receipts of over $1.5 billion during FY2014, Office of Management and Budget, *Budget of the U.S. Government, Fiscal Year 2014: Appendix*, at 718 (2013). The Treasury Department (Treasury) anticipated receipts of $595 million in the Treasury Forfeiture Fund for the same period, *id.* at 975. A year later, DOJ confirmed that its Fund had received $2.05 billion in FY2013, would receive an estimated $3.078 billion in FY2014, and would receive $1.375 billion in FY2015, Office of Management and Budget, *Budget of the U.S. Government, Fiscal Year 2015: Appendix*, at 747 (2014). At the same time, Treasury reported receipts of $1.713 billion in FY2013, and estimates of $600 million and $550 million in fiscal years 2014 and 2015, respectively, *id.* at 1041.

A third fund, the Special Forfeiture Fund, at one time used to fund the drug czar's office, no longer exists. A fourth, the Crime Victims Fund, which technically is fed by federal "Son of Sam" and espionage forfeitures, in fact is supported primarily by receipts from a source other than forfeiture—the proceeds from the collections of criminal fines—which are used to support a grant program for the relief of victims of crime.

References to the Postal Service Fund, 39 U.S.C. 2003, which might be considered a fifth forfeiture fund, have been omitted as general matter for several reasons. Although it receives the Postal Service's share of equitably distributed forfeitures, it was not created solely or even primarily for that purpose. It is instead a general operational fund into which all or virtually all Postal Service receipts are deposited and which is available, not merely for law enforcement or related purposes, but for the general operational needs of the Postal Service, 39 U.S.C. 2003(e)(1)("The Fund shall be available for the payment of all expenses incurred by the Postal Service in carrying out its functions as provided by law ..."). As a practical matter it is much more closely analogous to the general fund than to any of the forfeiture funds under discussion.

Forfeitures, fines, and civil penalties, collected for violation of various federal wildlife protection statutes make their way to two additional forfeiture funds: the Fisheries Enforcement Asset Forfeiture Fund and the Sanctuaries Enforcement Asset Forfeiture Fund, 16 U.S.C. 1861 note. Deposits in those Funds amount to approximately $6 million per year. Office of Management and Budget, *Budget of the U.S. Government, Fiscal Year 2015: Appendix*, at 211-12 (2014).

[133] 28 U.S.C. 524(c).

[134] 98 Stat. 2052, 2193.

[135] 28 U.S.C. 524(c)(4). The proceeds from three forfeiture provisions are expressly excluded from the Fund, those pursuant to: (1) section 11(d) of the Endangered Species Act (16 U.S.C. 1540(d)), (2) section 6(d) of the Lacey Act Amendments of 1981(16 U.S.C. 3375(d)), and (3) section 2003(b)(7) of title 39 of the United States Code dealing with the Postal Service, *id.*

[136] *E.g.*, 21 U.S.C. 881(e); 19 U.S.C. 1616a; 21 U.S.C. 853(i); 18 U.S.C. 981(d),(e); 18 U.S.C. 982(b); 18 U.S.C. 1963(g).

[137] Rewards may not exceed $500,000, 28 U.S.C. 524(c)((2).

[138] Rewards may not exceed the lesser of $500,000 or 25% of the amount realized from the confiscation without the personal approval of the Attorney General and notification of the chairmen and ranking minority members of the Appropriations and Judiciary Committees, *id.*

[139] The amount paid here may not exceed $100,000 without the approval of the agency head, 28 U.S.C. 524(c)(3).

[140] The "drug czar's" office was originally supported by the Special Forfeiture Fund, and the Fund continued in existence even after the office secured a more regular, more reliable source of support. Deposits in the Special Forfeiture Fund extended only through FY1997, 28 U.S.C. 524(c)(8). The Special Forfeiture Fund has since been abolished, P.L. 109-469, 120 Stat. 3539 (2006).

[141] 28 U.S.C. 524(c). The Department of Justice's annual forfeiture fund report anticipated FY2015 expenditures of:
$87.4 million for management of seized assets;
$2.14 billion to settle liens, mortgages, and petitions for remission and mitigation;
$149.8 million for automation-related contract costs;
$39.9 million for automation;
$4.8 million for training and printing;
$15.2 million for information leading to forfeiture;
$20.19 million for the purchase of evidence;
$53.7 million for contract to identify assets;
$.310 million to equip cars, boats and planes for law enforcement use;
$64.4 million for investigative costs leading to seizure;
$154.7 million for joint state, local and federal cooperative law enforcement operations;
$314.6 million transferred to state, local and tribal entities;
$9.4 million for storage, protection, and destruction of controlled substances; and
$58.468 million for other program management expenses.
U.S. Department of Justice, *Asset Forfeiture Fund: FY 2015 Performance Budget*, at 10-4, available at http://www.justice.gov/sites/default/files/jmd/legacy/2014/03/17/aff-justification

[142] *E.g.*, 28 U.S.C. 524(c)(1)(I)(2000 ed.) making the Fund available during FY1989 to pay expenses related to prison construction; Anti-Drug Abuse Act, §9310, P.L. 100-690, 102 Stat. 4540 (1988) granting access to the Fund to pay U.S. Attorney salaries and expenses during FY1989 for purposes authorized in the Omnibus Drug Initiative Act.
In the comprehensive appropriations measure for FY2015, Congress appropriated $1.1 billion from the super surplus for the Marshals Service support of federal prisoners in non-Federal institutions, and rescinded $193 million from the Fund's surplus, P.L. 13-235, 128 Stat. 2198, 2214 (2014).

[143] "... [A]ny excess unobligated balances remaining in the Fund on September 30, 1997, and thereafter shall be available to the Attorney General, without fiscal year limitation, for any federal law enforcement, litigative/prosecutive, and correctional activities, or any other authorized purpose of the Department of Justice ..." 28 U.S.C. 524(c)(8)(E).
In FY2008, the Attorney General authorized recourse to the super surplus in the Fund in the amount of $57.149 million; recipients included the Bureau of Alcohol, Tobacco, Firearms and Explosives ($105,000); the Civil Division ($338,000); the Criminal Division's Office of the Organized Crime Drug Enforcement Task Force ($138,000); the Drug Enforcement Administration ($118,000); the Executive Office of United States Attorneys ($330,000); the National Security Division ($6.120 million); the Bureau of Prisons ($30 million); and the Office of the Federal Detention Trustee ($20 million), U.S. Department of Justice, Office of the Inspector General, Audit Division, *Asset Forfeiture Fund and Sized Assets Deposit Fund Annual Financial Statement Fiscal Year 2008*, Audit Report 097-19, at 72 (Mar. 2009), http://www.usdoj.gov/jmd/afp/01progamaudit/fy2008/fy2008_afs_report.pdf.
Thereafter, the Attorney General authorized super surplus allocations for the Civil Division ($338,000 for each of fiscal years 2011, 2012, and 2013), the Executive Office for U.S.

Attorneys ($32,000 for FY2011, $30,000 for FY2012, and $19 million for FY2013) and the Bureau of Prisons ($151 million for FY2012), U.S. Department of Justice, Office of Inspector General, Audit Division, *Assets Forfeiture Fund and Seized Assets Deposit Fund Annual Financial Statements: Fiscal Year 2012*, Audit Report 13-07, n.18 (Jan. 2013); *Fiscal Year 2013,* Audit Report 14-08 (February 2014), http://www.justice.gov/oig /reports/2013/a1307.pdf, and http://www.justice.gov/oig/reports/2014/a1408.pdf.

Congress, however has subject the DOJ Asset Forfeiture Fund to rescissions over the last three fiscal years; $722.687 million in FY2013; $83.6 million in FY2014; and $193 million in FY2015, P.L. 113-6, 127 Stat. 275 (2013); P.L. 113- 76, 128 Stat. 83 (2014); P.L. 113-235, 128 Stat. 2214 (2014).

[144] 28 U.S.C. 524(c)(1).

[145] *Id.*

[146] U.S. Department of Justice, Criminal Division, *Asset Forfeiture: Law and Practice Manual*, 10-26 n.115 (June, 1998); *Department of Commerce, Justice, and State, the Judiciary, and Related Agencies Appropriations: Hearings Before a Subcomm. of the House Comm. on Appropriations*, 100th Cong., 2d Sess. 734-35 (1988) (Marshals Service response to questions submitted for the record); U.S. Department of Justice, Executive Office of Asset Forfeiture, *The Attorney General's Guidelines on Seized and Forfeited Property*, 19 (July, 1990), reprinted in, U.S. Department of Justice, *U.S. Attorneys Manual*, tit.9, ch. 118, http://www.usdoj.gov/usao/eousa/foia_reading 118mcrm.htm.

[147] U.S. Department of Justice, Office of Inspector General, Audit Division, *Assets Forfeiture Fund and Seized Assets Deposit Fund Annual Financial Statements: Fiscal Year 2013*, Audit Report 14-08, [3] (Feb. 2014), http://www.justice.gov/oig/reports/2014/a1408.pdf.

[148] P.L. 98-473, §§317, 2304, 98 Stat. 2054, 2193 (1984). In fact, in the hectic days at the end of the Ninety-Eighth Congress, the Fund was established twice, P.L. 98-573, §213(a)(11), 98 Stat. 2986 (1984), and continued its dual existence for a couple of years, see 19 U.S.C. 1613a, 1613b (Supp. II, 1984); (Supp. III. 1985). In 1986 and 1987, Congress repealed both and then revived one of the sections, P.L. 99-514, § 1888 (7), 100 Stat. 2925 (1986); P.L. 99- 570, §1152(b)(1), 100 Stat. 3207-12 (1986); P.L. 100-71, 101 Stat. 438 (1987). To further complicate matters, the provision was assigned to a previously occupied section 9703 of Title 31 of the United States Code (the first section 9703 and an accompanying section 9704 are unrelated to the forfeiture fund and addressed managerial flexibility generally).

The Treasury Department estimates that the Treasury Forfeiture Fund will receive $550 million in forfeiture deposits and recoveries in FY2015, Office of Management and Budget, *Budget of the U.S. Government, Fiscal Year 2015: Appendix*, 1041 (2014).

As with the DOJ super surplus, Congress has subject the Treasury Forfeiture Fund to rescissions over the last three fiscal years; $950 million in FY2013; $736 million in FY2014; and $769 million in FY2015, P.L. 113-6, 127 Stat. 417(2013); P.L. 113-76, 128 Stat. 186 (2014); P.L. 113-235, 128 Stat. 2339 (2014).

[149] 31 U.S.C. 9703(d). Tax enforcement is exempted generally, 31 U.S.C. 9703(a), (d) and during FY1993, the transition period between the Customs Service and the Department of the Treasury Funds, deposits are those from laws administered or enforced by the Customs Service and equitable shares earned by the Customs Service rather than the entire Department, 31 U.S.C. 9703(d).

[150] *Budget of the U.S. Government, Fiscal Year 2004: Appendix*, 770 (2004); *Departments of Commerce, Justice, and State, the Judiciary, and Related Agencies Appropriations for*

2005: Hearings Before a Subcomm. of the House Comm. on Appropriations (Pt.2), 108th Cong. 2d Sess. 937 (2004).

[151] The Government Accountability Office (GAO) noted in recent testimony that it had "recommended that DOJ and Treasury conduct a study to determine the feasibility of consolidating potentially duplicative asset management activities [relating to their respective forfeiture funds].... As of March 2013, DOJ officials reported that DOJ and Treasury representatives had met several times in the fall of 2012 and thereafter agreed upon an approach to conduct the study and assess potential costs," *Luxury Jets and Empty Prisons: Wasteful and Duplicative Spending at the Department of Justice: Hearing Before the Subcomm. on Crime, Terrorism, Homeland Security and Investigations of the House Comm. on the Judiciary*, 113 Cong., 1st Sess. (2013)(prepared statement of GAO Director David C. Maurer, at 10), http://judiciary.house.gov/hearings/113th/04102013/Maurer %2004102013.pdf.

[152] 19 U.S.C. 1616a.

[153] "The Secretary shall make available to the United States Coast Guard, from funds appropriated under subsection (g)(2)* in excess of $10,000,000 for a fiscal year, an amount equal to the net proceeds in the Fund derived from seizures by the Coast Guard," 31 U.S.C. 9703(c).

* "There are authorized to be appropriated from the Fund to carry out the purposes set forth in subsections (a)(2) and (c) not to exceed—(A) $25,000,000 for fiscal year 1993; and (B) $50,000,000 for each fiscal year after fiscal year 1993." 31 U.S.C. 9703(g)(2).

[154] 31 U.S.C. 9703(c).

[155] 31 U.S.C. 9703a)(1)(A).

[156] 31 U.S.C. 9703(a)(1)(F).

[157] 31 U.S.C. 9703(a)(1)(D). Payments to settle liens or mortgages or in remission or mitigation may not exceed the value of the property at the time of seizure, 31 U.S.C. 9703(b)(1).

[158] 31 U.S.C. 9703(a)(1)(E).

[159] 31 U.S.C. 9703(a)(1)(C). The amount paid as a reward may not be more than 25% of the amount realized in the forfeiture, 19 U.S.C. 1619(a)(2).

[160] 31 U.S.C. 9703(a)(2)(A).

[161] 31 U.S.C. 9703(a)(2)(D), (F).

[162] The offenses include money laundering, any of the money laundering predicate offenses, drug smuggling, credit card or computer fraud, counterfeiting, various firearms and explosives offenses, and fraud against certain financial institutions, 31 U.S.C. 9703(a)(2)(B).

[163] 31 U.S.C. 9703(a)(2)(G).

[164] 31 U.S.C. 9703(a)(1)(G). Equitable sharing payments may not exceed the value of the property at the time of disposal, 31 U.S.C. 9703(b)(2).

[165] 31 U.S.C. 9703(a)(1)(I).

[166] 31 U.S.C. 9703(a), (g)(3).

[167] 31 U.S.C. 9703(g)(1).

[168] Congress established the Special Forfeiture Fund in the Anti-Drug Abuse Act of 1988, P.L. 100-690, §6073, 102 Stat. 4323, 21 U.S.C.1509 (1988 ed.).

[169] P.L. 109-469, 120 Stat. 3539 (2006).

[170] P.L. 98-473, §1402, 98 Stat. 2170 (1984); see generally CRS Report R42672, *The Crime Victims Fund: Federal Support for Victims of Crime*, by Lisa N. Sacco.

[171] 42 U.S.C. 10601. It does not receive fines imposed under section 11(d) of the Endangered Species Act, 16 U.S.C. 1540(d); section 6(d) of the Lacey Act Amendments, 16 U.S.C. 3375(d); section 311 of the Federal Water Pollution Control Act, 33 U.S.C. 1321; or those

deposited in the Postal Service Fund, 39 U.S.C. 2601(a)(2), 2003; or in the railroad unemployment insurance account, 45 U.S.C. 351 et seq., 42 U.S.C. 10601.

[172] 18 U.S.C. 794.

[173] 18 U.S.C. 3681. Section 3681 (special forfeiture of collateral profits of crime) establishes an escrow account within the Crime Victims Forfeiture Fund to receive the proceeds that those convicted of certain espionage or violent federal offenses are paid under contracts for publications depicting their crimes. The account is available for five years to satisfy judgments in favor of the victims of such crimes, criminal fines, and, to a limited extent to pay for the defendant's attorneys' fees. After five years, the court may order the residue paid out of escrow and into the Fund. The section is not likely to have accounted for any substantial contributions to the Fund since the Fund could not have begun to receive unrestricted deposits under section 3681 until after the fifth anniversary of the section's enactment in November, 1991 and shortly thereafter the prospect of future receipts was clouded by the Supreme Court's opinion in *Simon & Schuster v. New York Crime Victims Bd.*, 502 U.S. 105 (1991), holding the comparable New York State "Son of Sam" statute inconsistent with the First Amendment, Cohen, CRS Report 92-56, *The "Son of Sam" Case: First Amendment Analysis and Legislative Implications.*

[174] 42 U.S.C. 10601 to 10603a. As of September 30, 2012, the Fund had a balance of approximately $8 billion and distributions were capped at $705 million per year. U.S. Department of Justice, Office of Justice Programs, *About OVC: Crime Victims Fund*, http://www.ojp.usdoj.gov/ovc/about/victimsfund.html.

[175] *Austin v. United States*, 509 U.S. 602, 622 (1993); *Alexander v. United States*, 509 U.S. 544, 559 (1993)(holding eighth amendment excessive fines standards applicable to civil and criminal forfeitures, respectively); *United States v. 92 Buena Vista Avenue*, 507 U.S. 111, 129 (1993)(a seemingly tortured statutory construction that could be read as driven by due process concerns for the property rights of innocent owners); *Republic National Bank v. United States*, 506 U.S. 80 (1992)(a case in which all nine members of the Court rejected application of the strict in rem legal fiction that the government sought to employ and in which one justice went so far as to observe that "I am surprised that the Government would make such a transparently fallacious argument in support of its unconscionable position in this case," 506 U.S. at 99 (Stevens, J., concurring in part and concurring in the judgment)).

[176] *United States v. Ursery*, 518 U.S. 267, 270-71 (1996)(rejecting the suggestion that the double jeopardy clause precludes consecutive forfeiture proceedings and criminal prosecutions); *Bennis v. Michigan*, 516 U.S. 442, 446 (1996) (refusing, at least under the facts before it, to find that due process bars the confiscation of the property of an innocent owner); *Libretti v. United States*, 516 U.S. 29, 48-51 (1995)(holding that neither the promise of a jury trial found in the Sixth Amendment nor that in the Federal Rules of Criminal Procedure extended to questions of fact in criminal forfeiture proceedings).

[177] *United States v. James Daniel Good Real Property*, 510 U.S. 43, 62 (1993)(generally requiring pre-seizure notice and hearing in real property cases); *United States v. Bajakajian*, 524 U.S. 321, 337 (1998)(holding criminal forfeitures to a grossly disproportionate standard under the excessive fines clause); see also *Degen v. United States*, 517 U.S. 820, 828-29 (1996)(declining the request to extend the common law doctrine of fugitive disentitlement so as to bar fugitive claimants from contesting the forfeiture of their property)(CAFRA subsequently extended the doctrine as a matter of statute, 28 U.S.C. 2466).

[178] *United States v. Sarbello*, 985 F.2d 716, 722 (3d Cir. 1993); *United States v. Bucuvalas*, 970 F.2d 937, 945-46 (1st Cir. 1992); *United States v. Smith*, 966 F.2d 1045, 1056 (6th Cir. 1992).

[179] *E.g., United States v. Santoro*, 866 F.2d 1538, 1544 (4th Cir. 1989); *United States v. One 107.9 Acre Parcel of Land*, 898 F.2d 396, 400-1 (3d Cir. 1990).

[180] *Alexander v. United States*, 509 U.S. 544 (1993); *Austin v. United States*, 509 U.S. 602 (1993).

[181] *Austin v. United States*, 509 U.S. 602, 622 (1993); *Alexander v. United States*, 509 U.S. 544, 559 (1993).

[182] *United States v. Bajakajian*, 524 U.S. 321, 334 (1998). Bajakajian had tried to leave the United States with $357,144 in cash and pled guilty to willfully failing to accurately report the fact (as required by 31 U.S.C. 5316 and made punishable under 18 U.S.C. 5322). The cash was neither criminally acquired, used, nor destined. Bajakajian's "crime was solely a reporting offense," 524 U.S. at 337; one for which the applicable federal sentencing guidelines made him liable to a maximum term of imprisonment of six months and a maximum fine of $5,000. The harm ... caused was also minimal. Failure to report this currency affected only one party, the Government, and in a relatively minor way. There was no fraud on the United States, and [he] caused no loss to the public fisc. Had his crime gone undetected, the Government would have been deprived only of the information that $357,144 had left the country," 524 U.S. at 338-39. The Court was unpersuaded by the government's claim that early statutes which set the fine for various customs evasion offenses at twice the value of the goods demonstrated historic acceptance of proportional penalties. These "early monetary forfeitures ... were considered not as punishment for an offense, but rather as serving the remedial purpose of reimbursing the government for the losses accruing from the evasion of customs duties," 524 U.S. at 342. Consistent with this observation, several lower federal courts have rejected Excessive Fines Clause arguments because the statutes in question were purely remedial rather than punitive, *e.g., United States v. Land [in] Winston Country (Wood)*, 221 F.3d 1194, 1199 (11th Cir. 2000);(18 U.S.C. 1955(d)); *United States v. $273,963.94 (Puzo)*, 164 F.3d 462, 466 (9th Cir. 1999)(19 U.S.C. 1497); *United States v. An Antique Platter of Gold (Stenhardt),* 184 F.3d 131, 139-40 (2d Cir. 1999), and one did so because although arising under the same statute as *Austin* the court was convinced that the purpose of confiscation in the case before it was remedial and not punitive, *United States v. 1948 South Martin Luther King Drive (Locher)*, 270 F.3d 1102, 1114-115 (7th Cir. 2001); see also *United States v. Betancourt*, 422 F.3d 240, 250 (5th Cir. 2005)("The forfeiture of drug proceeds [under criminal forfeiture provisions of 21 U.S.C. 853] does not constitute punishment, and thus neither the Eighth Amendment prohibition nor double jeopardy analysis is applicable").

[183] *United States v. $132,245.00 in U.S. Currency (Cyr)*, 764 F.3d 1055, 1057-58 (9th Cir. 2014)("If the amount of the forfeiture is grossly disproportional to the gravity of the defendant's offense, it is unconstitutional.... While we are not restricted to any rigid set of factors, we have typically considered four factors in weighing the gravity of the defendant's offense: (1) the nature and extent of the crime, (2) whether the violation was related to other illegal activities, (3) the other penalties that may be imposed for the violation, and (4) the extent of the harm caused"); *United States v. Sepulveda-Hernandez*, 752 F.3d 22, 36-7 (1st Cir. 2014)("The question, then, is whether the forfeiture judgment is grossly disproportional to the offenses of conviction. In responding to this question, we consider: (1) whether the defendant falls into the class of persons for whom the criminal statute was principally directed; (2) other penalties authorized by the legislature (or the Sentencing Commission); and (3) the harm caused by the defendant"); *United States v. Blackman*, 746 F.3d 137, 144 (4th Cir. 2014)("Under *United States v. Bajakajian*, 'a punitive forfeiture violates the Excessive Fines Clause if it is grossly disproportional to the gravity of a defendant's

offense.' Our court has distilled this standard to four factors: (1) the amount of the forfeiture and its relationship to the authorized penalty; (2) the nature and extent of the criminal activity; (3) the relationship between the crime charged and other crimes; and (4) the harm caused by the charged crime"); *United States v. Abair*, 746 F.3d 260, 267 (7th Cir. 2014)("Applying *Bajakajian*, an unconstitutionally excessive fine can be identified by looking to: (1) the nature of the defendant's crime and its relation to other criminal activity; (2) whether the criminal statute is principally meant to reach people like the defendant; (3) the maximum punishment that could have been imposed; and (4) the harm caused by the defendant's conduct"); see also *United States v. Chaplin's Inc.*, 646 F.3d 846, 851 & n.16 (11th Cir. 2011); *United States v. Castello*, 611 F.3d 116, 120 (2d Cir. 2010); *United States v. Cheeseman*, 600 F.3d 270, 283-84 (3d Cir. 2010).

184 *United States v. Smith*, 656 F.3d 821, 828-29 (8th Cir. 2011)("Smith was highly culpable; he participated in a large drug conspiracy, storing over ten pounds of methamphetamine at his residence for distribution.... The $10,000 money judgment [in the forfeiture order] representing proceeds from Smith's drug trafficking offenses, is not grossly disproportional to those same offenses"); *United States v. $79,650.00 Seized from Bank of America Account Ending in 8247(Girma Afework)*, 650 F.3d 381, 388 (4th Cir. 2011)("A proper assessment of whether a specific forfeiture contravenes the Excessive Fines Clause typically requires an analysis of several factors. This appeal, however, turns on only one of those factors: the amount of the forfeiture and its relationship to the authorized penalty"); *United States v. Segal*, 495 F.3d 826, 840 (7th Cir. 2007)("It is true that the forfeiture is large. It is only excessive, however, if it is disproportional to the offense. We cannot say that it was. This was massive fraud. When a defendant commits a multimillion-dollar crime, he can be required to forfeit assets also running into the millions"); *United States v. OrtizCintron*, 461 F.3d 78, 81-2 (1st Cir. 2006)(confiscation of property in drug dealing case with a relatively low value compared to the authorized fine).

185 *United States v. Olguin*, 643 F.3d 384, 398 (5th Cir. 2011)("Olguin played a part in transporting six loads of marijuana, each valued at approximately $600,000, which exceeds the $2 million forfeiture amount for which Olguin was held liable.... Contrary to Olguin's argument, this is not a case where a small player in a massive conspiracy is held liable for a grossly excessive sum ... "); *United States v. Hull*, 606 F.3d 524, 529-30 (8th Cir. 2010)("[I]f the value of the property forfeited is within the permissible range of fines using the sentencing guidelines, then it is presumptively not excessive.... Nor can it be said that the harm caused by Hull's conduct was minimal. The damage done by child pornography offenses is well documented"); *United States v. Elfgeeh*, 515 F.3d 100, 139 (2d Cir. 2008)("The order for a forfeiture of $22,435,467 is not disproportional. The essence of defendants' offenses was the unlicensed transmission of money, and neither defendant received the statutory maximum prison term allowed.... [T]he evidence showed that defendants in fact transmitted the moneys to 25 different countries. Plainly, defendants were persons at whom §1960(a) was aimed"); *United States v. Ely*, 468 F.3d 399, 403 (6th Cir. 2006)(noting in dicta that the amount confiscated was less than the advisory fine under the sentencing guidelines); *United States v. Puche*, 350 F.3d 1137, 1154 (11th Cir. 2003)("defendant's reliance on *Bajakajian* is misplaced as the defendant in that case was not a money launderer and was convicted only for a reporting offense"); but see *von Hofe v. United States*, 492 F.3d 175, 191 (2d Cir. 2007)("Mrs. von Hofe's offensive conduct boils down to her joint ownership ... and silence in the face of her husband's decision to grow marijuana in their basement almost thirty years into their marriage. And yet she is being punished as if she were distributing drugs, when the district court concluded as a matter of

fact that she had no knowledge of any distribution or remuneration. The government cannot justify forfeiture of Mrs. von Hofe's interest in [the family home], for the punishment bears no reasonable correlation either to her minimal culpability or any harm she caused").

[186] The double jeopardy clause which declares that no one shall "be subject for the same offence to be twice put in jeopardy of life or limb, U.S.Const. Amend.V, prohibits both successive punishment and successive prosecutions of the same individual for the same criminal offense," *United States v. Dixon*, 509 U.S. 688, 696 (1993).

[187] *One Lot Emerald Cut Stones v. United States*, 409 U.S. 232, 235-37 (1972); *United States v. One Assortment of Firearms*, 465 U.S. 354, 366 (1984) ("We accordingly conclude that the forfeiture mechanism set forth in §924(d) is not an additional penalty for the commission of a criminal act, but rather a separate civil sanction, remedial in nature. Because the §924(d) forfeiture proceeding brought against Mulcahey's firearms is not a criminal proceeding, it is not barred by the Double Jeopardy Clause").

[188] *Austin v. United States*, 509 U.S. 602, 608 n.4 (1993).

[189] *United States v. Ursery*, 518 U.S. 267 (1996).

[190] *Id.* at 278; see also *United States v. Williams*, 720 F.3d 674, 703 n. 23 (8th Cir. 2013)(" ... This argument is foreclosed by *United States v. Ursery*, in which the Supreme Court held that 'in rem civil forfeitures are neither punishment nor criminal for purposes of the Double Jeopardy Clause'"); *United States v. Leyland*, 277 F.3d 628, 633 (2d Cir. 2002) (criminal prosecution following civil forfeiture does not raise double jeopardy concerns); *United States v. 817 N.E. 29th Drive*, 175 F.3d 1304, 1311 (11th Cir. 1999) (civil forfeiture following conviction; "a forfeiture action cannot serve as the basis for a claim under the Double Jeopardy Clause"); *United States v. Candelaria-Silva*, 166 F.3d 19, 43-4 (1st Cir. 1999) (criminal forfeiture following initiation of civil forfeiture proceedings; "a completed civil forfeiture of property does not constitute 'jeopardy' under the Double Jeopardy Clause, and does not bar the subsequent criminal prosecution and punishment of the defendant whose property was forfeited").

[191] *United States v. $40,955 (el Fara)*, 554 F.3d 752, 758 (9th Cir. 2009), citing *United States v. Zucker*, 161 U.S. 475, 481 (1896).

[192] *Caplin & Drysdale v. United States*, 491 U.S. 617, 632 (1989); *United States v. Bonventre*, 720 F.3d 126, 130 (2d Cir. 2013); *United States v. Farmer*, 274 F.3d 800, 802 (4th Cir. 2001).

[193] *United States v. Monsanto*, 491 U.S. 600, 614-15 (1989); *Kaley v. United States*, 134 S.Ct. 1090, 1105 (2014).

[194] *United States v. Saccoccia*, 564 F.3d 502, 505 (1st Cir. 2009).

[195] *United States v. 6 Fox Street*, 480 F.3d 38, 45 (1st Cir. 2007); *United States v. 817 N.E. 29th Drive*, 175 F.3d 1304, 1311 no.13 (11th Cir. 1999); *United States v. Michelle's Lounge*, 39 F.3d 684, 698 (7th Cir. 1994). CAFRA, however, permits the appointment of counsel for an indigent civil forfeiture claimant for whom counsel has already been appointed in connection with a related criminal case, 18 U.S.C. 983(b).

[196] *Libretti v. United States*, 516 U.S. 29, 49 (1995), quoting *McMillan v. Pennsylvania*, 477 U.S. 79, 93 (1986).

[197] *Southern Union Co. v. United States*, 132 S.Ct. 2344, 2357 (2012).

[198] *United States v. Sigillito*, 759 F.3d 913, 936 (8th Cir. 2014), citing in accord, *United States v. Wilkes*, 744 F.3d 1101, 1109 (9th Cir. 2014); *United States v. Simpson*, 741 F.3d 539, 560 (5th Cir. 2014); *United States v. Day*, 700 F.3d 713, 733 (4th Cir. 2012); see also *United States v. Saccoccia*, 564 F.3d 502, 507 (1st Cir. 2009); *United States v. Capoccia*, 503 F.3d 103, 116 n.18 (2d Cir. 2007); *United States v. Leahy*, 438 F.3d 328, 331-33 (3d Cir. 2006);

United States v. Hall, 411 F.3d 651, 654 (6th Cir. 2005); *United States v. Cabez*, 258 F.3d 1256, 1257 (11th Cir. 2001).

[199] *United States v. James Daniel Good Real Property*, 510 U.S. 43, 48 (1993); *United States v. Shakur*, 691 F.3d 979, 988 (8th Cir. 2012); *United States v. Erpenbeck*, 682 F.3d 472, 476 (6th Cir. 2012); *United States v. Ritchie*, 342 F.3d 903, 910-11 (9th Cir. 2003); *Helton v. Hunt*, 330 F.3d 242, 247 (4th Cir. 2003); *Krimstock v. Kelly*, 306 F.3d 40, 51 (2d Cir. 2002).

[200] *Dusenbery v. United States*, 534 U.S. 161, 173 (2002)(quoting, *Mullane v. Central Hanover Bank & Trust Co.*, 339 U.S. 306, 314 (1950)); see also *United States v. Alvarez*, 710 F.3d 565, 567 (5th Cir. 2013); *Taylor v. United States*, 483 F.3d 385, 388-89 (5th Cir. 2007); *Nunley v. Department of Justice*, 425 F.3d 1132, 1135-136 (8th Cir. 2005); *Lobzun v. United States*, 422 F.3d 503, 507-508 (7th Cir. 2005); *Mesa Valderrama v. United States*, 417 F.3d 1189, 1196-197 (11th Cir. 2005).

[201] *Calero-Toledo v. Pearson Yacht Leasing Co.*, 416 U.S. at 678-79 ("*Fuentes* [*v. Shevin*, 407 U.S. 67 (1972)] reaffirmed, however, that, in limited circumstances, immediate seizure of a property interest, without an opportunity for prior hearing, is constitutionally permissible. Such circumstances are those in which the seizure has been directly necessary to secure an important governmental or general public interest. Second, there has been a special need for prompt action. Third, the State has kept strict control over its monopoly of legitimate force: the person initiating the seizure has been a government official responsible for determining, under standards of a narrowly drawn statute, that it was necessary and justified in the particular instance." [407 U.S.] at 91 ... The considerations that justified postponement of notice and hearing in those cases are present here. First, seizure under the Puerto Rican statutes serves significant governmental purposes: Seizure permits Puerto Rico to assert *in rem* jurisdiction over the property in order to conduct forfeiture proceedings, thereby fostering the public interest in preventing continued illicit use of the property and in enforcing criminal sanctions. Second, preseizure notice and hearing might frustrate the interests served by the statutes, since the property seized—as here, a yacht—will often be of a sort that could be removed to another jurisdiction, destroyed, or concealed, if advance warning of confiscation were given. And finally, unlike the situation in *Fuentes*, seizure is not initiated by self-interested private parties; rather Commonwealth officials determine whether seizure is appropriate under the provisions of the Puerto Rico statutes"); see also *United States v. Melrose East Subdivision*, 357 F.3d 493, 502 (5th Cir. 2004); *United States v. Any and All Radio Station Transmission Equipment (Perez)*, 218 F.3d 543, 550-51 (6th Cir. 2000); *Yskamp v. DEA*, 163 F.3d 767, 774 (3d Cir. 1998); *United States v. Lot 41, Berryhill Farm Estates*, 128 F.3d 1386, 1392 (10th Cir. 1997); *United States v. Down*, 68 F.3d 1030, 1038-39 (8th Cir. 1995).

[202] *United States v. James Daniel Good Real Property*, 510 U.S. 43 (1993).

[203] *United States v. Monsanto*, 491 U.S. 600, 615 (1989)("[A]ssets in a defendant's possession may be restrained in the way they were here based on a finding of probable cause to believe that the assets are forfeitable"); *United States v. Melrose East Subdivision*, 357 F.3d 493, 499-500 (5th Cir. 2004), *citing inter alia*, *United States v. Jones*, 160 F.3d 641, 645-48 (10th Cir. 1998); *United States v. Moya-Gomez*, 860 F.2d 760, 729-30 (7th Cir. 1988); *United States v. Farmer*, 274 F.3d 800, 805 (4th Cir. 2001); *United States v. Michelle's Lounge, 39 F.3d 684, 700-01 (7th Cir. 1994).*

[204] *Kaley v. United States*, 134 S.Ct. 1090, 1105 (2014).

[205] Due process bars forfeiture either (1) where the property has "been taken from [its owner] without his privity or consent" and used in a manner which would ordinarily give rise to confiscation, or (2) where the owner was "not only ... uninvolved in and unaware of the

wrongful activity, but also that he had done all that reasonably could be expected to prevent the proscribed use of the property," *Calero-Toledo v. Pearson Yacht Leasing Co.*, 416 U.S. at 689.

[206] 516 U.S. 442 (1996). *Bennis* also reaffirmed that the takings clause stands as no impediment to an otherwise valid forfeiture: "Petitioner also claims that the forfeiture in this case was a taking of private property for public use in violation of the Takings Clause of the Fifth Amendment, made applicable to the States by the Fourteenth Amendment. But if the forfeiture proceeding here in question did not violate the Fourteenth Amendment, the property in the automobile was transferred by virtue of that proceeding from petitioner to the State. The government may not be required to compensate an owner for property which it has already lawfully acquired under the exercise of governmental authority other than the power of eminent domain," *Bennis v. Michigan*, 516 U.S. at 452; see also *United States v. $7,990 (Fiorentino)*, 170 F.3d 843, 845 (8th Cir. 1999).

[207] *Bennis v. Michigan*, 516 U.S. at 457-58 ("I join the opinion of the Court and highlight features of the case key to my judgment.... First, it bears emphasis that the car in question belonged to John Bennis as much as it did to Tina Bennis.... The sole question, then, is whether Tina Bennis is entitled not to the car, but to a portion of the proceeds (if any there be after deduction of police, prosecutorial, and court costs) as a matter of constitutional right. Second, it was 'critical' to the judgment of the Michigan Supreme Court that the nuisance abatement proceedings is an 'equitable action.' ... That means the State's Supreme Court stands ready to police exorbitant applications of the statute.... Nor it is fair to charge the trial court with 'blatant unfairness' in the case at hand.... The court declined to order a division of sale proceeds ... for two practical reasons: the Bennises have 'another automobile' and the age and value of the forfeited car ... left practically nothing to divide after subtraction of costs. Michigan in short has not embarked on an experiment to punish innocent third parties. Nor do we conduct any such experiment. Michigan has decided to deter johns from using cars they own (or co-own) to contribute to neighborhood blight, and that abatement endeavor hardly warrants this Court's disapprobation").

[208] *United States v. $8,850 (Vasquez)*, 461 U.S. 555, 562-65 (1983); *United States v. Ninety Three Firearms*, 330 F.3d 414, 424-26 (6th Cir. 2003); (*United States v. $12,248 (Johnson)*, 957 F.2d 1513, 1518-519 (9th Cir. 1991); *United States v. Premises Located at Route 13*, 946 F.2d 749, 754-56 (11th Cir. 1991); but see *Smith v. City of Chicago*, 524 F.3d 834, 836-39 (7th Cir. 2008), vac'd and rem'd sub nom., *Alvarez v. Smith*, 130 S.Ct. 576 (2009).

[209] *United States v. Melrose East Subdivision*, 357 F.3d 493, 501 (5th Cir. 2004); *United States v. Property, Parcel of Aguilar*, 337 F.3d 225, 229-33 (2d Cir. 2003); *United States v. One "Piper" Aztec "F" DeLuxe Model 250 PA 23 Aircraft*, 321 F.3d 355, 360-61 (3d Cir. 2003); *United States v. Land [in] Winston County (Woods)*, 163 F.3d 1295, 1303 (11th Cir. 1998); *United States v. Santoro*, 866 F.2d 1538, 1544 (4th Cir. 1989).

[210] *United States v. McHan*, 345 F.3d 262, 269-70 (4th Cir. 2003).

[211] *United States v. Duboc*, 694 F.3d 1223, 1338-229 (11th Cir. 2012).

[212] *Collazos v. United States*, 368 F.3d 190, 202 (2d Cir. 2004); *United States v. $6,976,934.65, Plus Interest Deposited into Royal Bank of Scotland Int'l.*, 554 F.3d 123, 128 (D.C.Cir. 2009)("In *Collazos*, the Second Circuit distilled the statutory requirements for disentitlement into a five-element test: (1) a warrant or similar process has issued in a criminal case for the claimant's apprehension; (2) the claimant had notice or knowledge of the warrant or process; (3) the criminal case is related to the forfeiture action; (4) the claimant is not confined or otherwise held in custody in another jurisdiction; and (5) the claimant has deliberately avoided criminal prosecution by leaving the United States,

declining to enter or renter the country, or to otherwise evading the criminal court's jurisdiction. These five elements track the statutory requirements, and we adopt the same test")(internal citations omitted); see also *United States v. Technodyne LLC*, 753 F.3d 368, 377-87 (2d Cir. 2014); *Mastro v. Rigby*, 764 F.3d 1090, 1095-96(9th Cir. 2014).

213 *United States v. Shakur*, 691 F.3d 979, 988-89 (8th Cir. 2012) (internal citations omitted)("Here Shakur timely contested six of the government's forfeiture allegations, but his objections were entirely ignored. He was denied timely determination of the requisite nexus; a hearing on the contested allegations; the entry of a preliminary order directing the forfeiture of specific property; and entry of that order sufficiently in advance of sentencing to allow him to seek revisions. Finally, after sentencing, he was denied inclusion of a preliminary forfeiture order in his judgment of conviction, which deprived him of the right to have the entire sentence imposed as a package and reviewed in a single appeal. The wholesale violation of these Rule 32.2(b) mandates denied Shakur a meaningful opportunity to contest the deprivation if his property rights, as due process required").

214 *United States v. Marolf*, 173 F.3d 1213, 1216-218 (9th Cir. 1999); *Clymore v. United States*, 164 F.3d 569, 574 (10th Cir. 1999); *Small v. United States*, 136 F.3d 1334, 1338 (D.C.Cir. 1998); *United States v. Girealdo*, 45 F.3d 509, 512 (1st Cir. 1995).

215 *Adames v. United States*, 171 F.3d 728, 732 (2d Cir. 1999).

216 *United States v. 1184 Drycreek Rd.*, 174 F.3d 720, 727-28 (6th Cir. 1999); *United States v. Land [in] Winston County (Woods)*, 163 F.3d 1295, 1301-302 (11th Cir. 1998); *United States v. Marsh*, 105 F.3d 927, 931 (4th Cir. 1997); *United States v. 51 Pieces of Real Property (Nitsua Management)*, 17 F.3d 1306, 1319 (10th Cir. 1994).

Some circuits refuse to recognize the authority to permit such awards against the government, *United States v. $7,990 (Fiorentino)*, 170 F.3d 843, 844-46 (8th Cir. 1999); *Ikelionwu v. United States*, 150 F.3d 233, 238-39 (2d Cir. 1998).

217 18 U.S.C. 983(e).

218 *United States v. Monsanto*, 491 U.S. 600, 614-15 (1989); *Caplin & Drysdale v. United States*, 491 U.S. 617, 632-35 (1989).

219 *United States v. Monsanto*, 491 U.S. at 615 n.15.

220 *United States v. E-Gold, Ltd*, 521 F.3d 411, 416-19 (D.C.Cir. 2008), citing *inter alia, United States v. Property at 4492 S. Livonia Rd., Livonia*, 889 F.2d 1258, 1263 (2d Cir. 1989).

221 *Id.*

222 *United States v. Grande*, 620 F.2d 1026, 1038 (4th Cir. 1980) ("We would agree ... that if [18 U.S.C.] §1963 [RICO criminal forfeiture] revives forfeiture of estate as that concept was expressed in the Constitution it is almost certainly invalid because of the irrationality of a ruling that forfeiture of estate cannot be imposed for treason but can be imposed for a pattern of lesser crimes").

223 The confusion apparently stems from the congressional decision to authorize the use of criminal, in personam procedures rather than civil, in rem procedures to accomplish confiscation in RICO cases, see S.Rept. 617, 91st Cong., 1st Sess. 79 (1969). The character of the forfeiture, however, turns not upon the nature of the procedure selected but rather whether there is any required nexus between the property and the misconduct which provides the necessary predicate for confiscation.

224 *United States v. Grande*, 620 F.2d 1026, 1037-39 (4th Cir. 1980); *United States v. Thevis*, 474 F.Supp. 134, 140-41 (N.D.Ga. 1979), aff'd, 665 F.2d 616 (5th Cir. 1982); *United States v. Anderson*, 637 F.Supp. 632, 634 (N.D.Cal. 1986); *United States v. Pryba*, 674 F.Supp. 1504, 1517 (E.D.Va. 1987).

Under some interpretations, Article III or its due process shadow may limit the breadth or availability of the chemical weapons criminal forfeiture provisions and some of the terrorist civil forfeiture provisions, 18 U.S.C. 229B("Any person convicted under section 229A(a) shall forfeit to the United States ... (1) any property, real or personal, owned ... by a person involved in the offense")(note that like the forfeiture of estate condemned in Article III the only apparent nexus between the property and the crime is the property owner); 18 U.S.C. 981(a)(1)(G)(i); 50 U.S.C. 1702(a)(1)(C).

[225] U.S. Const. Art. III, §2.

[226] *Clapper v. Amnesty Int'l USA*, 133 S.Ct. 1138, 1146-147 (2013); *United States v. $304,980.00 in United States Currency (Davis)*, 732 F.3d 812, 818 (7th Cir. 2013)("[W]ithout a case or controversy under Article III, we have no authority to proceed to the merits").

[227] *United States v. Technodyne LLC*, 753 F.3d 368, 380 (2d Cir. 2014)("In general, in order to contest a governmental forfeiture action, claimants must have both standing under the statute or statutes governing their claims and standing under Article III of the Constitution ... "); *United States v. $196,969.00 United States Currency (Johnson)*, 719 F.3d 644, 646 (7th Cir. 2013)("The government moved the district court to strike the claim on the ground that it failed to establish Article III standing and also failed to comply with Supplemental Rule G(5), which a claim to property that the government is seeking forfeiture of must also do"); *United States v. $8,440,190.00 in U.S. Currency (Von BommelDuyzing)*, 719 F.3d 49, 57 n.11 (1st Cir. 2013)("Standing in forfeiture actions has both constitutional and statutory aspects").

[228] *United States v. $133,420.00 in United States Currency (Louis)*, 672 F.3d 629, 637-38 (9th Cir. 2012)(internal citations omitted); *United States v. $304,980.00 in United States Currency (Davis)*, 732 F.3d 812, 818 (7th Cir. 2013)(internal citations omitted)("The government argues that because the Davises have failed to prove their ownership of the seized cash, they do not have Article III standing. However, to have standing, a claimant ... must have a colorable claim to such a right. While it is true that the Davises have not proved their ownership of the case (indeed, they invoked the Fifth Amendment in response to the government's interrogatories on that subject), they do claim such ownership, and the money was found in Randy Davis's possession. This is sufficient to give them a colorable claim to the money. Therefore, the Davises have Article III standing ... ").

[229] The Fourth Amendment to the United States Constitution states in its entirety: "The right of the people to be secure in their persons, houses, papers and effects, against unreasonable searches and seizures shall not be violated, and no warrants shall issue but upon probable cause, supported by oath or affirmation, and particularly describing the place to be searched, and the persons or things to be seized."

[230] E.g., *Vernonia School District 47J v. Acton*, 515 U.S. 646, 653 (1995)("But a warrant is not required to establish reasonableness of all government [seizures]; and when a warrant is not required ... probable cause is not invariably required either ").

[231] E.g., *Virginia v. Moore*, 553 U.S. 164, 176 (2008)("We have recognized, however, that officers may perform searches incident to constitutionally permissible arrests in order to ensure their safety and safeguard evidence"); *Illinois v. McArthur*, 531 U.S. 326, 334 (2001)("[W]arrantless search of [an] automobile [is] constitutionally permissible').

[232] The Court noted some time ago that, "The seizure of stolen goods is authorized by the common law; and the seizure of goods forfeited for a breach of the revenue laws, or concealed to avoid the duties payable on them, has been authorized by English statutes for at least two centuries past; and the like seizures have been authorized by our own revenue acts from the commencement of the government. The first statute passed by Congress to

regulate the collection of duties, the act of July 31, 1789, 1 Stat. 19, 43, contains provisions to this effect. 'As this act was passed by the same Congress which proposed for adoption the original amendments to the constitution, it is clear that the members of that body did not regard searches and seizures of this kind as unreasonable,' and they are not embraced within the prohibitions of the [fourth] amendment," *Boyd v. United States*, 116 U.S. 616, 623 (1886), quoted in *United States v. Ramsey*, 431 U.S. 606, 617 (1977).

233 CAFRA authorizes a seizure pursuant to a warrant under the Federal Rules of Criminal Procedure, to the Supplemental Rules for Admiralty and Maritime Claims, 18 U.S.C. 981(b)(2), or to the alternative procedure it requires in real property cases, 18 U.S.C. 985(d). The language of Rule G(3)(b) of the Supplemental Rules may raise some question of whether probable cause and a warrant are always required: "If the defendant is not real property: (i) the clerk must issue a warrant to arrest the property if it is in the government's possession, custody, or control; (ii) the court—on finding probable cause—must issue a warrant to arrest the property if it is not in the government's possession, custody, or control and is not subject to a judicial restraining order; and (iii) a warrant is not necessary if the property is subject to a judicial restraining order;" see also *United States v. $304,980.00 in United States Currency (Davis)*, 732 F.3d 812, 818-19 (7th Cir. 2013)(explaining that consent stands an exception to any exclusionary rule, but noting that, "[a]s the district court in this case noted, there is some debate as to whether the common-law exclusionary rule should apply in civil forfeiture proceedings); *United States v. Marrocco*, 578 F.3d 627, 642-43 (7th Cir. 2009)(Easterbrook, J., concurring).

234 *One 1958 Plymouth Sedan v. Pennsylvania*, 380 U.S. 693, 697-98 (1965); *United States v. $45,000.00 in United States Currency (Martins)*, 749 F.3d 709, 714 (8th Cir. 2014); *United States v. $291,828 in United States Currency (Braddy)*, 536 F.3d 1234, 1237 (11th Cir. 2008); *United States v. $493,850 in U.S. Currency(Bruno)*, 518 F.3d 1159, 1165 (9th Cir. 2008); *United States v. Ninety-Two Thousand Four Hundred Twenty-Two Dollars and Fifty-Seven Cents (Kim's Warehouse)*, 307 F.3d 137, 142 (3d Cir. 2002); *United States v. $557,933.80 More or Less (Mercado-Filpo)*, 287 F.3d 66, 80 (2d Cir. 2002); *United States v. $404,905 (Alexander)*, 182 F.3d 643, 646 (8th Cir. 1999); *United States v. 9844 S.Titan Court*, 75 F.3d 1470, 1492 (10th Cir. 1996).

235 *One 1958 Plymouth Sedan v. Pennsylvania*, 380 U.S. 693 (1965); *INS v. Lopez-Mendoza*, 468 U.S. 1032, 1039-40 (1984)("[T]he body or identity of a defendant or respondent in a criminal or civil proceeding is never itself suppressible as a fruit of an unlawful arrest, even if it is conceded that an unlawful arrest, search or interrogation occurred. *Gerstine v. Pugh*, 420 U.S. 103, 119 (1975); *Frisbie v. Collins*, 342 U.S. 519, 522 (1952).... [a] similar rule applies in forfeiture proceedings directed against contraband or forfeitable property"); *United States v. $291,828 in United States Currency (Braddy)*, 536 F.3d 1234, 1237 (11th Cir. 2008); *United States v. 51 Pieces of Real Property*, 17 F.3d 1306, 1315-316 (10th Cir. 1994); *United States v. $12,390.00 (Dorsey)*, 956 F.2d 801, 806 (8th Cir. 1992); *United States v. $277,000.00 (Montes)*, 941 F.2d 899, 902 (9th Cir. 1991); *United States v. 415 East Mitchell Ave.*, 149 F.3d 472, 476 (6th Cir. 1998); *Krimstock v. Kelly*, 306 F.3d 40, 50 (2d Cir. 2002)("[T]he seizure and forfeiture of property are two distinct events under the federal civil forfeiture laws. While both events require the government to have probable cause, the government is not required to demonstrate probable cause until the forfeiture trial unless a claimant challenges the validity of the seizure before trial. If the government, once challenged, cannot establish probable cause for the initial seizure or offer post-seizure evidence to justify continued impoundment, retention of the seized property runs afoul of the Fourth Amendment").

[236] U.S. Const. Art. I, §10, cl.1; Art. I, §9, cl.3.

[237] *California Dept. of Corrections v. Morales*, 514 U.S. 499, 504-505 (1995).

[238] *United States v. Kalish*, 626 F.3d 165, 168 (2d Cir. 2010); *United States v. Valladares*, 544 F.3d 1257, 1270-271 (11th Cir. 2008)(the application of a forfeiture statute to conduct which began before the statute became effective and continued on past its effective date did not constitute an ex post facto violation); *United States v. Jennings*, 487 F.3d 564, 585 (8th Cir. 2007)("In the case of continuing offenses ... the Ex Post Facto clause is not violated by application of a statute to an enterprise that began prior to, but continued after the effective date of the statute" in this case a mail fraud scheme).

[239] 489 U.S. 46 (1989).

[240] *Alexander v. United States*, 509 U.S. 544, 552 (1993).

[241] *United States v. Any and All Radio Station Transmission Equipment (Perez)*, 218 F.3d 543, 549-51 (6th Cir. 2000).

[242] This list does not include statutes which are probably more accurately considered fines or penalties since they make no reference to specific property, i.e., "whoever violates this chapter shall forfeit an amount equal to three times the value of the goods." Nor does it include statutes where the forfeiture is essentially a lien against payment of a fine or penalty, e.g., 18 U.S.C. 3681. It does however include both criminal and civil forfeiture statutes. It also includes statutes (marked an *) listed because CAFRA declared proceeds traceable to violation of their provisions subject to confiscation either by identified them individually or as predicate offenses for 18 U.S.C. 1956 (money laundering) or for 18 U.S.C. 1961 (RICO), 18 U.S.C. 981(a)(1).

In: Federal Forfeiture Law
Editor: Jerald Diaz

ISBN: 978-1-63483-310-3

Chapter 2

ASSET FORFEITURE: SELECTED LEGAL ISSUES AND REFORMS*

Richard M. Thompson

SUMMARY

From its beginning in the First Congress, Congress has viewed asset forfeiture as an integral part of federal crime fighting: It takes contraband off the streets, ensures that "crime doesn't pay," and deprives criminals of their "tools of the trade." In short, asset forfeiture is the process of confiscating money or property from a person because it is illegal to possess, it constitutes proceeds of a crime, or it was used to facilitate a crime. Asset forfeiture became a major tool in combating organized crime, drug trafficking, and other serious federal offenses throughout the mid-to-late 20th century and continues to play a major role in federal prosecutions.

In recent years, however, there has been growing opposition to the expanding scope of asset forfeiture, both civil and criminal, with objections primarily coming in two forms: procedural and structural. The procedural objections are based on the idea that the current rules pertaining to asset forfeiture heavily favor the government. With civil asset forfeiture, the property owner need not be convicted nor even prosecuted for a crime before the government can confiscate his or her

* This is an edited, reformatted and augmented version of a Congressional Research Service publication R43890, prepared for Members and Committees of Congress dated February 2, 2015.

property. Unlike criminal prosecutions, the property owner is not constitutionally entitled to an attorney or many other safeguards found in the Bill of Rights. The burden of proof is set at the preponderance-of-the-evidence standard, lower than the traditional criminal standard of beyond a reasonable doubt. If the property owner is claiming innocence, he has the burden of proving either that he had no knowledge of the criminal activity or that he tried to stop the activity if he did know about it. Structural objections pertain to how property and money are allocated once forfeited. The Department of Justice (DOJ) is permitted by law to keep most of the forfeited assets, creating what some view as a profit motive. Recently, DOJ stopped its practice of "adoptive forfeitures," which allowed it to adopt property seized by state and local law enforcement as part of its "equitable sharing" program. Some saw this as a way of bypassing more stringent state forfeiture laws.

Asset forfeiture faced comparable criticism several decades ago, leading Congress to enact the Civil Asset Forfeiture Reform Act of 2000 (CAFRA), the first major overhaul in federal forfeiture law in 200 years. While this law brought about significant reform to federal forfeiture policy and procedures, some have questioned whether CAFRA went far enough to rein in what they characterize as overzealous police forfeiture tactics. Recent concerns about the current legal framework are evidenced in new reports of possible police misuse of federal forfeiture laws. Contemporaneously, reform legislation has been introduced in the 113th and 114th Congresses.

With these proposals in mind, this report will provide an overview of selected legal issues and reforms surrounding asset forfeiture, including the burden-of-proof standard and innocent-owner defense in civil asset forfeiture cases, access to counsel in both civil and criminal forfeiture cases (including a discussion of the 2014 Supreme Court asset forfeiture decision *Kaley v. United States*), allocation of profits from confiscated assets, and DOJ's equitable sharing program.

INTRODUCTION

Asset forfeiture has a long and storied history in Anglo-Saxon law, beginning hundreds of years ago in the common law of England and developing in the United States into a complex body of federal statutes.[1] For purposes of this report, "asset forfeiture" is the process of confiscating either property or money from a person because it is illegal to possess (contraband), constitutes the proceeds of a crime, or was used to facilitate a crime. Asset forfeiture comes in two forms, civil and criminal, each with its own set of intricate rules.

> In civil forfeiture cases, the guilt of the property owner is not in question. In fact, in many cases, there is no criminal prosecution at all. Rather, these cases turn on whether the property was sufficiently connected to a federal crime.

In civil asset forfeiture, the government proceeds against the offending property, not the property owner, in what is known as an *in rem* proceeding (which results in awkward case captions such as *United States v. $52,000.00, More or Less, in United States Currency*).[2] In civil forfeiture cases, the guilt of the property owner is not in question. In fact, in many cases, there is no criminal prosecution at all. Rather, these cases turn on whether the property was sufficiently connected to a federal crime. Because these are civil proceedings, many of the constitutional safeguards accorded to criminal defendants in the Bill of Rights have been held not to apply. Criminal forfeiture, on the other hand, is an *in personam* proceeding that follows a criminal prosecution. The defendant does not forfeit his property unless he is convicted of a qualifying crime.

While civil asset forfeiture began with the very first Congress, it took on a much greater role during the War on Drugs in the 1970s and 1980s. The efficacy of the program, however, soon created concerns of overreach, prompting Congress to take up forfeiture reform in the 1990s.[3] After considerable hearings and debate, Congress enacted the Civil Asset Forfeiture Reform Act of 2000 (CAFRA), the first major overhaul in federal forfeiture law in 200 years.[4] While this law brought about significant reform to federal forfeiture policy and procedures, some have questioned whether CAFRA went far enough to rein in what they characterize as overzealous police forfeiture tactics.[5] Others have questioned the legitimacy of the institution of civil forfeiture itself.[6] The Department of Justice (DOJ), on the other hand, has asserted that asset forfeiture plays a "critical and key role in disrupting and dismantling illegal enterprises, depriving criminals of the proceeds of illegal activity, deterring crime, and restoring property to victims."[7]

Concerns about the current legal framework are evidenced in new reports of possible police misuse of federal forfeiture laws.[8] Contemporaneously, a new round of reform proposals have been introduced, including two identical bills introduced in the 114th Congress, the Fifth Amendment Integrity Restoration Act of 2015, or FAIR Act (S. 255 and H.R. 540),[9] and the Civil Asset Forfeiture Reform Act of 2014 (H.R. 5212), introduced in the 113th Congress.[10]

With these proposals in mind, this report will provide an overview of select legal issues and reforms surrounding asset forfeiture, including the burden of proof standard and innocent owner defense in civil asset forfeiture cases, access to counsel in both civil and criminal forfeiture cases (including a discussion of the 2014 Supreme Court asset forfeiture decision *Kaley v. United States*), allocation of profits from confiscated assets, and DOJ's equitable sharing program. Before addressing these issues, a brief history and overview of civil and criminal asset forfeiture will put these legal issues and reforms into context.

OVERVIEW OF CIVIL ASSET FORFEITURE

Asset forfeiture comes in two forms: civil and criminal. The most significant legal distinction surrounding *civil* asset forfeiture is the principle that the defendant in the case is property— whether a vehicle, a house, or money—rather than a person. This "legal fiction" that property should be "held guilty and condemned" allows the government to proceed against people's property without ever bringing charges against them.[11] This practice can be traced back to English law, which permitted the forfeiture of property that killed a person (known as a deodand), forfeitures at common law for the property of those convicted of a felony or treason, and statutory forfeitures of offending property in violation of customs laws.[12]

Whatever the original rationale,[13] the concept of forfeiture was adopted in American customs laws beginning with the first Congress. It applied to ships and cargoes in violation of customs laws,[14] vessels used to deliver slaves to other countries,[15] and vessels used to deliver slaves to the United States.[16] While Congress enacted various civil forfeiture statutes over the subsequent 150 years, this practice became a major part of federal law and federal law enforcement policy during the War on Drugs, beginning with the Comprehensive Drug Abuse Prevention and Control Act of 1970.[17] This law permitted the confiscation of any substances manufactured or distributed in violation of federal drug laws and any conveyances—such as aircraft, vehicles, and vessels—used to facilitate the transportation and sale of these drugs. In 1978, civil forfeiture was extended to include the forfeiture of money, negotiable instruments, and other proceeds connected to a drug transaction.[18] In 1984, Congress added real property to the list of forfeitable property.[19]

While drug crimes may constitute the bulk of federal forfeitures, federal law permits forfeitures in a host of other areas.[20]

One of the major complaints of these civil asset forfeiture laws was how the procedural rules generally favored the government. The government was not required to prove guilt of the property or its owner beyond a reasonable doubt, nor even by a preponderance of the evidence. Instead, probable cause to believe that the property was connected to the prescribed federal crimes was enough to confiscate the property.[21] If the government made this showing, the burden would shift to the property owner to prove that the property was not implicated in the alleged crime. Additionally, claimants had to file a bond with the court in order to contest a forfeiture of their property.[22]

Although these statutes were a favored tool during the zenith of the War on Drugs, in the 1990s, Congress took up various legislative proposals to reform the civil forfeiture system.[23] After years of legislative debate, Congress enacted the Civil Asset Forfeiture Reform Act of 2000 (CAFRA).[24] This legislation was not a comprehensive overhaul of the asset forfeiture system based upon "first principles" but instead constituted a set of discrete legislative fixes.[25] These changes included shifting the burden of proof to the government and raising it to the preponderance of the evidence standard,[26] creating a uniform innocent owner defense,[27] eliminating the bond requirement,[28] imposing stricter filing deadlines for the government and the claimant,[29] creating a statutory hardship provision,[30] and authorizing appointment of counsel in certain cases.[31]

The civil forfeiture process generally begins when the government seizes someone's property that was connected to a criminal offense. At that point, the government must provide notice to any interested persons. If no one makes a claim on the property, the property can be forfeited under a process known as "administrative" or "nonjudicial" forfeiture without the government having to file a case in district court (so long as it meets the statutory class of property).[32] The rationale for this streamlined process is that requiring the government to obtain a default judgment for uncontested forfeitures is too time consuming and expensive.[33] If anyone makes a claim to the property, however, or if the property does not fall within the statutorily defined categories of property subject to administrative forfeiture, the case must be referred to the U.S. attorney to be handled in a judicial forfeiture proceeding.

Prior to the passage of CAFRA, administrative forfeitures were primarily governed by customs laws.[34] With CAFRA, Congress consolidated many of the procedural rules for administrative forfeitures in 18 U.S.C. § 983; however, the customs laws still apply as a gap filler when the new rules are silent on a particular issue.[35] Because CAFRA does not delineate what categories of property are subject to administrative forfeiture, this facet of forfeiture is still governed by customs laws. Under 19 U.S.C. § 1607, the government can use the administrative process to forfeit any property that does not exceed $500,000; any vehicle or other conveyance that was involved in a drug crime, regardless of value; and all monetary instruments, including U.S. currency, regardless of value.[36] Real property, such as a home or business, is not subject to administrative forfeiture.[37]

The civil forfeiture process generally begins when the government seizes someone's property that was connected to a criminal offense. If no one makes a claim on the property, the property can be forfeited under a process known as "administrative" or "nonjudicial" forfeiture without the government having to file a case in district court.

Under pre-CAFRA law, there were no strict deadlines governing when the government had to file an administrative or judicial forfeiture claim. The law required only that cases be commenced and prosecuted "without delay."[38] CAFRA altered this by placing time restrictions on both the government and claimants. It requires that "in any nonjudicial civil forfeiture, with respect to which the Government is required to send written notice to interested parties, such notice shall be sent in a manner to achieve proper notice as soon as practicable, and in no case more than 60 days after the date of the seizure."[39] This time limit is extended to 90 days in "adoptive forfeiture" cases where the property was seized by a state or local law enforcement agency and turned over to a federal law enforcement agency.[40] If the government fails to provide notice of the seizure in accordance with these rules and fails to get an extension, it must return the property to the owner "without prejudice to the right of the Government to commence a forfeiture proceeding at a later time."[41] DOJ reads this provision, and the majority of courts have accepted, that even if DOJ misses the deadline, it may still initiate a judicial or criminal forfeiture without first having to return the property.[42]

If notice is sent to an interested party, he has 35 days after the date the letter is mailed to file a claim. If the letter is not received, he has 30 days after the date of final publication of the notice of seizure.[43] Filing such a claim is where the property owner gets his or her "day in court." A claim must identify the specific property being claimed and the claimant's interest in the property and must be made under oath, subject to penalty of perjury.[44] To simplify the process of making a claim, CAFRA mandated that each federal agency conducting administrative forfeitures make claim forms available upon request and ensure that they are "written in an easily understandable language."[45]

If no one makes a claim to the property within the time specified,[46] the government can issue a declaration of forfeiture and sell the property at public auction.[47] While claimants cannot seek judicial review of the merits of the administrative forfeiture,[48] CAFRA created a mechanism to ensure that the government followed the required procedural safeguards. Under Section 983(e), a property owner can file a motion in district court to have the court set aside an administrative forfeiture on the grounds that he or she was not provided notice of the forfeiture proceeding.[49] To satisfy the Due Process Clause, the government need not provide actual notice, but its efforts must be "reasonably calculated" to provide notice to interested parties.[50] Section 983(e) is the "exclusive remedy" to set aside a declaration of forfeiture, and it must be filed within five years of the date of final publication of the seizure.[51] If the court sets aside the forfeiture, the government is permitted to commence a subsequent forfeiture proceeding against that person.[52] It has 60 days to file an administrative action or six months to file a judicial action.

If a claim is filed, the administrative forfeiture process is terminated and the case is referred to the U.S. attorney's office for initiation of judicial forfeiture proceedings.[53] The government has 90 days to file its complaint.[54] At this point, any person claiming an interest in the property may file a claim pursuant to the Supplemental Rules for Certain Admiralty Claims not later than 30 days after the date of service of the government's complaint or, if applicable, not later than 30 days after the date of final publication of the filing of the complaint.[55] The claimant then has an additional 20 days after filing the claim to file an answer to the government's complaint.[56]

As will be discussed in detail below, the burden of proof is on the government to prove that the property is forfeitable by a preponderance of the evidence.[57] If the government meets its burden, the property owner can then raise an affirmative defense, such as the innocent owner defense, again, discussed more thoroughly below.[58] Under the Seventh Amendment, claimants have a constitutional right to a jury trial as to any issue of fact.[59] At this point, the case will proceed like other civil suits: Both sides will conduct discovery under the Federal Rules of Civil Procedure, one or both sides will move for summary judgment, and, like many forfeiture cases, it is likely to be resolved without a full-blown trial.[60]

OVERVIEW OF CRIMINAL FORFEITURES

Unlike civil forfeitures, which are *in rem* actions brought directly against the offending property, criminal forfeitures are *in personam* actions in which the government proceeds against the person as part of a criminal prosecution,[61] and only property owned by the defendant—and not third parties—is subject to forfeiture. Until 1984, there were only two criminal forfeiture statutes on the books: the Racketeer Influenced and Corrupt Organizations Act (RICO)[62] and Continuing Criminal Enterprise (CCE) statutes.[63] Congress expanded criminal forfeitures as part of the Comprehensive Crime Control Act of 1984 to cover all federal drug crimes, not just CCE violations.[64] And in an effort to shift more forfeiture cases from the civil to the criminal side, Congress enacted 28 U.S.C. § 2461(c) as part of CAFRA. This so-called "bridge statute" allows the government to confiscate any property in a criminal proceeding that is forfeitable under the civil forfeiture provisions.[65]

As with the civil forfeitures, the first task of the government in criminal forfeitures is generally to secure the property subject to confiscation. The government can seek a pretrial restraining order by alleging that the property sought to be restrained would be subject to forfeiture upon conviction.[66] As will be discussed in more detail below,[67] the Supreme Court has held that probable cause is the appropriate standard for such a pretrial restraining order and that this determination can conclusively be made by the grand jury.[68] If the government seeks a pretrial restraining order *before* obtaining an indictment, it must meet the more stringent standard of demonstrating that there is a "substantial probability" that the government will prevail on the issue of forfeiture, that failure to issue the restraining order will result in the destruction or removal of the property, and that the need to preserve the availability of the property outweighs the hardship on the property owner.[69] Alternatively, under Section 853(f), the government can request the issuance of a warrant authorizing the seizure of the property in question.[70] To issue a warrant, the court must find that there is probable cause that the property will be subject to forfeiture in the event of a conviction and that a pretrial restraining order as provided under Section 853(e) would be insufficient to assure the availability of the property.

In addition to securing the property, the government must provide notice to the defendant. Prior to 2000, the Federal Rules of Criminal Procedure required that an indictment state with specificity "the extent of the interest or property subject to forfeiture."[71] Rule 32.2 was amended in 2000 to require only that the government inform the defendant that it will seek forfeiture generally but "need not identify the property subject to forfeiture or specify the amount of any forfeiture money judgment that the government seeks."[72] Today, instead of listing the specific property to be forfeited in an indictment, the defendant can seek a bill of particulars from the prosecutor listing the property subject to forfeiture.[73] The courts that have addressed this issue disagree about the appropriate timing and scope of the government's disclosure.[74]

> In criminal forfeiture proceedings, the majority of courts apply the preponderance standard of proof, not the reasonable-doubt standard, reasoning that forfeiture is part of the criminal sentence and not the substantive offense

Like any other criminal prosecution, at the guilt phase of the trial the elements of the offense must be proven beyond a reasonable doubt.[75] Upon securing a conviction, the court will then proceed to the forfeiture phase of the trial.[76] The majority of courts apply the preponderance standard of proof in these proceedings, reasoning that forfeiture is part of the criminal *sentence* and not the substantive offense.[77] For federal narcotics crimes, property will be presumed forfeitable if the government proves by a preponderance of the evidence that the property was acquired during the time of the violation (or within a reasonable time after) and there was not a lawful source for such property.[78] If the government meets its burden, the court will issue a preliminary order of forfeiture.[79] Any third party alleging claim to an interest in the property is resolved through a post-judgment ancillary hearing.[80]

SELECT LEGAL ISSUES

Standing

One legal issue that frequently arises in civil forfeiture cases is whether the claimant has sufficient legal standing to challenge the forfeiture of the property. The federal courts have held that a claimant must have constitutional, statutory, and prudential standing to mount a challenge to the forfeiture of his property.[81] It must be noted from the outset that while Congress has the authority to alter the statutory requirements for filing a forfeiture claim—including which party bears the burden of proof and what standard should apply—it cannot alter the constitutional requirement of standing.[82] Nonetheless, standing has become a major issue in asset forfeiture cases, especially when the property being seized is cash.

The federal courts have developed a set of rules to determine whether a claimant has constitutional standing to challenge the forfeiture of his assets. The claimant bears the burden to establish standing by a preponderance of the evidence.[83] To establish standing under Article III of the Constitution,[84] the claimant must demonstrate a "legally cognizable interest in the property that will be injured if the property is forfeited to the government."[85] This can be established by demonstrating a "colorable ownership, possessory or security interest in at least a portion of the defendant property."[86] If the claimant fails to establish standing, there is no case or controversy. Statutory standing is met through compliance with the applicable asset forfeiture statutes and rules, and prudential standing is established if the claimant's legal interest is within the zone of interests to be protected by the forfeiture statutes.[87]

The issue of standing frequently arises in forfeiture cases when the ownership of cash is in question. Beyond the technical requirements of the forfeiture statutes, many of these cases resort to complicated state property and gift laws. The lower courts are generally in agreement that the "unexplained naked possession [of cash] does not constitute a sufficient possessory interest to confer standing on a claimant."[88]A few representative cases can demonstrate how this standing requirement is applied in cash confiscation cases.

In *United States v. $119,030.00 in U.S. Currency*, a Virginia state trooper stopped Jonte Hamilton and two passengers in his car for speeding.[89] Upon questioning by the trooper, Hamilton stated that they were traveling to Houston, Texas, to attend a rap concert and shoot a music video. The trooper became suspicious because the rental car was due back in two days, clearly a short time to make it from Virginia to Texas and back. After giving Hamilton a verbal warning and telling Hamilton he was free to leave, the trooper then asked if there were weapons or drugs or large amounts of currency in the vehicle. One of the passengers said no. The trooper then asked to search the car, and the passenger again said no. After this refusal, the trooper did an exterior scan with a drug-sniffing dog that made a positive alert. Upon searching the car, the trooper found no drugs but did find $119,030.00 in U.S. currency (hence, the case name). Although Hamilton and the passengers denied ownership of the cash at the scene of the search and later signed affidavits to this effect, Hamilton later claimed ownership upon receiving a DEA forfeiture notice. Hamilton claimed that the money was a gift from a family friend that was being held by his mother until his 30th birthday. (He was 28 at the time of the seizure.)

Because possession alone is insufficient to demonstrate dominion and control, the district court assessed other indicia of an ownership or possessory interest.[90] Looking to the law concerning *inter vivos* gifts, the court rejected the idea that this was a valid gift, as it was conditioned on a future event (Hamilton turning 30 years old). The court also rejected the argument that he had a possessory interest in the cash, as he was not entitled to possess it until his 30th birthday. Based on the lack of either an ownership or possessory interest, coupled with his initial disclaimer of ownership at the time of seizure, the court held that Hamilton did not have Article III standing to contest the forfeiture of the money.[91] As an alternative theory, the court assessed but rejected the theory that Hamilton's mother was the owner of the money. She claimed to have been holding the money in trust for her son, but the court found that she had not met the clear and convincing burden of proving a valid oral trust.[92]

In a similar case, *United States v. $39,557.00, More or Less, in U.S. Currency*, a patrolman pulled over a van for allegedly traveling above the speed limit and appearing to not have valid registration.[93] After smelling burnt marijuana, the officer searched the vehicle, where he found a bag beneath the passenger seat that contained "a black bag with a large quantity of United States currency bundled in black rubber bands" and a purse under the back seat that also contained a large amount of money. The officer questioned the occupants of the van about the origins of the money. The driver refused to answer any questions, and the passenger, Richard Harold, claimed that he "was unaware of any money in the van."[94] Although originally disclaiming ownership, Harold filed a claim for the money after the government initiated forfeiture proceedings. The district court concluded that Harold did not have Article III standing to bring this claim. The court reasoned that he did not have a possessory interest in the cash, as it was not found on his person and he did not have an ownership interest in the van.[95] The court likewise rejected Harold's claim that the money was an inheritance from his deceased grandmother, finding that he had not overcome his initial renouncement of the money by a preponderance of the evidence. Thus, without Article III standing, Harold was precluded from proceeding with his claim for the money.

Burden of Proof in Civil Forfeitures

In large measure, debate surrounding possible civil asset forfeiture reform has centered on the burden of proof standard. Beginning with the first federal statutes, and for the first 200 years of civil forfeitures, the burden of proof was on the property owner to prove the "innocence" of the seized property.[96] CAFRA shifted the burden to the government based upon a preponderance of the evidence standard, but some have questioned whether it is sufficiently rigorous in relation to the substantial property interests at stake.[97] All the bills introduced in the 113th and 114th Congresses—S. 255, H.R. 540, and H.R. 5212—would raise the government's burden to "clear and convincing evidence." Whether for legal or policy reasons, some have called for raising the standard to beyond a reasonable doubt,[98] a standard currently employed by four states.[99]

Pre-CAFRA Standard

Prior to CAFRA, the government needed only prove probable cause that there was a nexus or substantial connection between the seized property and the underlying criminal activity.[100] This was the same probable cause standard found in other criminal law settings.[101] Probable cause was established if the government could show that it had "reasonable grounds, more than mere suspicion, to believe that property [was] subject to forfeiture."[102] The government was not required to prove that a crime actually occurred but needed only to demonstrate the "probability or substantial chance" of such activity.[103] In addition to posing a low evidentiary threshold, probable cause could be demonstrated by inadmissible hearsay evidence.[104] Moreover, some cases held that the government was not required "to show a relationship between the property and a *particular* drug transaction—only that the property was related to some illegal drug transaction."[105]

Once the government met its burden, the burden would shift to the property owner to rebut the government's evidence and show that the property seized was not used to facilitate the crime[106] or that he did not consent to the illegal use,[107] the latter known as the innocent owner's defense, which will be explored below.[108] The claimant's burden was by a preponderance of the evidence—that is, whether it was more probable than not that the alleged facts were true.[109] If the claimant failed to rebut the government's case, the property was subject to forfeiture.[110]

While constitutional challenges to placing the burden of proof on the claimant were wholly unsuccessful,[111] some federal judges voiced concern about the fairness of this standard. For instance, in a dissenting opinion, Judge Beam of the Eighth Circuit Court of Appeals analyzed the probable cause standard under the *Mathews v. Eldridge* balancing test used to assess the adequacy of procedural rules under the Due Process Clause.[112] Noting the importance of property rights in the American constitutional structure, he argued that placing the burden of proof on the claimant was a denial of due process:

> [T]he current allocation of burdens and standards of proof requires that the claimant prove a negative, that the property was not used in or to facilitate illegal activity, while the government must prove almost nothing. This creates a great risk of an erroneous, irreversible deprivation. The function of a standard of proof, as that concept is embodied in the Due Process Clause and in the realm of factfinding, is to instruct the factfinder concerning the degree of confidence our society thinks he should have in the correctness of factual conclusions for a particular type of adjudication. The allocation of burdens and standards of proof implicates similar concerns and is of greater importance since it decides who must go forward with evidence and who bears the risk of loss should proof not rise to the standard set. In civil forfeiture cases, where claimants are required to go forward with evidence and exculpate their property by a preponderance of the evidence, all risks are squarely on the claimant. The government, under the current approach, need not produce any admissible evidence and may deprive citizens of property based on the rankest of hearsay and the flimsiest evidence. This result clearly does not reflect the value of private property in our society, and makes the risk of an erroneous deprivation intolerable.[113]

Likewise, Judge Kozinksi, writing for a majority in a Ninth Circuit Court of Appeals forfeiture case, observed, albeit in dicta, that allowing the government to confiscate property based on probable cause was a "constitutional anomaly."[114] He noted that a burden of proof is indicative of the importance society places on a certain legal decision. Because the "stakes are exceedingly high" when a person is threatened with the loss of property, he found it "surprising were the Constitution to permit such an important decision to turn on a meager burden of proof like probable cause."[115]

Legislative History and CAFRA Standard

Whether the standard of proof should be raised to preponderance of the evidence or clear and convincing evidence was "one of the most hotly contested issues as CAFRA moved through Congress."[116] H.R. 1916, introduced by Representative Hyde in the 104th Congress, proposed the clear and convincing standard[117]; however, a compromise bill introduced by Representatives Hyde and Conyers in the 105th Congress lowered it to the preponderance standard.[118] The following Congress, Representative Hyde reintroduced his bill, reverting to the clear and convincing standard.[119] The House Judiciary Committee noted in its report accompanying this bill that civil asset forfeiture, in the view of the committee, "did not merely serve a remedial function," as was previously asserted by DOJ, but rather was sufficiently punitive to warrant raising the standard to the intermediate clear and convincing evidence standard.[120] In June 1999, the House debated and passed Representative Hyde's bill, which contained the clear and convincing standard.[121] However, the two bills introduced in the Senate later that year, which were ultimately enacted into law, settled on the preponderance standard.[122]

Under this standard, found at 18 U.S.C. § 983(c), the government now bears the burden of proving that the property is subject to forfeiture by a preponderance of the evidence. This means that the government, and not the claimant, must proffer sufficient facts at trial to connect the property to the crime. While CAFRA elevated the burden of proof, courts continue to look to preCAFRA cases for guidance when deciding whether to approve the forfeiture.[123] In reviewing the evidence, courts apply a totality-of-the-circumstances approach to determine if there is a sufficient connection between the property and the crime.[124] The property need not actually be used in the crime, but merely intended to be used.[125] Moreover, the property's role in the crime need not be "integral, essential or indispensable."[126] For forfeiture under the federal drug laws, property "facilitates" a crime when it makes the crime "less difficult or more or less free from obstruction or hindrance."[127] And although CAFRA shifted the burden of proof to the government, the courts still find that the claimant's failure to explain a legitimate source of the money as probative of illegal drug activity.[128]

If the government is proceeding under a facilitating theory, Section 983(c)(3) requires the government to demonstrate a "substantial connection" between the property and the offense.[129] This resolved a prior split in the circuit courts as to whether the government had to show a "substantial connection" or a more limited "nexus" between the seized property and the criminal activity.[130] Courts have found the following as factors in determining whether there is a substantial connection between the property and the alleged federal crime: large sums of cash,[131] inconsistent statements,[132] bundling and hiding cash,[133] drug odor on cash,[134] and one-way flight purchased with cash and containing a different passenger's name.[135] In some cases, even where no money or drugs were transported in a vehicle, it was enough that the vehicle transported a "pivotal figure in the transaction."[136] In one case, the circuit court upheld the forfeiture of a vehicle that was used to drive to the scene of an anticipated drug deal, not the actual drug deal.[137]

However, some courts have required a stricter connection between the property and the crime. For instance, the New Hampshire District Court rejected the forfeiture of several thousand dollars in cash that was found in a lockbox with several grams of cocaine, holding that the government failed to specify under which of the three theories described in Section 881(a) it was relying: money used to facilitate the drug crime, money to purchase drugs, or money as the proceeds of a drug crime.[138] Likewise, the District Court for the District of Nebraska held that the possession of "lots of money" and an alert by a drug dog alone were not enough to find a substantial connection between the seized money and alleged drug activity, especially where the claimant claimed a legitimate business purpose for the money.[139]

Reform Proposals

Many observers have argued that the clear and convincing standard would be the appropriate burden of proof in civil forfeiture cases.[140] Following this approach, all three reform bills—S. 255 and H.R. 540, introduced in the 114th Congress, and H.R. 5212, introduced in the 113th Congress—would raise the burden of proof on the government to the clear and convincing standard.[141] Additionally, S. 255 and H.R. 540 would add an element to the government's case-inchief when it proceeds on a facilitating theory by requiring it to prove by clear and convincing evidence that "(A) there was a substantial connection between the property and the offense," (B) the owner of any interest in the seized property—(i) used the property with the intent to facilitate the offense; or (ii) knowingly consented or was willfully blind to the use of the property by another in connection with the offense[.]"

Beyond policy considerations, some have contended that a heightened standard beyond the current preponderance standard is constitutionally compelled. In a pre-CAFRA case concerning the forfeiture of a public housing unit, District Court Judge Jack Weinstein of the Southern District of New York argued that:

> on constitutional as well as policy grounds there is doubt about the propriety of shifting the burden of proof in quasi-criminal proceedings to

> leaseholders. Characterizing this action as civil by statute does not negate its essentially punitive nature as part of the broad initiatives taken to combat drugs. The law would be much more comfortable with a forfeiture scheme that, at least in the case of homes, placed the entire burden on the Government to establish that forfeiture is warranted *with a standard that is higher than a preponderance.*[142]

Although this statement was dicta, as the case was resolved on other grounds, Judge Weinstein argued that, similar to other quasi-criminal contexts—such as parental rights proceedings and deportation proceedings—this higher standard "may be constitutionally mandated" for certain civil asset forfeiture proceedings, particularly when a person's home is at stake.[143]

DOJ, on the other hand, took the position during debates on CAFRA that the burden of proof in civil forfeiture cases should be treated like any other civil case in federal court—that is, under the preponderance standard.[144] Speaking through then-Deputy Attorney General Eric Holder, DOJ argued that raising the standard to clear and convincing evidence "would have a devastating effect on the government's ability to establish the forfeitability of the property in complex money laundering and drug cases. We are concerned that too high a burden of proof will result in inappropriate losses of cases by the government, leading to a windfall for undeserving criminals."[145]

The innocent owner defense applies when the property may have been connected to a federal crime, but the owner had no knowledge of such use, or if he did have knowledge, attempted to prevent such use.

Straddling these competing views, one commentator recommends applying alternative burdens of proof depending on the nature of the property seized.[146] He suggests that contraband could be confiscated under the lower probable cause standard due to its inherent illegality.[147] Discerning the criminal origins of proceeds, on the other hand, is a more difficult endeavor, so he maintains that proceed forfeitures should remain at the preponderance standard.[148] However, property that the government claims was used to facilitate a crime would be forfeited only under the reasonable-doubt standard. He argues that unlike contraband and proceeds—property to which the owner never had a legal right—forcing forfeiture of facilitating property "is particularly grave because it involves depriving individuals of their hard-earned and legally acquired property."[149]

Innocent Owner Defense

If the government meets its burden of proof, the property owner then has the opportunity to present an affirmative defense, such as the innocent owner defense.[150] Generally speaking, the innocent owner defense applies when the property may have been connected to a federal crime, but the owner had no knowledge of such use or, if he did have knowledge, attempted to prevent such use. Prior to CAFRA, an innocent owner defense could be found in several federal statutes, but the scope of these statutes was ambiguous and created confusion in the lower courts.[151] CAFRA resolved this by creating a uniform innocent owner defense that applies to all forfeitures except customs violations. Some have called for overhauling this provision once again by placing the burden on the government to prove that the owner knew of the illegal activity or that he had consented to its use.[152]

Pre-CAFRA Rule

Prior to CAFRA, several federal statutes contained innocent owner defenses. Under 21 U.S.C. § 881(a)(6) and (7), no money or real property could be forfeited "by reason of any act or omission established by that owner to have been committed or omitted without the knowledge or consent of that owner."[153] Similarly, conveyances were not subject to forfeiture "by reason of any act or omission established by that owner to have been committed or omitted without the knowledge, consent, or willful blindness of the owner."[154]

Characterized in one decision as being "[f]illed with negatives" and "nearly impenetrable" language,[155] courts disagreed as to whether these statutes should be read in the conjunctive (requiring a claimant to demonstrate both a lack of knowledge and consent) or in the disjunctive (permitting a showing of one or the other).[156] Under the majority approach, a claimant had to prove by a preponderance of the evidence "either a lack of knowledge of the activity or the lack of consent to it."[157] Where the claimant had knowledge of the crime, consent was "inferred unless the claimant [could] prove that he took all reasonable measures to rid the property of the illegal conduct."[158]

CAFRA Rule

CAFRA created a uniform innocent owner defense providing that "an innocent owner's interest in property shall not be forfeited under any civil forfeiture statute."[159] Like affirmative defenses in other contexts, the "claimant shall have the burden of proving that the claimant is an innocent owner by a preponderance of the evidence."[160] This defense was bifurcated, with different rules applying to property interests existing when the offense was committed and those interests arising after the offense was committed.

With respect to a property interest in existence at the time the crime took place, an innocent owner is someone who "(i) did not know of the conduct giving rise to forfeiture; or (ii) upon learning of the conduct giving rise to the forfeiture, did all that reasonably could be expected under the circumstances to terminate such use of the property."[161] This was an adoption of the disjunctive test in which a claimant could show either lack of knowledge *or* consent. Congress clarified that claimants could show that "they did all they reasonably could" to terminate such use by demonstrating that they "(I) gave timely notice to an appropriate law enforcement agency of information that led the person to know the conduct giving rise to a forfeiture would occur or has occurred; *and* (II) in a timely fashion revoked or made a good faith attempt to revoke permission for those engaging in such conduct to use the property or took reasonable actions in consultation with a law enforcement agency to discourage or prevent the illegal use of the property."[162] Notice that it is not sufficient to merely report the activity to the police. The claimants must also take additional steps to revoke or discourage such further illegal use, unless they reasonably believe such actions will put them or others in danger.[163]

With respect to property interests that arise after the illegal activity, an "innocent owner" is someone who "(i) was a bona fide purchaser or seller for value (including a purchaser or seller of goods or services for value); and (ii) did not know and was reasonably without cause to believe that the property was subject to forfeiture." There is a carve out of this "purchaser" requirement for residences obtained through marriage, divorce, or inheritance if the following elements are met:

I. the property is the primary residence of the claimant;
II. depriving the claimant of the property would deprive the claimant of the means to maintain reasonable shelter in the community for the claimant and all dependents residing with the claimant;
III. the property is not, and is not traceable to, the proceeds of any criminal offense; and
IV. the claimant acquired his or her interest in the property through marriage, divorce, or legal separation, or the claimant was the spouse or legal dependent of a person whose death resulted in the transfer of the property to the claimant through inheritance or probate, except that the court shall limit the value of any real property interest for which innocent ownership is recognized under this subparagraph to

the value necessary to maintain reasonable shelter in the community for such claimant and all dependents residing with the claimant.164

Reform Proposals

While CAFRA extended the innocent owner defense to most civil forfeitures, it has been critiqued mainly for leaving the burden on the alleged innocent owner. All of the reform proposals introduced in the 113th and 114th Congresses would have amended the innocent owner provision. H.R. 5212 would have amended Section 983(d) to shift the burden of proof to the government:

> (1) The innocent owner defense should be available to a claimant. Where a prima facie case is made for such a defense, the Government has the burden of proving that the claimant knew or reasonably should have known that the property was involved in the illegal conduct giving rise to the forfeiture.[165]

Several interpretative issues should be noted concerning this language. First, the term "prima facie case" is somewhat ambiguous in this context. In the general forfeiture context, the courts have used the term "prima facie" to describe the burden of proof: "Probable cause refers to 'reasonable ground for belief of guilt, supported by less than prima facie proof but more than mere suspicion.'"[166] The Eleventh Circuit acknowledged that it did not know what "prima facie proof" meant in that context.[167] The court noted that traditionally "prima facie proof" is that proof "sufficient to establish a fact or raise a presumption unless disproved or rebutted."[168] But, as the court and others have noted, "probable cause *is* prima facie proof" because the government can prevail in an uncontested forfeiture case based on probable cause.[169] The court then assumed that this usage of prima facie proof presumably meant that the government need not meet the traditional civil standard of preponderance but instead need only satisfy the lesser probable cause standard. However, the court finished by noting that "such usage of the term 'prima facie proof' seems to be an unfortunate misuse of legal terminology with no significance."[170]

Based on this understanding of the use of the term "prima facie proof," it appears that H.R. 5212 attempted to create a burden shifting scheme in which the claimant must make some initial showing for the defense but need not prove it by a preponderance of the evidence. If this showing is made, the burden would shift to the government to prove that the claimant knew or reasonably should have known that the property was involved in the illegal conduct.

Second, under H.R. 5212, the government would have been permitted to demonstrate that the claimant "*reasonably should have known* that the property was involved in the illegal conduct." Prior to CAFRA, there was some disagreement in the lower courts concerning the willful blindness standard in the prior innocent owner defense provided under Section 881(a)(4)(c). Some courts applied an objective standard, in which the claimant not only had to prove he was actually unaware of the activity but also that he did everything he reasonably could to prevent the unlawful activity.[171] Under this objective approach, willful blindness existed when the owner failed to exercise due care to ensure that the property was not being used for an illegal purpose— in effect, a negligence standard.[172] Other courts applied a subjective approach where willful blindness would be found if the owner was aware of a high probability that the property was being used for criminal activity and failed to make reasonable inquiries to determine if the property was so used.[173] It appears that by employing the "reasonably should have known language," H.R. 5212 would employ the objective, negligence approach.

Under current law, Section 983(d)(2)(B) illustrates the types of evidence claimants can offer to demonstrate that, *upon learning of the illegal conduct*, they did all they reasonably could to prevent the illegal use of the property:

> (I) gave timely notice to an appropriate law enforcement agency of information that led the person to know the conduct giving rise to a forfeiture would occur or has occurred; and (II) in a timely fashion revoked or made a good faith attempt to revoke permission for those engaging in such conduct to use the property or took reasonable actions in consultation with a law enforcement agency to discourage or prevent the illegal use of the property.[174]

Because H.R. 5212 would have shifted the burden to the government, it would amend subsection (B) to permit the government to show "that the property owner should have had knowledge of the criminal activity by showing that the property owner did not" fulfill the requirements of subsection (d)(2)(B)—that is, inform the police and revoke use of the property. Unlike the current version which uses these factors as proof of steps taken once the claimant *learns* of the illegal activity, H.R. 5212 would have used these factors to demonstrate that the claimant *should have known* of the illegal activity. It is uncertain, however, how demonstrating that a person did not inform the police or take steps to prevent the illegal use of their property necessarily proves that he should have *known* of the illegal use of the property. The fact that a person did not notify the police of the illegal use or take actions to stop such use could, to the contrary, indicate that the person simply had no knowledge of such illegal use. In any event, subsection (d)(2)(B) indicates that these two factors are ways in which the government "may" demonstrate that the owner should have known of the illegal conduct. Other proof of this requirement would be permissible.

S. 255 and H.R. 540 appear to convert the innocent owner defense from an affirmative defense into an element of the government's case-in-chief by requiring the government to prove by clear and convincing evidence that "(A) there was a substantial connection between the property and the offense," (B) the owner of any interest in the seized property—(i) used the property with the intent to facilitate the offense; or (ii) knowingly consented or was willfully blind to the use of the property by another in connection with the offense[.]" It appears that it would apply only to interests in existence at the time of illegal conduct, as an owner with an after-acquired interest could not have intentionally used the property or given consent for another to use the property. S. 255 and H.R. 540 would not strike out the existing innocent owner defense at Section 983(d)(2)(A) but instead would amend the language to redefine an innocent owner as "an owner who upon learning of the conduct giving rise to the forfeiture, did all that reasonably could be expected under the circumstances to terminate such use of the property."

Access to Counsel

Another recurring issue surrounding asset forfeiture is the extent to which property owners should be accorded access to counsel to contest confiscation of their property. This issue has arisen in both the criminal context, in which a defendant's assets are frozen pretrial and he cannot use them to pay for counsel of his choice, and in civil asset forfeitures, in which indigent property owners cannot afford to contest the government's confiscation of their property.

Challenging Asset Freeze to Pay Legal Fees in Criminal Prosecution

Under the federal criminal forfeiture statute, 21 U.S.C. § 853, the government may seek to freeze the assets of a criminal defendant pending trial if it can demonstrate that those assets will be forfeitable upon conviction.[175] There have been a series of Supreme Court and lower court cases assessing what constitutional protections must be accorded to a defendant whose property is subject to this restraint. The most recent case, *Kaley v. United States*, rejected the claim that defendants are entitled to an independent judicial evaluation of probable cause upon which a Section 853(e) restraining order is based.[176]

Prior to *Kaley*, the Supreme Court issued two key rulings relating to Section 853(e)'s pretrial restraining order. In the 1991 case *Caplin & Drysdale, Chartered v. United States*, the Court assessed whether the Fifth and Sixth Amendments require an exemption from forfeiture for assets that a defendant wishes to use to pay for an attorney—essentially, a constitutional carve out of Section 853(e) for legal fees.[177] Acknowledging that "there will be cases where a defendant will be unable to retain the attorney of his choice," the Court nonetheless rejected this claim, finding that "a defendant has no Sixth Amendment right to spend another person's money for services rendered by an attorney, even if those funds are the only way that that defendant will be able to retain the attorney of his choice."[178] And handed down that same day, the Court in *United States v. Monsanto* held that the government can constitutionally freeze assets under Section 853(e) before trial based upon a finding of probable cause: "[I]f the Government may, post-trial, forbid the use of forfeited assets to pay an attorney, then surely no constitutional violation occurs when, after probable cause is adequately established, the Government obtains an order barring a defendant from frustrating that end by dissipating his assets prior to trial."[179] In a footnote, the *Monsanto* Court reserved the question that was ultimately addressed in *Kaley*—that is, whether a judicial hearing was required to assess the grand jury's probable cause determination before a restraint of property can be effectuated.[180]

Both before and after the *Monsanto* ruling, the majority of lower courts held that the combination of the Fifth and Sixth Amendments requires a post-seizure, pretrial hearing as to probable cause that "(a) the defendant committed the crimes that provide a basis for forfeiture, and (b) the properties specified as forfeitable in the indictment are properly forfeitable."[181] These cases relied primarily on the three-part balancing test from *Mathews v. Eldridge*, which assesses (1) the private interest at stake; (2) "the risk of an erroneous deprivation" of this interest and the value of additional procedural protections; and (3) the government's interest and the burdens of providing these additional protections.[182] Unlike the Court in *Kaley*, these courts held that the *Mathews* balance tipped in favor of the defendant. In assessing the defendant's interest, the Second Circuit in *Monsanto*, echoed by the D.C. Circuit, noted that the private interest at stake is "not merely a defendant's wish to use his property in whatever manner he sees fit," but "that interest is augmented by an important liberty interest: the qualified right, under the sixth amendment, to counsel of choice."[183] Put more directly by the Seventh Circuit, "[t]he defendant needs the attorney *now* if the attorney is to do him any good."[184] As to the value of this added process above and beyond the grand jury determination, the D.C. Circuit acknowledged that it was not sure what evidence a defendant may offer at such a hearing. However, it was "precisely that lack of knowledge on the part of the court and the prosecution that makes it apparent that there is 'considerable worth in a post-indictment, pre-trial adversarial hearing' on the issue of the restraint of the seized property."[185] Finally, while the government's interest in maintaining the secrecy of the grand jury proceedings was considered weighty, the courts found that there were sufficient procedural mechanisms in place—such as *in camera* review and the admission of hearsay evidence—that softened this concern.[186] Recognizing the government's interest in grand jury secrecy, they found nothing that outweighed the defendants' constitutional rights to due process and counsel under the Fifth and Sixth Amendments. The Eleventh Circuit, on the other hand, has applied the four-part speedy trial test from *Wingo v. Barker* to hold that the district courts may decide on a case-by-case basis whether a hearing is warranted.[187] However, at this hearing, a defendant is entitled to challenge only "the nexus between those assets and the charged crime, but not the sufficiency of the evidence supporting the underlying charge."[188]

The Supreme Court granted review in *Kaley* to resolve the split in the circuits and to address the question left open by the *Monsanto* footnote: whether the criminally accused are entitled to judicial review of a grand jury's determination of probable cause prior to full restraint of their property.[189] In *Kaley*, the government secured a grand jury indictment charging Kerry Kaley and her husband Brian with transporting stolen medical devices across state lines and laundering the proceeds of that activity.[190] Upon obtaining the indictment, the government sought a restraining order under 21 U.S.C. § 853(e)(1) to prevent the Kaleys from transferring any assets traceable to or involved in the alleged offenses.[191] Included in the Kaleys' seized assets was a $500,000 certificate of deposit that they intended to use to pay for an attorney. The district court denied the Kaleys' request for a hearing to challenge the grand jury's determination of probable cause, and the Eleventh Circuit affirmed.[192]

Writing for a six-member majority, Justice Kagan posited that the Court's holdings in *Caplin & Drysdale* and *Monsanto* all but resolved the question before it.[193] The Kaleys, the Court noted, were not contesting *Monsanto*'s holding that probable cause was sufficient to effectuate a pretrial seizure of assets. Instead, their challenge was about who should make the probable cause determination—the grand jury or a judge. The Kaleys argued that the Due Process Clause entitled them to an independent judicial determination of probable cause beyond that of the grand jury.[194] Justice Kagan wrote that the resolution to this question "has a ready answer, because a fundamental and historic commitment of our criminal justice system is to entrust those probable cause findings to grand juries."[195] Applying the theory that the greater includes the lesser, because a grand jury determination of probable cause is constitutionally sufficient to support the pretrial restraint of a person's liberty, the Court found that it should also support the lesser interest of temporarily freezing a defendant's assets. A different result, Justice Kagan wrote, could have "strange and destructive consequences" on the criminal justice system by permitting opposite conclusions from the grand jury and judge on this probable cause determination. The majority reserved the question of whether *Mathews* was the appropriate test to apply in this criminal setting. Nonetheless, the majority applied *Mathews* and held that the balance weighed against permitting a judicial hearing to contest the seizure of a defendant's assets.[196]

In a somewhat unusual lineup, Chief Justice John Roberts, joined by Justices Breyer and Sotomayor, dissented, arguing that "few things could do more to undermine the criminal justice system's integrity than to allow the Government to initiate a prosecution and then, at its option, disarm its presumptively innocent opponent by depriving him of counsel of his choice—without even an opportunity to be heard."[197] The Chief Justice challenged the majority's greater-includesthe-lesser argument by noting that it is "far from clear" which interest is greater when a defendant is subject to serious federal charges: "the interest in temporary liberty pending trial, or the interest in using one's available means to avoid imprisonment for many years after trial."[198] Responding to the argument that permitting possibly differing probable cause determinations would create "legal dissonance," Chief Justice Roberts observed that such a hearing would not disrupt the traditional role of the grand jury to decide whether a defendant should be required to stand trial and the role of the judge to decide pretrial matters.[199] Unlike the majority, the dissenters concluded that *Mathews* was the appropriate Due Process test to apply to this "collateral issue of the pretrial deprivation of property" and would have held that the balance weighed in favor of permitting a pretrial hearing.

Proposed Amendments

If Congress decided to craft a legislative response to the *Kaley* decision, the question then becomes what procedures and standards should govern such a hearing. There do not appear to be any existing legislative proposals to create this type of hearing, but the pre-*Kaley* circuit decisions offer some guidance:

- The proposal might establish what is required to initiate this judicial hearing. In several of the circuits, it appears that a preliminary showing that the defendant is otherwise without assets to hire an attorney is sufficient to trigger a full adversarial hearing before the district court.[200] Others have applied more stringent requirements, noting that "Due process does not automatically require a hearing and a defendant may not simply ask for one."[201] The Tenth Circuit has required that a defendant make "a prima facie showing of a bona fide reason to believe the grand jury erred in determining that the restrained assets" were traceable to the alleged criminal activity.[202]
- The proposal might address *when* a defendant would be entitled to a hearing. The Second Circuit in *Monsanto* held that the government's interest in protecting potentially forfeitable property justified the absence of a *pre*-restraining order hearing under Section 853(e)(1)(A).[203] The D.C. Circuit agreed, noting that "[i]t may well be that in the case of criminal proceeding in which the government may ultimately have rights in the property at issue, immediate protective measures must be taken in order to prevent dissipation or deterioration of the assets before the time of trial is reached."[204] Thus, the government could be allowed to secure an initial seizure of the property with a post-restraint hearing to follow.
- The proposal could include provisions addressing concerns by the Supreme Court and several of the lower courts that permitting such a hearing might jeopardize the government's case and trial strategy.[205] Moreover, there is some fear that requiring the government to announce its witnesses before trial might lead to "witness tampering or jeopardize witness safety."[206] Following the suggestion of the Second Circuit's *Monsanto* ruling,[207] this concern could arguably be alleviated by ensuring that, like other procedures under Section 853, the Rules of Evidence will not apply, allowing hearsay evidence to

be admitted. Additionally, permitting *in camera* review of sensitive material could assuage concerns that a prosecutor's trial strategy will be jeopardized.

- The proposal could address which party should bear the burden of proof and what exactly that party must prove. In earlier rulings, the Second Circuit held that the government should bear the burden and that it must demonstrate "by evidence independent of the indictment, a probability of convincing a jury beyond a reasonable doubt both that the defendant has violated the statute and that the assets are subject to forfeiture[.]"[208] However, in its more recent ruling, it held that government need only establish probable cause as to the defendant's guilt and the forfeitability of the specified assets.[209] This approach was followed by other circuits, including the Ninth[210] and the D.C. Circuit.[211] The Fourth Circuit placed the burden on the defendant, requiring him to prove "by a preponderance of the evidence that the government seized untainted assets without probable cause and that he needs those same assets to hire counsel."[212] As described above, the Tenth Circuit provided that once the defendant makes a prima facie showing that the grand jury erred, the burden then shifts to the government to demonstrate that there is probable cause to believe that the assets are traceable to the alleged offense.[213]

In certain instances, the government may determine that engaging in a pretrial hearing is inadvisable. The Seventh Circuit has stated that in this instance, the government could be required to "consent to the exemption of reasonable attorneys' fees, as determined by the district court in its supervisory role, from the property otherwise subject to forfeiture."[214] Alternatively, the Second Circuit has stated that the government can simply forgo restraint and obtain forfeiture after the conviction.[215]

While the Court rejected an outright exemption from forfeiture for a certain amount of funds for an attorney as a constitutionally compelled requirement in *Caplin & Drysdale*,[216] Congress could create such an exemption.[217] Similar to the limitation of assets a defendant could contest in the post-restraint, pretrial hearing, this proposal could limit the amount of seized assets the defendant can unfreeze to an "amount necessary to pay reasonable attorneys' fees for counsel of sufficient skill and experience to handle the particular case."[218]

Indigent Access to Counsel in Civil Asset Forfeitures

The issue of adequate access to counsel has also arisen in the context of civil forfeitures. There are two provisions of federal law providing for the appointment of counsel in civil asset forfeiture proceedings. Section 983, Title18, provides that indigent claimants are entitled to counsel in cases involving residences and permits attorneys who are representing defendants in criminal cases to also represent them in the civil forfeiture cases.[219] Section 2465(b), Title 28, provides that in any civil forfeiture proceeding in which the claimant "substantially prevails," the United States shall be liable for "reasonable attorney fees and other litigation costs reasonably incurred by the claimant."[220] These provisions were scaled back from the version that passed the House in 1999, which would have provided for appointment of counsel in any case in which the claimant was indigent.[221] S. 255 and H.R. 540 would mirror this approach by expanding the current access to indigent counsel to any civil proceeding in which a claimant has standing to contest the forfeiture, not only when his primary residence is in jeopardy of being forfeited. They would also place the responsibility on appointing counsel on the court rather than requiring the claimant to request counsel himself. H.R. 5212 would have amended Section 983(a)(1)(A)(i) to require the government to inform recipients of a forfeiture notice that they "may be able to obtain free or reduced rate legal representation under subsection(b)."

STRUCTURAL REFORMS

In addition to procedural reforms, considerable attention has been given to the structural aspects of civil asset forfeiture. One issue in this context is what some perceive as the misallocation of forfeiture revenues directly back to law enforcement agencies rather than into the general fund of the United States.[222] Another issue is the program referred to as "equitable sharing," in which the federal government either assists state and local law enforcement in seizing assets or "adopts" a seizure made solely by local entities and remits up to 80% of the revenue upon completion of a federal forfeiture proceeding.

ALLOCATION OF FORFEITURE REVENUES

In its 2010 report *Policing for Profit: The Abuse of Civil Asset Forfeiture*, the Institute for Justice stated its view that "the most troubling aspect of modern civil asset forfeiture laws is the profit incentive at their core."[223] Part of the concern is that law enforcement agencies are utilizing revenues from asset forfeiture to supplement their shrinking budgets,[224] a power that is somewhat anomalous for a government agency.[225] Another concern is that the government has been subsuming other law enforcement priorities in an "overzealous pursuit of forfeiture."[226] Some federal courts have also expressed concern about the "corrupting incentives" that arise from the current arrangement.[227] By contrast, the Treasury Department noted during debate on CAFRA that allowing law enforcement agencies to keep the profits of asset forfeiture helps pay for its own property management costs, relieves burdens that would otherwise fall on taxpayers, and overall "strengthens law enforcement by rechanneling forfeited value back into this most fundamental societal purpose.... "[228]

Prior to 1984, this issue of profit motive was largely nonexistent or, at best, indirect, since the proceeds from forfeited assets were deposited directly in the general fund of the United States Treasury.[229] However, as part of the Comprehensive Crime Control Act of 1984, codified at 28 U.S.C. § 524, Congress diverted these funds into the newly created Department of Justice Assets Forfeiture Fund.[230] As initially established, any amount in the fund in excess of $5 million not appropriated that fiscal year was required to be deposited in the Treasury's general fund.[231] However, in 1986 this cap was eliminated.[232]

Funds are deposited into the Assets Forfeiture Fund via several statutes. Section 524(c)(4) of Title 28 provides that "all amounts from the forfeiture of property under any law enforced or administered by the Department of Justice" (except for several limited carve outs) and all funds received through the federal equitable sharing program shall be deposited into the Assets Forfeiture Fund.[233] Section 881(e) of Title 21 provides that the proceeds of any sale of forfeited property and forfeited moneys must also be deposited in the Assets Forfeiture Fund.[234]

Section 524 of Title 28 establishes how money from the Assets Forfeiture Fund can be spent. Section 524(c) provides that money in the fund is available to the attorney general for the following purposes:

- Forfeiture-related expenses
- Payment to informants in drug-related cases
- Awards for information leading to civil or criminal forfeitures
- Payment of liens or mortgages against property that has been forfeited
- Remission and mitigation payments related to forfeited property
- Equipping vehicles, vessels, or aircrafts of federal agencies participating in the fund, or state or local law enforcement agencies engaged in a joint law enforcement operation with a federal agency
- Payments for other equipment directly related to seizure or forfeiture, including laboratory equipment, protective equipment, communications equipment, and the operation and maintenance costs of such equipment
- Purchase evidence of federal drug or money laundering offenses
- Payment of state and local real estate taxes on forfeited property
- Payment of overtime salaries, travel, fuel, training, equipment, and other similar costs of state and local law enforcement officers that are incurred in a joint law enforcement operation with a federal law enforcement agency participating in the fund
- Federal correctional construction costs[235]

Additionally, Section 524(c)(8) provides that any excess unobligated balance remaining in the fund "shall be available to the Attorney General, without fiscal year limitation, for any Federal law enforcement, litigative/prosecutive, and correctional activities, or any other authorized purpose of the Department of Justice."[236]

Also established in the Comprehensive Crime Control Act of 1984 is the Department of the Treasury Forfeiture Fund, then called the "Customs Forfeiture Fund."[237] This fund is administered by the Secretary of the Treasury and receives deposits of currency and proceeds from forfeitures under laws enforced or administered by the Treasury or the Coast Guard, amounts received by the Treasury or the Coast Guard as an equitable share of a forfeiture conducted by other authorities, or income realized from investments on behalf of the fund.[238] Similar to DOJ's fund, this statute establishes how these funds can be used.[239]

Proposed Legislative Amendments

Some have suggested that the most appropriate method of removing the profit motive from forfeiture cases would be to stop diverting assets to the very law enforcement agencies conducting the seizures.[240] S. 255 and H.R. 540 would take this general approach by requiring confiscated funds to be deposited back into the Treasury's General Fund and would eliminate the various provisions that allow property to be transferred to another federal agency or to any state and law enforcement agency that participated directly in the seizure of the property. Congress may also consider allocating such funds for a specific program. During the debates on asset forfeiture reform in the 1990s, Representative John Conyers introduced H.R. 3347, which would have required that not less than 50% of funds disbursed from the Assets Forfeiture Fund be spent on a "community-based crime control program (including private, nonprofit programs) for drug education, prevention, and treatment." Various states have employed a similar approach of diverting funds to specific programs, such as substance abuse programs[241] or public education.[242]

Equitable Sharing

> "Equitable sharing" is a policy in which federal law enforcement agencies can share forfeiture revenues with participating state and local law enforcement agencies.

In addition to the issue of allocation of forfeiture revenues, some have voiced concern about the appropriateness of the "equitable sharing" program.[243] Equitable sharing is a policy in which federal law enforcement agencies can share forfeiture revenues with participating state and local law enforcement agencies. Some federal courts and commentators had expressed concern that this policy allows law enforcement agencies to circumvent local laws that might impose more stringent procedural requirements, such as higher burdens of proof, or laws that do not funnel assets directly into law enforcement budgets.[244] DOJ has lauded equitable sharing generally for "fostering cooperation among federal, state, and local law enforcement agencies" and allowing the federal government "to provide valuable additional resources" to local police.[245] On January 16, 2015, Attorney General Holder issued new guidelines pertaining to one of the more controversial aspects of equitable sharing known as "adoptive seizures," which might alleviate some apprehensions about this program.[246]

Equitable sharing is authorized and regulated by several federal statutes. Section 881(e)(1)(A) of Title 21 provides that "[w]henever property is civilly or criminally forfeited under this subchapter the Attorney General may ...

transfer the property ... to any State or local law enforcement agency which participated directly in the seizure or forfeiture of the property."[247] Subsection (e)(3) provides that:

> Attorney General shall assure that any property transferred to a State or local law enforcement agency ... has a value that bears a reasonable relationship to the degree of direct participation of the State or local agency in the law enforcement effort resulting in the forfeiture, taking into account the total value of all property forfeited and the total law enforcement effort with respect to the violation of law on which the forfeiture is based; and (B) will serve to encourage further cooperation between the recipient State or local agency and Federal law enforcement agencies.[248]

Likewise, 18 U.S.C. § 981(e)(2) provides that "notwithstanding any other provision of the law, except Section 3 of the Anti Drug Abuse Act of 1986, the Attorney General, the Secretary of the Treasury, or the Postal Service, as the case may be, is authorized to retain property forfeited pursuant to this section, or to transfer such property on such terms and conditions as he may determine to ... to any State or local law enforcement agency which participated directly in any of the acts which led to the seizure or forfeiture of the property." Under 19 U.S.C. § 1616a, the Secretary of the Treasury may "transfer any of the [forfeited] property to ... any State or local law enforcement agency that participated directly or indirectly in the seizure or forfeiture of the property."[249]

Presumably based on this statutory authority, the Attorney General has issued guidelines to regulate the equitable sharing program. These guidelines were first issued in 1985 as part of the U.S. Attorneys Manual entitled "Guidelines on Seized Forfeited Property"[250] and were recently updated in 2009 as the "Guide to Equitable Sharing for State and Local Law Enforcement Agencies."[251]

Prior to Attorney General Holder's announcement, agencies participated in the equitable sharing program in two ways. The first is "joint investigations," in which federal agencies work with state or local agencies to enforce federal law.[252] A state or local agency's share is based on "a reasonable relationship to the agency's direct participation in the investigation or law enforcement effort resulting in the forfeiture.[253] In some instances, joint task forces involving federal, state, and local law enforcement agencies have written equitable sharing agreements based upon numbers of personnel and other contributions to the task force.[254] DOJ's new rules do not alter this part of equitable sharing—the sharing of proceeds when both federal and local law enforcement agencies are involved. The second method, called "adoptive forfeitures," which has been curtailed by the new DOJ guidelines, allowed federal authorities to "adopt" assets that were seized *solely* by a local law enforcement agency.[255]

DOJ's new order prohibits "the federal adoption of property seized by state or local law enforcement under state law in order for the property to be forfeited under federal law."[256] While generally ending the practice of adoptive forfeitures, the new order creates an exception for property "that directly relates to public safety concerns, including firearms, ammunition, explosives, and property associated with child pornography." It also creates three additional exceptions: "(1) seizures by state and local authorities working together with federal authorities in a joint task force; (2) seizures by state and local authorities that are the result of joint federal-state investigations or that are coordinated with federal authorities as part of ongoing federal investigations; or (3) seizures pursuant to federal seizure warrants, obtained from federal courts to take custody of the assets originally seized under state law."[257] Notably, the first two exceptions allow the continued practice of sharing assets that are the result of joint participation between federal and state/local authorities.

Reform Proposals

Notwithstanding DOJ's new policy, the three recent bills addressing asset forfeiture would amend the various equitable sharing provisions. If enacted, S. 255 and H.R. 540 would appear to completely end equitable sharing—both adoptive forfeitures and forfeitures obtained through joint investigations. H.R. 5212 would not have eliminated equitable sharing altogether but would have instead prohibited the use of federal forfeiture laws to circumvent state or local laws: "The Attorney General shall assure that any equitable sharing between the Department of Justice and a local or state law enforcement agency was not initiated for the purpose of circumventing any State law that prohibits civil forfeiture or limits use or disposition of property obtained via civil forfeiture by State or local agencies." Based on comments by incoming Senate Judiciary Committee chairman Chuck Grassley and other lawmakers, it is apparent that asset forfeiture, including equitable sharing, will remain on the congressional radar in the 114th Congress.[258]

End Notes

[1] For a general history and analysis of federal asset forfeiture law, see CRS Report 97-139, Crime and Forfeiture, by Charles Doyle.

[2] United States v. $52,000.00, More or Less, in United States Currency, 508 F. Supp. 2d 1036 (S.D. Ala. 2007).

[3] See DAVID B. SMITH, 1-1 PROSECUTION AND DEFENSE OF FORFEITURE CASES § 1.02 (2014).

[4] Civil Asset Forfeiture Reform Act of 2000, P.L. 106-185, 114 Stat. 202.

[5] INSTITUTE FOR JUSTICE, POLICING FOR PROFIT: THE ABUSE OF CIVIL ASSET FORFEITURE 11 (2010) (hereinafter "POLICING FOR PROFIT").

[6] Todd Barnet, Legal Fiction and Forfeiture: An Historical Analysis of the Civil Asset Forfeiture Reform Act, 40 DUQ. L. REV. 77, 100 (2001) ("The lack of protection provided to forfeiture victims raises many questions about the appropriate place of forfeiture law in a just society. Both civil and criminal forfeiture laws were intended to target Mafiosi and drug kingpins, but this is not the effect these laws have had."); Richard Rahn, Abusive Civil Asset-Forfeiture Laws, CATO INSTITUTE (Apr. 14, 2014) available at http://www.cato.org/publications/commentary/abusivecivil-asset-forfeiture-laws.

[7] See DEP'T OF JUSTICE, NATIONAL ASSET FORFEITURE STRATEGIC PLAN 2008-2012 5 (2008), available at http://www.justice.gov/criminal/afmls/pubs/pdf/ strategicplan.pdf.

[8] See, e.g., Michael Sallah, Robert O'Harrow Jr. & Steven Rich, Stop and Seize, WASH. POST (Sept. 6, 2014), available at http://www.washingtonpost.com/sf/investigative/2014/09/06/stop-and-seize/; Sarah Stillman, Taken, NEW YORKER (Aug. 12, 2013), available at http://www.newyorker.com/magazine/2013/08/12/taken.

[9] S. 255, H.R. 540, 114th Cong. (2015).

[10] H.R. 5212, 113th Cong. (2014).

[11] Various Items of Personal Property v. United States, 282 U.S. 577, 581 (1931).

[12] Calero-Toledo v. Pearson Yacht Leasing Co., 416 U.S. 663, 680-82 (1974).

[13] As Justice Holmes noted in The Common Law, the rationale for a law can evolve to fit the times. OLIVER WENDELL HOLMES, JR., THE COMMON LAW 5 (Little, Brown and Co. 1938). While forfeiture may have begun as a penalty against the offending property, it has come to be rationalized under both remedial and punitive theories of punishment against the property owner, and, perhaps most importantly, as a source of government revenue. See U.S. DEP'T OF JUSTICE, U.S. ATTORNEY'S MANUAL, THE ATTORNEY GENERAL'S GUIDELINES ON SEIZED AND FORFEITED PROPERTY § 9-118.010 ("The Department of Justice asset forfeiture program has three primary goals: (1) to punish and deter criminal activity by depriving criminals of property used or acquired through illegal activities; (2) to enhance cooperation among foreign, federal, state and local law enforcement agencies through the equitable sharing of assets recovered through this program, and, as a by-product, (3) to produce revenues to enhance forfeitures and strengthen law enforcement.").

[14] See Act of July 31, 1789, § 13, 1 Stat. 39, 47.

[15] See Act of Mar. 22, 1794, 1 Stat. 347.

[16] See Act of Mar. 2, 1807, 2 Stat. 426.

[17] See Comprehensive Drug Abuse Prevention and Control Act of 1970, P.L. 91-513, § 511, 84 Stat. 1236, 1276 (codified at 21 U.S.C. § 881(a)); see generally H.Rept. 106-192, at 3.

[18] See Psychotropic Substances Act of 1978, P.L. 95-633, § 301(a), 92 Stat. 3768, 3777 (codified at 21 U.S.C. § 881(a)(6)).

[19] P.L. 98-473, 98 Stat 1837, 2050 (1984) (codified at 21 U.S.C. § 881(a)(7)).

[20] See, e.g., 18 U.S.C. § 1082 (illegal gambling); 18 U.S.C. § 1963(a) (RICO violations); 18 U.S.C. § 3666 (bribery); 18 U.S.C. § 3667 (liquor violations); 19 U.S.C. § 1453 (customs violations); 47 U.S.C. § 782 (vessels that transport contraband); see CRS Report 97-139, Crime and Forfeiture, supra note 1, at pp. 76-87, for a complete list of federal forfeiture statutes.

[21] 19 U.S.C. § 1615 (1994).

[22] 19 U.S.C. § 1623 (1994).

[23] Smith, supra note 3.

[24] P.L. 106-185, 114 Stat. 202; Stefan D. Cassella, The Civil Asset Forfeiture Reform Act of 2000: Expanded Government Forfeiture Authority and Strict Deadlines Imposed on All Parties, 27 J. LEGIS. 97 (2001) (providing legislative history of CAFRA).

[25] Smith, supra note 3 ("CAFRA does not replace, but is superimposed upon, the existing procedures in the customs laws, the Supplemental Rules, and the forfeiture statutes themselves.").

[26] 18 U.S.C. § 983(c).

[27] Id. §983(d)

[28] Id. §983(a).

[29] Id. §983(a)

[30] Id. §983(f).

[31] Id. §983(b), (h), 28 U.S.C. § 2465.

[32] CAFRA refers to forfeitures that do not require filing a case in a district court as "nonjudicial forfeitures." See id. § 983(a)(1)(A)(i).

[33] See United States v. Ninety-Three Firearms, 330 F.3d 414, 422 (6th Cir. 2003).

[34] Before CAFRA, the rules governing notice, the filing of a claim, and the cost bond requirement were provided under 19 U.S.C. §§ 1607-1609. See, e.g., 19 U.S.C. § 1609 ("If no such claim is filed or bond given within the twenty days hereinbefore specified, the appropriate customs officer shall declare the vessel, aircraft, merchandise, or baggage forfeited, and shall sell the same at public auction ...").

[35] H.Rept. 106-192, at 21 (1999) ("To the extent these procedures are inconsistent with any preexisting federal law, these procedures apply and supercede preexisting law."); Cassella, supra note 24, at 103.

[36] 19 U.S.C. 1607. Beginning in 1844, Congress first authorized administrative forfeitures in cases where the property seized did not exceed $100. Act of Apr. 2, 1844, ch.8, 5 Stat. 653. Over the years, this limit was sporadically raised. In 1954, it was raised to $2,500, Tariff Act of 1930, P.L. 768, § 506, 68 Stat. 1141; in 1978, it was raised to $10,000, Customs Procedural Reform and Simplification Act of 1978, P.L. 95-410, 92 Stat. 897; in 1984, it was raised to $100,000, Comprehensive Crime Control Act of 1984, P.L. 98-473, 98 Stat. 1837, 2053; and, in 1990, it was raised to its current limit of $500,000. Customs and Trade Act, P.L. 101-382, § 122, 104 Stat. 629, 641. The limit on administrative forfeitures under federal tax law is $100,000. 26 U.S.C. § 7325.

[37] 18 U.S.C. § 985 ("Notwithstanding any other provision of law, all civil forfeitures of real property and interests in real property shall proceed as judicial forfeitures.").

[38] 19 U.S.C. § 1604 (2000 ed.).

[39] 18 U.S.C. § 983(a)(1)(A)(i). Although this notice requirement explicitly applies to any "nonjudicial civil forfeiture proceeding," the courts have held that these deadlines also

apply to judicial forfeitures. See United States v. 475 Martin Lane, 545 F.3d 1134, 1141 (9th Cir. 2008); United States v. Misc. Firearms, 399 F. Supp. 2d 881, 882 (C.D. Ill. 2005).

[40] Id. § 983(a)(1)(A)(iv). The time limit for sending notice can be extended in two ways. A "supervisory official in the headquarters office of the seizing agency" may extend the period for sending notice up to 30 days if there is reason to believe notice might have adverse consequences such as endangering human life or risking flight from prosecution. Id. § 983(a)(1)(B). Any further extension of the notice period must be extended by the court. Id. § 983(a)(1)(C).

If the seizure imposes a hardship on the owner, a claimant may file for immediate release of the property if the claimant can demonstrate a possessory interest in the property; sufficient ties with the community to provide assurance that the property will be available at the time of the trial; that the continued possession by the government will cause substantial hardship to the claimant; and the hardship outweighs the risk that the property will not be available if forfeiture is ultimately granted. 18 U.S.C. § 983(a)(3)(B).

[41] Id. § 983(a)(1)(F).

[42] See Smith, supra note 3, at § 6.02; see, e.g., Return of Seized Prop. v. United States, 625 F. Supp. 2d 949, 954 (C.D. Cal. 2009) ("Release of the seized motorcycles to Claimants would therefore be academic. The Government's properly-filed civil forfeiture action would allow it to immediately re-seize the property."); United States v. $ 114,031.00 in United States Currency, No. 06-21820, 2007 U.S. Dist. LEXIS 74362, *9 (S.D. Fla. Oct. 4, 2007) ("The plain language of the statute says that returning the property would not prevent the Government from later bringing a forfeiture proceeding. It does not say that the Government is required to return the property before it can bring a forfeiture proceeding."); but see United States v. Assorted Jewelry with an Approximate Value of $ 219,860.00, 386 F. Supp. 2d 9, 13 (D.P.R. 2005) (dismissing forfeiture action with prejudice for failing to meet notice deadline).

[43] Id. § 983(a)(2)(B).

[44] Id. § 983(a)(2)(C).

[45] Id. § 983(a)(2)(D).

[46] There has been some debate on when a case is considered "filed" with the appropriate agency.

[47] 19 U.S.C. § 1609.

[48] See Mesa Valderrama v. United States, 417 F.3d 1189, 1196 (11th Cir. 2005).

[49] Id. § 983(e).

[50] Taylor v. United States, 483 F.3d 385, 388 (2007) (quoting Mullane v. Central Hanover Bank & Trust Co., 339 U.S. 306, 314 (1950)).

[51] Id. § 983(e)(3).

[52] Id. § 983(e)(2)(B).

[53] Id. § 983(a)(3)(A). As an alternative to filing a judicial claim, the government can proceed against the property by obtaining a criminal indictment and taking the steps necessary to preserve its right to maintain custody of the property. Id. § 983(a)(3)(B)(ii). If the government does not file a complaint for judicial forfeiture as required, the government must promptly release the property and "may not take further action to effect the civil forfeiture of such property in connection with the underlying offense." § 983(a)(3)(B)(ii).

[54] Id. § 983(a)(3)(A).

[55] Id. § 983(a)(4)(A).

[56] Id. § 983(a)(4)(B).

[57] See 18 U.S.C. § 983(c); see "Burden of Proof," infra p. 9.

[58] § 983(d); see "Innocent Owner Defense," infra p.14.

[59] United States v. One 1976 Mercedes Benz, 618 F.2d 453, 469 (7th Cir. 1980).

[60] See Smith, supra note 3, at § 2.05.

[61] See United States v. Tit's Cocktail Lounge, 873 F.2d 141, 143 (7th Cir. 1989).

[62] 18 U.S.C. § 1961.

[63] 21 U.S.C. § 848.

[64] Comprehensive Crime Control Act of 1984, P.L. 98-47, 98 Stat. 1976, 2044.

[65] 28 U.S.C. § 2461(c).

[66] 21 U.S.C. § 853(e)(A).

[67] See "Challenging Asset Freeze to Pay Legal Fees in Criminal Prosecution," infra pp. 20-22.

[68] See United States v. Monsanto, 491 U.S. 600, 616 (1989); Kaley v. United States, 134 S. Ct. 1090, 1094 (2014).

[69] 21 U.S.C. § 853(e)(B).

[70] 21 U.S.C. § 853(e).

[71] FED. R. CRIM. P. 7(c)(2) (1).

[72] FED. R. CRIM. P. 32.2(a).

[73] United States v. Galestro, No. 06-285, 2008 U.S. Dist. LEXIS 53834, *31 (E.D.N.Y. July 15, 2008) ("Although item-specific notice need not be provided in the indictment itself, the defendant is nonetheless entitled to have the government identify the particular assets that it is seeking to forfeit so that the defendant can prepare his defense.") (citation and internal quotation marks omitted).

[74] See, e.g., United States v. Palfrey, 499 F. Supp. 2d 34, 52 (D.D.C. 2007) (ordering government to disclose to defendant within 30 days of trial details regarding the nexus between the property sought and the crimes alleged and to identify within 60 days the proceeds of specified unlawful activity); United States v. Vasquez-Ruiz, 136 F. Supp. 2d 941, 944 (N.D. Ill. 2001) (ordering government to disclose within 30 days of trial a bill of particulars "identifying the specific items of property ... that it claims are subject to forfeiture."); United States v. Diaz, 190 F.3d 1247, 1258 (11th Cir. 1999) (holding that no bill of particulars needed where defendant had actual knowledge of government's intent to confiscate defendant's interest in home).

[75] United States v. Sandini, 816 F.2d 869, 873 (3d 1987).

[76] FED. R. CRIM. P. 32.2(b)(1)(A) ("As soon as practical after a verdict or finding of guilty, or after a plea of guilty or nolo contendere is accepted, on any count in an indictment or information regarding which criminal forfeiture is sought, the court must determine what property is subject to forfeiture under the applicable statute.").

[77] See, e.g., United States v. Cherry, 330 F.3d 658, 670 (4th Cir. 2003); United States v. Gasanova, 332 F.3d 297, 301 (5th Cir.); United States v. Vera, 278 F.3d 672, 673 (7th Cir. 2002); United States v. Cabeza, 258 F.3d 1256, 1257 (11th Cir. 2001); but see United States v. Pelullo, 14 F.3d 881, 906 (3d Cir. 1994).

[78] 21 U.S.C. § 853(d).

[79] Fed. R. Crim. P. 32.2(b).

[80] 18 U.S.C. § 1963(l); 21 U.S.C. § 853(n).

[81] United States v. $119,030.00 in U.S. Currency, 955 F. Supp. 2d 569, 576 (W.D. Va. 2013).

[82] See Raines v. Byrd, 521 U.S. 811, 820 n.3 (1997) ("It is settled that Congress cannot erase Article III's standing requirements by statutorily granting the right to sue to a plaintiff who would not otherwise have standing.").

[83] United States v. 7,000.00 in U.S. Currency, 583 F. Supp. 2d 725, 729-30 (M.D.NC. 2008).

[84] The Supreme Court has interpreted Article III to require three elements to establish standing: (1) an injury in fact that is concrete and particularized; (2) the injury is caused by

defendant's conduct; and (3) the injury is redressable by court action. See Lujan v. Defenders of Wildlife, 504 U.S. 555, 560-61 (1992).

[85] United States v. $515,060.42 in U.S. Currency, 152 F.3d 491, 497 (6th Cir. 1998).

[86] Id.

[87] United States v. $500,000.00 in U.S. Currency, 591 F.3d 402, 404 (5th Cir. 2009); see generally SUPP. RULE FOR ADMIRALTY OR MARITIME CLAIMS AND ASSET FORFEITURE ACTIONS RULE G.

[88] Munoz-Valencia v. United States, 169 F. App'x 150, 152 (3d Cir. 2006); United States v. $321,470.00, U.S. Currency, 874 F.2d 298, 304 (5th Cir. 1989); United States v. $515,060.42 in U.S. Currency, 152 F.3d 491, 498 (6th Cir. 1998).

[89] 119,030.00 in U.S. Currency, 955 F. Supp. 2d at 572.

[90] Id. at 579.

[91] Id. at 581.

[92] Id. at 582.

[93] United States v. $39,557.00, More or Less, in U.S. Currency, 683 F. Supp. 2d 335, 337 (D.N.J. 2010).

[94] Id. at 337-38.

[95] Id. at 341.

[96] Act of July 31, 1789, 1 Stat. 29, 43-44.

[97] See infra note 76.

[98] See, e.g., David Pimental, Forfeitures Revisited: Bringing Principle to Practice in Federal Court, 13 NEV. L. J. 1, 55 (2012); Rachel L. Stuteville, Reverse Robin Hood: The Tale of How Texas Law Enforcement Has Used Civil Asset Forfeiture to Take from Property Owners and Pad the Pockets of Local Government-the Righteous Hunt for Reform Is on, 46 TEX. TECH L. REV. 1169, 1200 (2014).

[99] POLICING FOR PROFIT, supra note 5, at 22.

[100] See 18 U.S.C. § 981 (cross-referencing 19 U.S.C. § 1615) (1996); United States v. $3,000 in Cash, 906 F. Supp. 1061, 1065 (E.D. Vir. 1995).

[101] United States v. $506,231 in U.S. Currency, 125 F.3d 442, 451 (7th Cir. 1997).

[102] In re Seizure of All Funds in Accounts in Names Registry Pub. Inc., 68 F.3d 577, 580 (2d Cir. 1995) (quoting Marine Midland Bank, N.A. v. United States, 11 F.3d 1119, 1124 (2d Cir. 1993)).

[103] United States v. Certain Real Prop., Commonly Known as 6250 Ledge Rd., Egg Harbor, Wis., 943 F.2d 721, 725 (7th Cir. 1991) (quoting United States v. Edwards, 885 F.2d 377, 389–390 (7th Cir.1989)).

[104] United States v. $3,000 in Cash, 906 F. Supp. 1061, 1065 (E.D. Vir. 1995).

[105] United States v. $242,484.00, 389 F.3d 1149, 1160 (11th Cir. 2004) (emphasis added); see also United States v. Four Parcels of Real Prop. in Greene & Tuscaloosa Counties in State of Ala., 941 F.2d 1428, 1440 (11th Cir. 1991).

[106] United States v. Three Hundred Sixty Four Thousand Nine Hundred Sixty Dollars ($364,960.00) in United States Currency, 661 F.2d 319, 325 (5th Cir. 1981).

[107] United States v. One Parcel of Real Estate Located at 7715 Betsy Bruce Lane Summerfield, N.C., 906 F.2d 110, 111 (4th Cir. 1990).

[108] See "Innocent Owner's Defense," infra p. 9.

[109] United States v. $52,000.00, More or Less, in United States Currency, 508 F. Supp. 2d 1036, 1040 (S.D. Ala. 2007).

[110] United States v. Certain Real Prop. 566 Hendrickson Blvd., Clawson, Oakland Cnty., Mich., 986 F.2d 990, 995 (6th Cir. 1993) ("It is well settled that the government is entitled to a judgment of forfeiture upon an unrebutted showing of probable cause.").

[111] See, e.g., United States v. One Beechcraft King Air 300 Aircraft, 107 F.3d 829, 829 (11th Cir. 1997); United States v. $94,000.00 in U.S. Currency, Along With Any Interest Earned Thereon in First Fin. Sav. Ass'n Account No. 79- 70063411, 2 F.3d 778, 783 (7th Cir. 1993); United States v. 228 Acres of Land & Dwelling Located on Whites Hill Rd. in Chester, Vt., 916 F.2d 808, 814 (2d Cir. 1990).

[112] United States v. Twelve Thousand, Three Hundred Ninety Dollars ($12,390), 956 F.2d 801, 810 (8th Cir. 1992) (Beam, J., dissenting); Mathews v. Eldridge, 424 U.S. 319, 335 (1976).

[113] 956 F.2d at 811 (Beam, J., dissenting) (internal quotation marks and citations omitted).

[114] United States v. $49,576.00 United States Currency, 116 F.3d 425, 429 (9th Cir. 1997).

[115] Id.

[116] Cassella, supra note 24, at 108.

[117] H.R. 1916, 104th Cong. (1st Sess. 1995).

[118] H.R. 1965, 105th Cong. (2d Sess. 1998).

[119] H.R. 1658, 106th (1st Sess. 1999).

[120] H.Rept. 106-192, at 12-13.

[121] H.R. 1658 (engrossed in H.R.).

[122] S. 1701, 106th Cong. (1st Sess. 1999); S. 1931, 106th Cong. (1st Sess. 1999); P.L. 106-185 (codified at 18 U.S.C. § 983(c)).

[123] United States v. Funds in Amount of Thirty Thousand Six Hundred Seventy Dollars, 403 F.3d 448, 469 (7th Cir. 2005) ("The government's burden may have increased in the wake of CAFRA, but it did not become insurmountable. Factors that weighed in favor of forfeiture in the past continue to do so now-with the obvious caveat that the government must show more or stronger evidence establishing a link between forfeited property and illegal activity."); United States v. $21,510.00 In U.S. Currency, 144 F. App'x 888, 890 (1st Cir. 2005).

[124] United States v. $242,484, 389 F.3d 1149, 1160 (11th Cir.2004); United States v. One 2005 Dodge Magnum, 845 F. Supp. 2d 1361, 1370 (N.D. Ga. 2012).

[125] United States v. Schifferli, 895 F.2d 987, 990 (4th Cir. 1990).

[126] United States v. Schifferli, 895 F.2d 987, 990 (4th Cir. 1990).

[127] United States v. Premises Known as 3639-2nd St., N.E., Minneapolis, Minn., 869 F.2d 1093, 1096 (8th Cir. 1989; United States v. One 1977 Lincoln Mark V Coupe, 643 F.2d 154, 157 (3d Cir. 1981).

[128] United States v. $252,300.00 in U.S. Currency, 484 F.3d 1271, 1275 (10th Cir. 2007); United States v. $11,320.00 in U.S. Currency, 880 F. Supp. 2d 1310, 1325 (N.D. Ga. 2012).

[129] 18 U.S.C. § 983(c)(3) (emphasis added).

[130] Compare United States v. One 1986 Ford Pickup, 56 F.3d 118, 1187 (9th Cir. 1995), with United States v. Daccarett, 6 F.3d 37, 56 (2d Cir. 1993).

[131] United States v. $124,700 in U.S. Currency, 458 F.3d 822, 826 (8th Cir. 2006); United States v. $84,615 in U.S. Currency, 379 F.3d 496, 501 (8th Cir. 2004); United States v. $93,685.61 in U.S. Currency, 730 F.2d 571, 572 (9th Cir. 1984).

[132] United States v. $252,300.00 in U.S. Currency, 484 F.3d 1271, 1274 (10th Cir. 2007).

[133] $124,700 in U.S. Currency, 458 F.3d at 826.

[134] United States v. U.S. Currency, in Amount of $150,660.00, 980 F.2d 1200, 1206 (8th Cir. 1992); United States v. Ninety One Thousand Nine Hundred Sixty Dollars ($91,960.00), 897 F.2d 1457, 1463 (8th Cir. 1990).

[135] United States v. Ninety One Thousand Nine Hundred Sixty Dollars ($91,960.00), 897 F.2d 1457, 1463 (8th Cir. 1990).

[136] United States v. One 1979 Porsche Coupe, Vin 9289200514, 709 F.2d 1424, 1427 (11th Cir. 1983); United States v. One 1977 Cadillac Coupe DeVille VIN: 6D47S7Q234771, 644 F.2d 500, 503 (5th Cir. 1981).

[137] United States v. One 1974 Cadillac Eldorado Sedan, Serial No. 6L47S4Q407966, 548 F.2d 421, 426 (2d Cir. 1977).

[138] United States v. Ten Thousand Six Hundred Forty-Eight, 975 F. Supp. 2d 163, 169 (D.N.H. 2013); 21 U.S.C. § 881(a)(6).

[139] United States v. $1,074,900.00 in U.S. Currency, 932 F. Supp. 2d 1053, 1064 (D. Neb. 2013).

[140] See, e.g., POLICING FOR PROFIT, supra note 5, at 14; Eric Moores, Reforming the Civil Asset Forfeiture Reform Act, 51 ARIZ. L. REV. 777 (2009) ("While the increased burden has not had the intended effect, a standard of clear and convincing evidence would require the government to present a stronger case before depriving citizens of their property."); Barclay Thomas Johnson, Restoring Civility-the Civil Asset Forfeiture Reform Act of 2000: Baby Steps Towards a More Civilized Civil Forfeiture System, 35 IND. L. REV. 1045, 1079 (2002) ("[T]he changes to the Act remedy the most glaring inequities, but do not go far enough. In a country based on the cry of life, liberty, and property, it is surprising that, barely two centuries after its founding, the government should be able to deprive its citizens of their core constitutional right to property based on a mere preponderance of the evidence.")

[141] S. 255, H.R. 540, 114th Cong. (2015); H.R. 5212, 113th Cong. (2014).

[142] United States v. Leasehold Interest in 121 Nostrand Ave., 760 F. Supp. 1015, 1032 (E.D.N.Y.1991) (emphasis added).

[143] Id.

[144] Oversight of Federal Asset Forfeiture: Its Role in Fighting Crime, Hearing before the Subcomm. on Criminal Justice Oversight of the S. Comm. on the Judiciary, 106th Cong. 23 (July 21, 1999) (prepared statement of Deputy Attorney General Eric Holder).

[145] Id.

[146] Pimental, supra note 98, at 55.

[147] Id. at 55.

[148] Id. at 56.

[149] Id. at 57.

[150] United States v. Real Prop. Located at 3234 Washington Ave. N., Minneapolis, Minn., 480 F.3d 841, 843 (8th Cir. 2007).

[151] See United States v. One 1973 Rolls Royce by & Through Goodman, 43 F.3d 794, 815 (3d Cir.1994); Smith, supra note 3, at § 4.02.

[152] S. 255, H.R. 540, 114th Cong. (2015); H.R. 5212, 113th Cong. (2014); POLICING FOR PROFIT, supra note 5, at 14.

[153] 21 U.S.C. § 881(a)(7) (1994).

[154] Id. § 881(a)(4).

[155] One 1973 Rolls Royce by & Through Goodman, 43 F.3d at 815

[156] Compare id. (conjunctive), with United States v. One Parcel of Land at Lot 111-B, 902 F.2d 1443, 1445 (9th Cir. 1990) (disjunctive).

[157] United States v. 121 Allen Place, 75 F.3d 118, 121 (2d Cir. 1996).

[158] Id.

[159] 18 U.S.C. § 983(d)(1).

[160] Id.

[161] Id. § 983(d)(2)(A).

[162] 18 U.S.C. § 983(d)(2)(B) (emphasis added).

[163] See, e.g., United States v. 19 & 25 Castle St., 31 F.3d 35, 40-41 (2d Cir. 1994); United States v. 1012 Germantown Rd.,963 F.2d 1496, 1504-05 (11th Cir. 1992).

[164] 18 U.S.C. § 983(d)(3).

[165] H.R. 5212.

[166] United States v. $4,255,625.39, 762 F.2d 895, 903 (11th Cir. 1985) (quoting United States v. One 1978 Chevrolet Impala, 614 F.2d 983, 984 (5th Cir. 1980)).

[167] United States v. $242,484.00, 351 F.3d 499, 504 n.8 (11th Cir. 2003).

[168] Id.(citing BLACK'S LAW DICTIONARY 1209 (7th ed. 1999)).

[169] Id.; see also PROSECUTION AND DEFENSE OF FORFEITURE CASES, supra note 3, at § 11.03.

[170] 351 F.3d at 504 n.8.

[171] United States v. One 1980 Bertram 58' Motor Yacht, Known as the M/V Mologa, Serial No. 138M80587-80, VIN: Berro 138M80B, 876 F.2d 884, 888 (11th Cir. 1989).

[172] One 1973 Rolls Royce by & Through Goodman, 43 F.3d at 806.

[173] Id. at 806; United States v. One 1989 Jeep Wagoneer, V.I.N. 1J4GS5874KP105300, 976 F.2d 1172, 1175 (8th Cir. 1992) ("[W]illful blindness involves an owner who deliberately closes his eyes to what otherwise would have been obvious and whose acts or omissions show a conscious purpose to avoid knowing the truth.").

[174] 18 U.S.C. § 983(d)(2)(B).

[175] 21 U.S.C. § 853(e).

[176] Kaley v. United States, 134 S. Ct. 1090, 1094 (2014).

[177] Caplin & Drysdale, Chartered v. United States, 491 U.S. 617, 619 (1989).

[178] Id. at 626.

[179] United States v. Monsanto, 491 U.S. 600, 616 (1989).

[180] Id. at 615 n.10.

[181] See, e.g., United States v. E-Gold, Ltd., 521 F.3d 411, 421 (D.C. Cir. 2008); United States v. Monsanto, 924 F.2d 1186, 1198 (2d Cir. 1991); United States v. Moya-Gomez, 860 F.2d 706, 730 (7th Cir. 1988); but see United States v. Bissell, 866 F.2d 1343, 1352 (11th Cir. 1989).

[182] Mathews v. Eldridge, 424 U.S. 319, 335 (1976).

[183] Monsanto, 924 F.2d at 1193; E-Gold, Ltd., 521 F.3d at 417.

[184] Moya-Gomez, 860 F.2d at 726 (emphasis in original).

[185] E-Gold, Ltd., 521 F.3d at 418 (quoting Monsanto, 924 F.2d at 1195).

[186] E-Gold, Ltd., 521 F.3d at 418-19; Monsanto, 924 F.2d at 1197-98.

[187] See United States v. Bissell, 866 F.2d 1343, 1353 (11th Cir. 1989); Wingo v. Barker, 407 U.S. 514 (1972). "The four Bissell/Barker factors are: '(1) the length of the delay before the defendants received their post-restraint hearing; (2) the reason for the delay; (3) the defendants' assertion of the right to such a hearing pretrial; and (4) the prejudice the defendants suffered due to the delay weighed against the strength of the United States's interest in the subject property.'" United States v. Kaley, 677 F.3d 1316, 1321 (11th Cir. 2012) (quoting United States v. Kaley, 579 F.3d 1246, 1254 (11th Cir. 2009)).

[188] United States v. Kaley, 677 F.3d 1316, 1327 (11th Cir. 2012).

[189] Kaley v. United States, 134 S. Ct. 1090, 1094 (2014).

[190] Kaley, 134 S. Ct. at 1095.

[191] 21 U.S.C. § 853(e).

[192] United States v. Kaley, 677 F.3d 1316, 1330 (2012).

[193] Caplin & Drysdale, Chartered v. United States, 491 U.S. 617 (1989); United States v. Monsanto, 491 U.S. 600, 615 (1989).

[194] Kaley, 134 S. Ct. at 1097.

[195] Id. at 1097.

[196] Id. at 1100.

[197] Id. at 1111 (Roberts, C.J., dissenting).

[198] Id.

[199] Id. at 1109 (Roberts, C.J., dissenting).

[200] See E-Gold, Ltd., 521 F.3d at 421; Monsanto, 924 F.2d at 1198.

[201] United States v. Farmer, 274 F.3d 800, 805 (4th Cir. 2001); United States v. Jones, 160 F.3d 641, 647 (10th 1998).

[202] Jones, 160 F.3d at 647.

[203] Monsanto, 924 F.2d at 1192.

[204] E-Gold, Ltd., 521 F.3d at 415-16.

[205] Kaley, 134 S. Ct. at 1101 ("Still more seriously, requiring a proceeding of that kind could undermine the Government's ability either to obtain a conviction or to preserve forfeitable property. To ensure a favorable result at the hearing, the Government could choose to disclose all its witnesses and other evidence. But that would give the defendant knowledge of the Government's case and strategy well before the rules of criminal procedure—or principles of due process—would otherwise require.") (internal citation omitted).

[206] Id. at 1101-02.

[207] Monsanto, 924 F.3d at 1198 ("As indicated hereinabove, however, the Federal Rules of Evidence would not be followed in the pretrial hearings that this opinion would require, thus allowing the use of hearsay testimony and precluding unwarranted exposure of government witnesses.").

[208] United States v. Monsanto, 836 F.2d 74, 83 (2d Cir. 1987).

[209] Monsanto, 924 F.3d at 1195.

[210] United States v. Roth, 912 F.2d 1131, 1133 (9th Cir. 1990).

[211] E-Gold, Ltd., 521 F.3d at 419.

[212] United States v. Farmer, 274 F.3d 800, 805 (4th Cir. 2001).

[213] Jones, 160 F.3d at 647.

[214] See United States v. Moya-Gomez, 860 F.2d 706, 731 (7th Cir. 1988); United States v. Michelle's Lounge, 39 F.3d 684, 696 (7th Cir. 1994).

[215] Monsanto, 924 F.2d at 1198.

[216] Caplin & Drysdale, 491 U.S. at 632.

[217] Contra United States v. Bissell, 866 F.2d 1343, 1351 (11th Cir. 1989) ("The appellants contend that the Sixth Amendment requires that enough funds be exempt from pretrial restraints and forfeiture to pay for counsel of choice and other litigation expenses. Specifically, they argue that the Sixth Amendment protects the individual's right to select and be represented by his preferred attorney with assets in his possession at the time of arrest. Thus, the appellants urge that to protect a Sixth Amendment interest in a vigorous adversarial process, as well as an individual's interest in selecting counsel of choice, the Constitution requires the exemption of funds which are sufficient to allow defendants to retain their preferred counsel. We disagree.").

[218] Moya-Gomez, 860 F.2d at 730.

[219] 18 U.S.C. § 983.

[220] 28 U.S.C. § 2465(b).

[221] H.R. 1658 (engrossed in H.R.).

[222] See Policing for Profit, supra note 5, at 9; Civil Asset Forfeiture Reforms: Hearing on H.R. 1916 before the H. Jud. Comm., 104th Cong., 2d Sess. 310 (1996) (prepared statement of E.E. Edwards, et al., Co-Chairs of the National Association of Criminal Defense Lawyers Asset Forfeiture Abuse Task Force) ("Decisions regarding whose property to seize, and how to deal with citizens whose property has been seized is too often dictated by the profit the agencies stand to realize from their seizures.").William Patrick Nelson, Should the Ranch Go Free Because the Constable Blundered— Gaining Compliance with Search and Seizure Standards in the Age of Asset Forfeiture, 80 CAL. L. REV. 1309, 1310 (1992).

[223] See POLICING FOR PROFIT, supra note 5, at 9.

[224] Sallah, et al., supra note 8.

[225] Nelson, supra note 159.

[226] PROSECUTION AND DEFENSE OF FORFEITURE CASES § 1.01, supra note 3, at § 1.01.

[227] United States v. Funds Held ex rel. Wetterer, 210 F.3d 96, 110 (2d Cir. 2000).

[228] Hearing on H.R. 1916, supra note 154, at 240 (prepared statement of Jan P. Blanton, Director, Executive Office for Asset Forfeiture, Department of the Treasury).

[229] See CRS Report 97-139, Crime and Forfeiture, supra note 1, at 21.

[230] Comprehensive Crime Control Act of 1984, P.L. 98-473, 98 Stat. 1837, 2052 (codified at 28 U.S.C. § 524(c)(4)).

[231] 98 Stat. 2053.

[232] Department of Justice Assets Forfeiture Fund Amendments Act of 1986, P.L. 99-570, § 1152, 100 Stat. 3207, 3207-12.

[233] 28 U.S.C. § 524(c).

[234] 21 U.S.C. § 881(e).

[235] 28 U.S.C. § 524(c).

[236] 28 U.S.C. § 524(c)(8).

[237] P.L. 98-473, § 317, 98 Stat. 1837, 2054.

[238] 31 U.S.C. § 9703.

[239] Id.

[240] POLICING THE POLICE, supra note 5, at 14; Shamoil Shipchandler, Asset Forfeiture: Knock it Off or I'm Stopping this Car!, NATIONAL LAW REVIEW (Dec. 9, 2014), available at http://www.natlawreview.com/article/asset-forfeiture-knockit-or-i-m-stopping-car.

[241] See, e.g., CONN. GEN. STAT. § 54-36I.

[242] See, e.g., N.C. GEN. STAT. ART. IX, § 7; NEB. CONST. ARTICLE VII-5.

[243] POLICING THE POLICE, supra note 5, at 14.

[244] See Scarabin v. Drug Enforcement Admin., 966 F.2d 989, 991 (5th Cir. 1992) (noting that it did not quarrel with claimant's description of adoptive seizures as a "scam," "shell game," and "money laundering"); United States v. One 1979 Chevrolet C-20 Van, 924 F.2d 120, 122 (7th Cir. 1991) (calling adoptive seizures a "questionable practice"); INSTITUTE FOR JUSTICE, HOW FEDERAL EQUITABLE SHARING ENCOURAGES LOCAL POLICE AND PROSECUTORS TO EVADE STATE CIVIL FORFEITURE LAW FOR FINANCIAL GAIN 1 (2011) ("[W]ith equitable sharing, state and local law enforcement can take profit from property they might not be able to under state law. If a state provides greater protections or bars law enforcement from directly benefitting from forfeitures, agencies can simply turn to federal law."); Stuteville, supra note 34, at 1185 (2014) ("Equitable sharing provides a way to get around state laws regarding forfeiture proceeds and, thus, is a scapegoat for states with stringent forfeiture laws."); Moores, supra note 74, at 794 ("While CAFRA applies to federal law enforcement agencies, states retain the power

to control their own state and local law enforcement agencies pursuant to their police power. Federal law, however, has undermined this power through a process called 'equitable sharing,' which allows state and local police to bypass their own laws when federal forfeiture terms are more favorable. This results in even less political accountability, as equitable sharing permits state and local police to bypass state legislation mandating how forfeiture money can be spent.").

[245] U.S. DEP'T OF JUSTICE, GUIDE TO EQUITABLE SHARING FOR STATE AND LOCAL LAW ENFORCEMENT AGENCIES (2009).

[246] U.S. DEP'T OF JUSTICE, PROHIBITION OF CERTAIN FEDERAL ADOPTIONS OF SEIZURES BY STATE AND LOCAL LAW ENFORCEMENT AGENCIES, available at http://www.justice.gov/sites/default/files/opa/press-releases/attachments/2015/ 01/16/attorney_general_order_prohibiting_adoptions.pdf.

[247] 21 U.S.C. § 881(e)(1)(A).

[248] Id. § 881(e)(3).

[249] 21 U.S.C. § 1616a(c).

[250] 7 Smith, supra note 3, at § 7.02.

[251] GUIDE TO EQUITABLE SHARING, supra note 246, at fwd., 1.

[252] Id. at 6.

[253] Id. at 12.

[254] Id. at 13.

[255] Id. at 6.

[256] PROHIBITION OF CERTAIN FEDERAL ADOPTIONS OF SEIZURES BY STATE AND LOCAL LAW ENFORCEMENT AGENCIES, supra note 250.

[257] Id. at 2.

[258] See Commentary from Senator Chuck Grassley, The Scoop: Asset Forfeiture Reforms Move Forward (Jan. 26, 2015), available at http://www.grassley.senate.gov/news/commentary/ scoop-asset-forfeiture-reforms-move-forward; Robert O'Harrow Jr., Defense lawyers, lawmakers and civil libertarians press for asset seizure reform, WASH. POST (January 27, 2015), available at http://www.washingtonpost.com/investigations/defense-lawyers-lawmakers-and-civillibertarians-press-for-asset-seizure-reform/2015/01/27/63bcf368-a66f-11e4-a7c2-03d37af98440_story.html.

INDEX

D

E

M

N

O

P

Q

R

U

V

W